Soviet Labour Ideology and the Collapse of the State

Soviet Labour Ideology and the Collapse of the State

Bobo Lo
Visiting Scholar
Wolfson College
Oxford

148513

First published in Great Britain 2000 by
MACMILLAN PRESS LTD
Houndmills, Basingstoke, Hampshire RG21 6XS and London
Companies and representatives throughout the world

A catalogue record for this book is available from the British Library.

ISBN 0–333–75167–1

 First published in the United States of America 2000 by
ST. MARTIN'S PRESS, INC.,
Scholarly and Reference Division,
175 Fifth Avenue, New York, N.Y. 10010

ISBN 0–312–22984–4

Library of Congress Cataloging-in-Publication Data
Lo, Bobo, 1959–
Soviet labour ideology and the collapse of the state / Bobo Lo.
p. cm.
Includes bibliographical references and index.
ISBN 0–312–22984–4 (cloth)
1. Labor policy—Soviet Union. 2. Labor productivity—Soviet Union.
3. Soviet Union—Economic policy—1981–1985. 4. Soviet Union—Economic
policy—1986–1991. I. Title.

HC340.L3 L6   1999
331.11'0947—dc21
                                                                99–048279

This book is printed on paper suitable for recycling and made from fully managed and sustained
forest sources.

10 9 8 7 6 5 4 3 2 1
09 08 07 06 05 04 03 02 01 00

Printed and bound in Great Britain by
Antony Rowe Ltd, Chippenham, Wiltshire

To Lyn, for ensuring that I'd be around to write this book

Contents

Acknowledgements

I owe an enormous debt to more people than I am able to name here. To Lyn and Bruce Minerds for being there for me during all the times in Moscow – good, bad and sometimes downright ugly. To Leslie Holmes, my former PhD supervisor, for his constant encouragement, indispensable advice and great contacts! To Linda Kouvaras and Richard Ward for their wonderful friendship and support over the years. To Stephen and Jen Wilson, without whom this book would never have happened. To Leonid Kuzmich and Peter Hawley for their life-saving medical interventions. To Ormond College for providing me with a splendid environment in which to live and work. To my mother and father for putting up with me all these years. To Helen, Hsiao, Boba and Ping. To Stephanie and to great friends – Lizzy, Steve and Nicola, H and Ros, Jane and Tim, Orme, Hilde and Julie.

The opinions expressed in this book are personal to the author and should not be interpreted in any way as representing the views of the Australian Government.

List of Abbreviations

AUCCTU	All-Union Central Council of Trade Unions
CDSP	Current Digest of the Soviet Press
CPSU	Communist Party of the Soviet Union
FBIS	Foreign Broadcast Information Service
GNP	Gross National Product
ILO	International Labour Organization
JPB	Job Placement Bureau
KOMSOMOL	Communist Youth League
KPSS	Kommunisticheskaya Partiya Sovetskogo Soyuza
NEP	New Economic Policy
PTU	Professionalno-tekhnicheskoe uchilishche
RAPO	Raionnoe agro-promyshlennoe obedinenie
SOL	Scientific Organization of Labour
STP	Scientific–Technological Progress
TPC	Territorial Production Complex
VPO	Vsesoyuznoe promyshlennoe obedinenie

Note on Transliteration

The particular transliteration system used in this book has been chosen for its simplicity. Consequently, hard signs, soft signs and diacritical marks have not been rendered. Soft and mixed adjective endings, as in *russkii*, have been transliterated as *ii* rather than *i*, *iy* or *y*, except in the case of certain well-known names such as Yavlinsky. Hard adjective endings have been transliterated as *y* instead of *yi*, for example, *novy*. No attempt has been made to transliterate the palatalized 'e' with *ye*, with the exceptions of Yevgenii and Yevtushenko which are more commonly recognizable with a *y* at the beginning of the word.

1
Introduction

'Experience shows that the most dangerous moment for a bad
government is generally that in which it sets about reform'

Alexis de Tocqueville, *L'Ancien Regime*,
(in Partington, 1992, p. 699).

The demise of the Soviet Union was the culmination of a decade of
remarkable political, economic and social change in that country. The
Soviet state's metamorphosis from apparently omnipotent monolith
into fragmented commonwealth reflected, in turn, one of the most
profound ideological revolutions witnessed this century. This transformation found especially dramatic expression in changing official
conceptions of the role and nature of labour in Soviet society. In less
than a decade, from the death of Brezhnev in November 1982 to the
Union's dissolution in December 1991, Soviet labour ideology degener-
ated from a seemingly timeless philosophy based on immutable principles, into a shifting set of *ad hoc* propositions dominated by
considerations of tactical expediency. Over the same period, a more or
less coherent economic system characterized by full and compulsory
employment gave way to a disintegrating structure in which unemployment became recognized as a permanent socioeconomic phenomenon.

This book sets out to examine the nature, dimensions and causes of
the transformation in Soviet labour ideology in the post-Brezhnev era. It
argues that this transformation was driven by the regime's search for
increased productivity, a project initiated in response to the Soviet
Union's mounting economic difficulties in the early 1980s. It will
be argued, further, that the reformulation of Soviet labour ideology
during 1982–91 reflected, to a very large extent, a series of unforeseen

1

and involuntary outcomes. In embarking on the quest for greater productivity, the regime little understood the impact this would have on fundamental labour dogma and the functioning of the USSR's economic system.

The Soviet leadership thought to control the direction and magnitude of economic reform, but instead found it increasingly difficult to manage its wider consequences – political, economic, ideological. Although Gorbachev (1988a, pp. 49–59) presented *perestroika* as a programme for the political, economic and social renewal of Soviet society, the transformations in the USSR were far greater than he and others in the regime ever imagined. Gorbachev, and Andropov before him, clearly believed in the manageability of change; for all the talk about a 'revolution from below' (ibid., p. 57), the regime continued to think and act in terms of a revolution from above, of the state at once directing the course of reform, mitigating its possible adverse consequences, and retaining effective political and economic control. What transpired, however, was a process that outgrew the intentions of its initiators to such an extent that the purported 'cure' for the Soviet Union's economic difficulties – increasing labour productivity – became instead the engine of ideological change in labour and the catalyst for the delegitimization and dismantling of the Soviet system. In the end, the collapse of the USSR testified to the extent to which the leadership was overtaken and overwhelmed by the very forces it had unleashed.

The transformation of Soviet labour ideology

In contrast to conventional Gorbachev-centric views of change, I argue that the transformation of Soviet labour ideology, propelled by the search for greater productivity, in fact began under Andropov and underwent three distinct phases – moderate intra-systemic, radical intra-systemic and extra-systemic. The first of these encompassed the 'intensification' (*intensifikatsiya*) of the economy following Brezhnev's death and, after a short hiatus under Chernenko, Gorbachev's 'acceleration' (*uskorenie*) campaign during 1985–87. *Intensifikatsiya* derived from a general consensus that falling economic growth rates and worsening labour shortages made unsustainable the 'extensive', resource- and labour-intensive, model of development that had served as the basis of Soviet economic policy since the 1930s. While there were differences of emphasis within the leadership, the regime believed at this stage that essentially fine-tuning reforms – a crackdown on worker indiscipline, more 'rational' norm-setting and planning methods, improved economic and social incentives – would be sufficient to stop the economic rot and revive the socialist vision. However, regime expectations were soon disabused. Although *intensifikatsiya* was not intended to undermine the command-administrative system or attack ideological icons such as the full employment doctrine, it highlighted massive waste, inefficiency and corruption throughout the Soviet economy. In the process, it asked searching questions about the nature and performance of labour in Soviet society. Genuine efforts were made to restore the productive content of labour and to counteract the notion of job as 'welfare entitlement' (Connor, 1991, p. 192). For the first time, notions of conditionality were introduced to the concept of full employment, as whole categories of redundant (or potentially redundant) labour were uncovered. In a stringent economic climate, unconditional, guaranteed full employment – long touted as one of the supreme achievements of Soviet socialism – became increasingly identified with overemployment, labour shortages and the non-fulfilment of economic objectives. The futility of attempting to implement 'normal', incremental, reforms in an abnormal (or distorted) system became increasingly apparent. There could be no significant improvements in labour productivity as long as existing economic mechanisms, structures and psychological habits remained unreformed. Confronted with the reality that Soviet economic difficulties could not be arrested by simple but superficial solutions, the Gorbachev regime came to recognize that the search for greater labour productivity entailed a wider quest for a more efficient economic system, capable of achieving socialism's ambitious social and economic objectives.

The enactment of the 1987 Law on the State Enterprise marked the beginning of the second, 'radical intra-systemic', phase in the transformation of Soviet labour ideology. Gorbachev sought to give new life to the search for labour productivity by returning to the fundamentals of what he termed Leninist democratic centralism.[1] Specifically, the leadership envisaged a better balance between central economic control and enterprise autonomy, based on the promotion of *chuvstvo khozyaina* – the citizen's sense of being master in work and life. At the same time, the renewed emphasis on principles of economic accountability (*khozraschet*) and self-financing (*samofinansirovanie*) was intended to introduce to enterprises heightened conceptions of responsibility and autonomy, as well as the need for greater responsiveness to consumer requirements. Although implementation of such ideas was half-hearted at best, their very introduction reflected the emergence of a much more critical attitude towards the use of labour resources. Whereas previously the debate over labour had been about restoring its productive content, now questions arose about its affordability within the enterprise and the need to release workers unable or unwilling to meet increased production demands. In sharp contrast to their symbiotic relationship in traditional Soviet ideology, there was now an increasing differentiation between labour (the performance of work) and employment (occupation of a work position). Recognition grew that the search for labour productivity necessitated proper consideration of the socioeconomic problems arising from large-scale labour release.

The emergence of new uncertainties and changing values brought out into the open two critical contradictions that were to have a decisive impact on the future of the Soviet Union. The first was the ever sharpening conflict between the state's persuit of equity and efficiency objectives. As it became clear that the quest for greater labour productivity must necessarily impact on the former, the radical intra-systemic period witnessed a marked decline in socialist paternalism, as the promise of an 'assured future' (Brezhnev, 1970, p. 3) was first diluted and then dissolved. The Soviet state's 'loyalty-solidarity' system (Lane, 1987, pp. 230–1), under which economic efficiency was subordinated to considerations of political stability and social welfare, gave ground to 'capitalist' notions of competition, freedom of enterprise, and individual self-reliance (including the idea that there must be 'losers' as well as 'winners' in a competitive society). The regime sought to alleviate these contradictions by redefining concepts of socialist social justice and by renegotiating the implicit social contract between the state and the people. However, it was unable to reconcile a renewed emphasis on productivity and accountability with its longstanding commitment to safeguard people's living standards and employment prospects. Instead, deteriorating economic performance was accompanied by increasingly serious shortages of consumer goods and services and a severely weakened social welfare net. By 1988, it was already evident that the regime was struggling to deliver on its socioeconomic promises, or even to ensure the continuation of the predictable (if often unattractive) rhythm of life that the Soviet citizen had 'enjoyed' under Brezhnev.

The second great contradiction during the latter years of the Gorbachev era was the tension between policies devolving rights and responsibilities to enterprises and the regime's desire to retain economic control. Although it by now recognized the ineffectualness of directive methods of economic management, it remained unwilling to cede the influence that accompanied the exercise of these powers. The outcome of such hesitancy and purposelessness was unfortunate if unsurprising:

the centre lost much of its capacity to manage economic policy and outcomes, while a new enterprise culture to replace command-administrative methods remained stillborn. Labour productivity declined further, and the mood of most workers during the last years of the Soviet era continued to be characterized by feelings of 'alienation' (*otchuzhdenie*) rather than *chuvstvo khozyaina*.

The political consequences of inconsistent economic direction, in which Soviet labour ideology became increasingly a set of *ad hoc* propositions, were all too evident: a regime in disarray, neither knowing its purpose (beyond a vague hope of economic recovery) nor how to achieve it; a declining economy; a growing lack of confidence, both within the regime itself, and by the general population in government. Regime prescriptions served not only to discredit specific policy proposals, but also Soviet socialist economic administration in general. What began as a circumscribed search for labour productivity was now exposing both the shallowness and fickleness of socialist dogma, and the impotence of the state in the face of mounting economic and political challenges. For the first time, a real sense arose of the state's vulnerability – that its authority could (indeed must) be successfully challenged.

The third, 'extra-systemic', phase (post-1990) coincided with the most overt signs of the transformation of Soviet labour ideology. In embracing market principles, albeit often tentatively, the regime effectively abandoned conventional socialist approaches to raising productivity. The evident failure of intra-systemic approaches (moderate and radical) stripped the Gorbachev administration of its 'ideological virginity' (Shmelev, 1987, p. 147), forcing it to search for a system – any system – that might offer solutions to arrest the Soviet Union's accelerating economic decline. In these circumstances, regime priorities changed from the quantitative maximization of labour resources – putting people to work – to minimizing and legitimizing the social consequences of rationalization – unemployment/non-employment. Official attitudes towards labour became dominated by short-term pragmatic considerations, as the regime's facade of ideological consensus broke down in an increasingly fractious political environment.

This last phase marked the effective, if protracted, surrender of the Soviet state. Although Gorbachev struggled to the bitter end, with hindsight it can be seen that his administration was mortally wounded as early as the 28th Party Congress in July 1990. By this time, it had lost any semblance of real control over the economy, a situation exacerbated by its continuing prevarication between 'market' prescriptions and the old command-administrative methods. Although the government continued to issue edicts and policy pronouncements, Soviet enterprises acted as they saw fit, free in the knowledge that the central authorities were unable and/or unwilling to impose their will through hard budget constraints. In the meantime, growing shortages led to increased autarkic tendencies within republics and regions, as local administrations sought to arrest plummeting living standards. The spectacle of economic anarchy in turn bred political chaos and social uncertainty. Faced by a Soviet leadership bereft of self-confidence and lacking the wherewithal or the will to reestablish its authority, new political forces emerged to fill the vacuum – Yeltsin in Moscow, and the republican power elites at the periphery.

Ideological transformation and the collapse of the state

It is a central thesis of this book that the regime's search for labour productivity was the major factor in the collapse of the Soviet state. However, this is not to argue that the USSR's pronounced economic decline from the late 1970s 'forced' the leadership to initiate wide-ranging reforms and, in so doing, 'proved' that the Soviet socialist/command-administrative system was intrinsically 'unviable'. In fact, there is every reason to suppose that, had the leadership not chosen to address the issue of declining labour productivity when it did, the Soviet Union could have muddled along for some time, albeit it with declining/negative growth rates, growing shortages of consumer and other goods, and chronic irresponsibility and apathy throughout society. There was nothing 'inevitable' about the choices Andropov and Gorbachev made, and the experience of post-Soviet Russia shows that the state or even an administration can survive even in the face of the most acute economic pressures and non-performance. The point is not that the situation in the Soviet Union in the early 1980s was 'objectively' unsustainable, but that the Soviet leadership believed (i) it should no longer be tolerated without some effort at redress; and (ii) it could be remedied 'intra-systemically' – that is, without touching upon the foundations of the system or impinging on the legitimacy of the CPSU's state rule.

Similarly, it needs to be emphasized from the outset that economic crisis *by itself* was insufficient to bring about the collapse of the state. The critical factor was the regime's increasingly chaotic and uncertain policy responses which, far more than the economic problems themselves, highlighted the vulnerability of the Soviet ruling caste and opened it up to the possibility of successful challenge. Unwittingly, the Gorbachev administration accelerated the pace of its demise by enlisting democratization and *glasnost* in the struggle to raise labour productivity. In bringing political liberalization into the equation, it fundamentally altered the nature of legitimacy in Soviet society. Whereas previously this had centred on the regime's ability to commit 'enormous powers of coercion, control and manipulation' (Bialer, 1988, pp. 269–70), it now became much more contingent on public popularity and support, itself dependent on the fulfilment of core socioeconomic objectives. Growing public awareness of poor government performance was matched by the Gorbachev administration's sense of its own weakness, as successive policy failures eroded its self-confidence and ability to rule. It was in this political–psychological context that the republics felt able to delink themselves from Moscow and that Yeltsin and the so-called 'pro-capitalist coalition' (Kotz and Weir, 1997, p. 8) developed the confidence to usurp many of the functions formerly the preserve of the central authorities and, eventually, to supersede the Soviet state.

The idea that the search for labour productivity acted as the engine of the Soviet state's delegitimization and dismantling challenges the popular explanation that gives primacy to the regime's progressive abdication of regime controls over information, assembly and expression, in response to mounting political, cultural and ethnic pressures. This theory suffers from much the same problem as the 'economic' explanation: it assumes the regime was 'forced' into behaving in the way it did, and ascribes disproportionate influence to popular forces for change.[2] A careful examination of the events of the last decade of the USSR reveals, however, that there was nothing inherently irresistible about such 'pressures'. For example, although the ethnic factor had been a constant throughout the Soviet era, it did not assume any particular urgency, let alone volatility, until well into the Gorbachev period – that is, some time after the search for labour productivity had been initiated. Indeed, as Moshe Lewin (1995, p. 271, cited in Kotz and Weir, 1997, p. 142) has pointed out, the growth of ethnic nationalism was more a product than a cause of the loosening of regime controls. Similarly, the according of political freedoms through *glasnost* and democratization was hardly made under duress. The impact of the dissident movement was feeble at this time, while the general population, although undoubtedly more politically aware than previous generations, by no means constituted a hotbed of sedition and revolt that needed to be placated. Just the opposite in fact. One of the tasks that Andropov and then Gorbachev set themselves was to galvanize an apathetic population into activity. Thus, democratization, *glasnost* and political liberalization were introduced, less for their intrinsic value, than because they were seen as critical to efforts to increase productivity through devolution of decision-making and the inculcation of *chuvstvo khozyaina*. It was only after their unsuccessful introduction to the workplace that the leadership upped the ante and extended the project of democratization to the wider political arena. Even then, as Gorbachev (1996, p. 569) has admitted, its rationale was principally economic: the successful introduction and implementation of 'innovative' measures was contingent on a 'a radical reconstruction of the political system'.[3]

Finally, it should be noted that the nexus outlined in this book between the search for higher productivity, ideological transformation, and the collapse of the Soviet state, seeks to modify two other common explanations of the USSR's demise: (i) the triumphalist view that the Soviet Union buckled in response to the arms race pressure exerted by the Reagan administration in the early 1980s;[4] and (ii) the assertion that the state socialist system was brought down by a 'pro-capitalist' section of the elite which deserted and deliberately dismantled it in a 'revolution from above'.[5]

Both these theories seem to me to be careless about timing and lacking in logic. The first rests on the highly dubious assumption that the Soviet leadership underwent a 'road to Damascus' conversion under duress, and ignores the fact that many of the economic prescriptions introduced under Andropov and Gorbachev were already being presented as state policy in the mid-1960s by then Soviet Prime Minister Kosygin. It also disregards the well-documented reality that the switch from extensive to intensive methods of economic development was prompted principally by the sharp decline in Soviet growth rates from the late 1970s and the accompanying depletion of labour and natural resources. Certainly, as Andropov himself observed (see Chapter 2), such internal strains acquired additional urgency in the circumstances of growing superpower tensions in the early 1980s. However, the leadership was less bothered about specifically competing with the American economy, than about the Soviet Union's failure to keep pace with past performance in accordance with the dictates of Stalinist 'forced growth strategy'.[6]

The 'revolution from above' theory ascribes excessive importance to the alleged deideologization of the Soviet governing elite. It is true that many members of the senior *nomenklatura* were profoundly cynical about many socialist ideological 'truths'. However, it is wrong to suggest that '[b]y the 1980s ideology had long since ceased to have any real significance for most of the Soviet elite' (Kotz and Weir, 1997, p. 6), for this underestimates the important instrumental role that ideology played in the Soviet polity – as a vital means of control and legitimacy. While Yeltsin and the 'pro-capitalist coalition' undoubtedly deserted the state socialist system and sought to undermine it, particularly during 1990–91, they clearly did so in the belief that the old regime no longer served their purposes and was ripe for the plucking. Although the full impact of Russia's economic disintegration had yet to be felt, the extent of the Gorbachev administration's loss of control was already widely apparent. It is significant that the pro-Yeltsin camp felt able to launch a public challenge to the Gorbachev administration only after the economy had fallen apart, and when the regime and its policies were in a state of rout. While the actions of Yeltsin and his political allies contributed to accelerating the end of the Soviet state, their political and economic opportunism was far from being the prime cause of its collapse.

The story of the regime's search for labour productivity, the transformation of labour ideology that accompanied it, and the decline and fall of the Soviet state system, was in many ways a story of tragic heroism. The Soviet leadership refused to accept, as it so easily could have done, the Brezhnevian status quo of declining growth rates, poor labour productivity, and growing irresponsibility and amorality in society. First Andropov, then Gorbachev, perceived a need to tackle these problems on the basis of improved labour productivity, hoping through this for a restoration of economic fortunes and socialist ethics and morality. Instead, however, their well-motivated efforts served only to expose the extent of the system's rottenness and corruption, thereby effectively undermining both the illusion and substance of Soviet power. Although other factors – the rise of ethnic nationalism, political liberalization, the ascent of Yeltsin and his supporters – all contributed to the USSR's demise, the original engine of change was the refusal of first Andropov and then Gorbachev to accept Brezhnevian 'stagnation' (*zastoi*) and mediocrity as the country's inevitable lot, and their consequent attempts to arrest what they considered to be an unacceptable economic situation. The search for labour productivity – and the ideological transformation it spawned – was the critical precursor that provided both the reason and the opportunity for other forces for change to come into play.

Methodological approach

I have adopted a mixed methodology incorporating functional categorizations within a largely chronological approach. For most of the period covered by this book, the labels 'socialist morality', 'planning–techno-cratic' and 'incentive–humanistic' have been used to describe general prescriptions introduced by the regime to raise labour productivity, rather than applied more specifically (and more arbitrarily) to individual personalities and their alleged reformist or conservative credentials.

'Socialist morality' equates to proposals whose underlying premise was that Soviet economic difficulties were primarily attributable to individual moral weakness – absenteeism, 'parasitism', drunkenness, general slackness on the job. The description, 'planning–technocratic', refers to prescriptions founded in the logic that 'better' (that is, more detailed and precise) central planning was the key to Soviet economic performance. The primacy of planning was, in turn, reinforced by an implicit faith in scientific–technological progress (STP) and the cultiva-tion of the 'new type of worker' through improved education and training. Finally, what I have called the 'incentive–humanistic' approach towards labour productivity derived from the notion of the Soviet worker as a social being with particular, if not especially heroic, needs and desires. It recognized the limitations (and eventually futility) of methods based on coercion and the 'communist vision', and instead sought to stimulate better work by appealing to the worker's material self-interest – through extra pay, the introduction of performance- and skill-based wage differentials, and greater availability of purchaseable goods and services.

These functional categorizations inform the structure of the chapters about labour ideology in the Andropov, Chernenko and early Gorba-chev periods (Chapters 2 to 4). The structure of Chapter 5 on labour ideology in Gorbachev's radical intra-systemic phase focuses much more directly on the regime's growing use of incentive–humanistic methods, and considers their implications for socialist social justice and employ-ment policy. In Chapter 6 – on labour ideology during the last 18 months of the Soviet era – various political–functional categorizations[7] will be used, in recognition of the emergence of a new brand of confrontational politics marked by open and bitter policy disagree-ments. The final chapter, on labour issues in the new Russia, reflects the particular political fractiousness of post-Soviet society by identifying and evaluating some of the principal issues and debates – macroeco-nomic stabilization versus structural policy, shock therapy versus gradu-alism, and the issue of political risk.

There are several obvious advantages to a broadly chronological approach. First, it brings out the essentially linear nature of the trans-formation of Soviet labour ideology during this period: from relative stasis under Brezhnev, through intensification during the Andropov period, to the momentous and accelerating changes under Gorbachev and Yeltsin. The framework such a chronology provides is sufficiently flexible and capacious to take account of the cross-sectional/class diversity in labour attitudes. Despite the existence of policy fluctuations and turnarounds that often marked the regime's approach, each of the periods covered by the chapters in this book gave rise to particular themes and trends that distinguished it from the others. At the same time, all of these periods are comprehensible as stages in the inexorable transformation of official attitudes towards the role and nature of labour in Soviet and post-Soviet society.

A chronological/functional approach also avoids the obvious pitfall of imposing inappropriate political and/or ideological labels to stereotype peculiarly Soviet phenomena. In focusing on concrete government policies and actions, rather than on tenuous generalized assumptions about the alleged ideological and institutional biases of key players, it treats contrasting prescriptions on their own merits (or demerits) and eschews the temptation to overestimate the degree of tension and conflict within the ruling elite. It is worth noting here that policy differences on various social and economic issues did not necessarily reflect particular ideological or political inclinations, and that many contemporary Soviet commentaries on labour questions offered policy prescriptions derived from apparently contradictory sources of inspiration. Furthermore, the *ad hoc* nature of policy formulation and implementation makes it hard to prove the existence of a conscious association between specific prescriptions and overall political orientation, certainly at least until the later Gorbachev period when ideas of *glasnost* and political democratization took firm root, and the centre's loss of political and economic control became evident to all.

Finally, a chronological approach lends itself naturally to portraying change; *ipso facto*, it is a dynamic rather than static paradigm. Because it does not seek to impose absolute definitions it does not suffer from the problem of time-specificity that dogs the use of inflexible and subjective categorizations such as 'liberal', 'reformist' and 'radical'. A chronological approach is more able to accommodate ideological inconstancies whereby the 'radicals' of one era became, in many cases, the 'reformists' or even the 'conservatives' of the next.[8] The inevitable policy contradictions within each period are reconciled by recognizing the existence of the numerous dichotomies that influenced practically every aspect of regime ideology and daily life. Indeed, it is possible to view the development of Soviet labour ideology from Andropov to Gorbachev as a series of outcomes resulting from the (largely unsatisfactory) resolution of fundamental tensions: equity and efficiency; central control versus devolution; plan and market; continuity and change.

Definitional note

One of the principal problems when discussing the transformation of Soviet labour ideology is that of definition: what do we understand by the 'social contract', the 'welfare state', 'legitimacy', 'power', 'the market'? Indeed, what is Soviet labour ideology? It is therefore useful to establish from the outset what we mean by such terms.

Soviet labour ideology

I have used this term to embrace official concepts of, and attitudes towards, the role, nature and performance of labour in Soviet society. More generally, I have followed Alex Pravda's (1988, p. 239) understanding of ideology as a 'predispositional influence' on decision-makers in policy-making, for example, in labour and welfare policy. Thus, the regime's 'ideological commitment to full employment' explained much of its reluctance to tackle the adverse economic consequences of 'absolute job security'.[9]

The question of ideology leads on naturally to the issue of the regime's ideological conviction. Most commentators have tended to impute a substantial measure of cynicism in the incantations of Soviet leaders, and with good reason. Moshe Lewin (1991, p. 238), for example, has denied that Soviet leaders over the previous 20 years or so were 'even remotely possessed' of a 'messianic' ideal: 'The Soviet Communist Party was an organisation dedicated to the maintenance of the status quo; one which used the founding fathers' terminology, but which took great care to ensure that terms like "Marxism" and "Socialism" were emasculated and completely destroyed as meaningful ideas.' On the other hand, other writers have credited the state with at least some ideological sincerity. Thus, David Lane (1987, pp. 11–12) uses the expression, 'the Protestant ethic of socialism', to describe the labour ideology of 'Soviet Marxism'.

In this book, the question of whether ideology was genuine or a sham is secondary. The key point is the extent to which ideological tenets 'predisposed' regime behaviour in favour of or against particular policies. It was entirely possible for members of the leadership to have lost affection for traditional socialist values, but nevertheless to understand the importance of ideology in rationalizing and consolidating political power. In the area of labour, for example, this would oblige the state to aid loss-making enterprises and prevent the laying-off of workers, even while the leadership remained privately dismissive about the fiction of the 'workers' state'.

The 'social contract' and the welfare state

The 'social contract' and the welfare state are not only significant ideas in themselves, but they also provide a broader ideological context in which to analyse the transformation of Soviet labour ideology from its traditional base of the full employment doctrine, to acceptance of 'capitalist-style' unemployment as a permanent feature of the socioeconomic landscape.

These concepts present particular definitional problems. The terms 'social contract' and 'welfare state' are foreign, imported by non-Soviet commentators to categorize phenomena for which Soviet literature had no ready-made labels.[10] Thus, Linda Cook (1992, p. 37) describes the 'social contract' as an arrangement whereby the regime provided the working class with 'full and secure employment, egalitarian wage policies and lax performance pressures in industry, state-controlled and heavily subsidised retail prices for essential goods, and socialised human services', in exchange for its 'political compliance and quiescence'.[11] By contrast, Ken Jowitt (1993, p. 27) debunks the notion of a 'social contract' as '[o]ne of the most misleading characterizations of the Brezhnev period,' asserting instead that the nexus between regime and society was that of a 'protection racket' in which the former played a 'parasitical' role and the latter that of 'scavenger'. The question of the existence (or otherwise) of a social contract is intimately linked to that of whether the Soviet Union could properly be called a welfare state. Ed Hewett (1988, p. 2) applied the term to describe the 'massive' economic security enjoyed by Soviet citizens. On the other hand, others (Kornai, 1992, pp. 326–7) have pointed out the undeniable fact that welfare expenditure in socialist economies tended to be residual (*ostatochny*) in nature, emphasized in periods of prosperity but neglected in difficult times.

Clearly the 'social contract' under Brezhnev bore no relation to the original Rousseauian ideal, freely entered into and based on equal exchange; it was imposed by the state and heavily biased towards state interests, delivering often uncertain benefits to the population. That said, Soviet social policy from Brezhnev to Gorbachev showed the imprint of key elements of an implicit social contract – full employment, job security, cheap (if often unavailable) consumer goods, a narrowing of income differentials, and a slackening of work pressure. The reluctance of Soviet leaders to countenance unemployment or the freeing of prices because of the destabilizing political and economic consequences of such actions, hints strongly at the existence of an informal social bargain and related expectations. Similarly, use of the term 'welfare state' in this book in no way implies a judgement as to its effectiveness or efficiency. The essential point is that the state considered itself responsible for providing these services. While it may have been motivated more by a perceived need to retain control than by feelings of philanthropy, it was overwhelmingly paternalist in its orientation and delivered (albeit often very poorly) welfare benefits touching nearly every aspect of daily life. The upshot was a 'cradle-to-grave social security' (Breslauer, 1991, p. 638) that provided the population, at a basic level, with a safety blanket unparalleled in Western experience.

Legitimacy and power

The question of legitimacy has always been contentious, perhaps nowhere more so than in the Soviet context. Stephen White (1979, p. 189) defined it as 'uncoerced support' for a regime or government, while on the other hand Seweryn Bialer (1988, pp. 269–70) argued that the Soviet version was characterized by the 'commitment of enormous powers of coercion, control and manipulation at the disposal of the regime'. In effect, the former definition understood legitimacy as a 'popular legitimacy' based on the acquisition and retention of public support, while the latter proposed a power–legitimacy nexus, in which regime stability was assured as long as the will to rule of the leadership and political elite remained strong.

In this book, the power–legitimacy nexus will be understood generally in terms of the regime's capacity to ensure substantial popular compliance with its wishes, whether through the exercise of state authority, the inculcation of an ideological vision, or the provision of socioeconomic benefits. Accordingly, the regime's loss of power and legitimacy during this period is understood simply as a growing inability to retain political and economic control. It follows from this that the nature of legitimation may be dynamic and unstable. If legitimacy and power depend on the leadership 'acting within the pattern of values of society and through the accepted norms of the political system' (Lane, 1991, p. 96), then it is equally true that as society's values change, so do forms of legitimation. In noting that the validity of many traditional sources of legitimacy may be undermined under the impact of modernization and growing consumerism, Lane (ibid., p. 96) correctly discerned a major shift in the organization of state socialist society from 'ideologically driven' to 'interest driven'.

The market, market socialism and the socialist market

According to Kornai (1992, p. 500), the market is based on the 'affinity between private property and market coordination', and functions on the basis of the 'discipline' of cut-throat competition in which the price of failure is bankruptcy. He (ibid., p. 477) asserted that a market without such discipline is no market at all, but rather 'market socialism' or 'plan-cum-market' – a hybrid of capitalism and socialism in which each is supposed to compensate for the other's shortcomings. Central planning and control intervene when the market needs to be corrected for social welfare reasons, while the market alerts central planners to faulty decisions that harm the interests of buyers and sellers.

However, many Soviet reformist economists used the term, 'market', simply to denote the existence of supply and demand relations (or 'commodity–money relations'), no matter how rudimentary or imperfect. Under this interpretation, the concept of 'market' was not only compatible with 'market socialism' (or the 'socialist market') with its multiple forms of ownership, but integral to it (Shmelev and Popov, 1990, p. 216). For simplicity's sake, therefore, I have used the word 'market' in a relatively narrow supply and demand sense, for example, 'labour market', unless specifically stated otherwise. Kornai's conception of the 'market' will be expressed as 'market economy'. 'Market socialism' will denote a mixed economy where market forces predominate, and 'socialist market' where these are subordinate to planning methods. Finally, the term 'marketization' describes progress towards a market economy.

Note on primary sources

This book focuses mainly on the views of the political, intellectual and bureaucratic elite, rather than of the population generally. In the case of the first named, the pronouncements of Soviet leaders from Brezhnev to Gorbachev have been carefully surveyed from various sources: daily newspapers (in particular, *Pravda* and *Izvestiya*), volumes of collected speeches, the proceedings of the Supreme Soviet and Congress of People's Deputies. The same sources have also been useful in providing the texts of various policy resolutions, decrees, laws, and other official documents.

Second, and mindful of the vital role played by academic economists in the reformulation of Soviet labour ideology, I have drawn extensively from specialist economics and sociological journals such as *Voprosy ekonomiki*, *EKO*, and *Sotsiologicheskie issledovaniya*, as well as from Party publications such as *Kommunist*.

Daily and weekly newspapers, as well as academic journals, were also a fertile ground for the frequently expressed views of bureaucrats whose role as propagandists and implementers of labour policies was critical. Within the ambit of the bureaucracy, I include the official trade union establishment which, for most of the period under review, played an integral role in economic and social administration.

2
Andropov and the Intensification of Labour

'[The Andropov phenomenon] was... a repudiation of all that was associated with Brezhnevism in the minds of the people, along with the conviction that reform was imperative and inevitable.'

Mikhail Gorbachev (1996, p. 153)

Introduction

Most analyses of Soviet reform focus overwhelmingly on the spectacular changes of the Gorbachev period. The rationale for this approach derives from one of two basic assumptions. The first argues that there was little attempt to reform the Soviet system before Gorbachev became General Secretary in April 1985. Gorbachev broke with his political heritage by embarking on a wide-ranging political and economic restructuring of the Soviet system. *Glasnost* and *perestroika* were emblematic of new directions in domestic and foreign policy, and Gorbachev himself emerged as a man of revolutionary rather than evolutionary bent. Consistent with the magnification of Gorbachev, the role of his immediate predecessors, Yurii Andropov and Konstantin Chernenko, is minimized. Jan Adam (1993, p. 193) dismisses them thus: 'In 1983 [sic], L. Brezhnev died and his two successors followed more or less in his footsteps.'

The other major premise underlying the Gorbachev-centric view of change in the Soviet Union was outlined by Ed Hewett (1988, p. 258). While giving greater weight to Andropov in the development of Soviet economic reform, he nevertheless concluded that his time 'was too short to do much more than register dissatisfaction. The significance of the brief Andropov period lay not in substance, but in the tone he set for his successors.' Similarly, Tatyana Zaslavskaya (1990, p. 46) has argued that Andropov 'succeeded only in engendering hope for the desired changes and creating a breath of spiritual fresh air in the stale social atmosphere'. In short, although Andropov's failure to engage in significant reforms was caused by lack of opportunity, and not lack of inclination, his influence on the reform process was nonetheless limited and peripheral.

This chapter seeks to qualify such Gorbachev-centric views of change. It argues that the Andropov era marked a critical stage in the development of regime ideology by creating a political environment that both facilitated and stimulated subsequent change. This was nowhere more evident than in the evolution of attitudes towards the nature and function of labour in society, on which the quintessential idea of the Soviet Union as workers' state was based. Under Andropov there was a radical departure from the formalism and complacency of the Brezhnev era. Far from following in his predecessor's footsteps, he made a concerted effort to revive labour values and restore meaning to the concept of *chuvstvo khozyaina* – the individual as master in work and life. While most of Andropov's socioeconomic agenda remained unfulfilled during his short term in office, his impact on the reform process extended far beyond the mere identification of economic weaknesses and 'setting the tone' for Gorbachev. The evolution in labour ideology over which he presided assisted the introduction of many Gorbachev policies by providing a more variegated, flexible and receptive context in which reformist ideas could be introduced and developed. By extending the boundaries of the ideologically permissible in the socioeconomic sphere, Andropov also indirectly (if unwittingly) challenged the existing system of economic management and relations, and labour's role in it. Within this paradigm, the imperatives of reformulating labour ideology and restructuring the economic mechanism in accordance with the requirements of a modern complex economy were closely intertwined. The need for a more flexible interpretation of the role of labour in Soviet society increased pressures to restructure the economy, while, in turn, the restructuring of economic relations served to undermine such traditional and previously largely unchallenged assumptions as the notion of job as 'welfare entitlement' (Connor, 1991, p. 192) and the full employment doctrine. The outcome of these mutually reinforcing tendencies did not emerge until well into the Gorbachev period, but their symptoms were already discernible under Andropov.

This chapter is divided into three sections. The first outlines the *status quo ante* of Soviet labour ideology before its transformation under

Andropov and Gorbachev. Second, I discuss the negative socioeconomic phenomena that pushed the Soviet leadership into embarking on the search for higher labour productivity. The final section examines the economic prescriptions introduced during the Andropov period, and assesses their importance in the transformation of Soviet labour ideology.

The place of labour in Soviet socialism

Labour's centrality as the dominant ethos of the Soviet state was perhaps best expressed by Brezhnev (1972, p. 5) on the occasion of the 50th anniversary of the USSR in December 1972: 'what we are building is not a realm of idlers where the land flows with milk and honey, but the most organized and most hard-working society in the history of mankind.' The idea of the Soviet Union as the 'workers' state', consisting 'only of working classes and social groups' (Brezhnev, 1977, p. 2),[1] was the philosophical foundation underpinning Soviet attitudes towards labour on the eve of reforms initiated by Andropov.

In its classical, pre-reform incarnation, Soviet labour ideology was based on several fundamental tenets, outlined most notably in the 1977 Soviet Constitution and the 1970 Principles of Labour Legislation. First, labour was viewed as the instrument which ensured the practical viability of socialism. Article 14 of the Constitution (*Konstitutsiya SSSR...*, 1982, p. 66) declared that '[t]he free, non-exploited labour of the Soviet people is the source of growth in social wealth, and of the welfare of the people and each Soviet person.' The second ideological pillar was the notion that labour was 'free' and could not be bought or sold like a commodity. Contrary to the case under capitalism where workers were 'oppressed' by the bosses in the latter's quest to maximize surplus value,[2] the socialist system ensured that Soviet workers enjoyed the 'freedom from exploitation' that was the 'basic condition' of the individual's 'genuine freedom' (Osnovy zakonodateltsva...o trude', Pravda, 17 July 1970, p. 1). The principle of 'freedom from exploitation' based on the non-commodification of labour was especially important, not only in differentiating socialist and capitalist modes of production, but also in supporting the overwhelming preponderance of state and collective forms of ownership in the Soviet economy.[3] Although 'individual labour activity' (*individualnaya trudovaya deyatelnost*) was permitted under Article 17 of the Constitution (*Konstitutsiya SSSR...*, 1982, p. 72), it was essentially restricted to the 'personal labour of citizens and family members' in handicrafts, individual farm plots, and services. The official political–legal commentary on the Constitution (ibid., p. 73) condemned the idea of hired labour as leading to its 'alienation' (*otchuzhdenie*) and thereby contradicting 'the very essence of the socialist social system'.

'Free' though it purported to be, the performance of labour in Soviet society was bound up with the universal obligation to work. Article 14 of the Constitution (ibid., p. 66) asserted that '[s]ocially useful labour and its results define the individual's position in society', and spoke of transforming labour into the 'prime life-need of each Soviet person'.[4] The requirement to work was outlined even more emphatically in Article 60 (ibid., p. 185): 'Conscientious labour in a freely chosen area of socially useful activity...is a duty and a matter of honour for each USSR citizen able to work. Avoidance of socially useful labour is incompatible with the principles of socialist society.' Non-employment was equated with 'parasitism' (*tuneyadstvo*), criminal behaviour, or educational and cultural backwardness (as in the case of the rural non-employed of Central Asia and the Caucasus) (Perevedentsev, 1976, p. 2).

The universal obligation to work derived logically from the linkage between labour performance and quality of life, individual and collective. Although the warning in Stalin's 1936 Constitution that 'he who does not work shall not eat' (*Konstitutsiya SSSR...*, 1982, p. 185) was softened in the 1977 version, the axiom, 'from each according to their ability, to each according to their work' (ibid., p. 66), remained a cornerstone of Soviet labour ideology. This dictum provided both the basis for socialist concepts of social equality and justice (ibid., p. 188), as well as a precept according to which the measure of accumulation (the production of national wealth) and the measure of consumption (the satisfaction of people's needs) were balanced (ibid., p. 66).

Just as the obligation to work arose naturally from the direct connection between the performance of labour and improved living standards, so the full employment doctrine stemmed from the unacceptability of non-work. If people had a duty to perform socially useful labour, then the state had an equal duty to ensure that this obligation could be fulfilled. Moreover, since income levels were tied to work performance, it followed that 'every member of society able to work must have the possibility of doing so' (Kotlyar, 1991, p. 108). Article 40 of the 1977 Constitution (*Konstitutsiya SSSR...*, 1982, pp. 140–1) reiterated the citizen's right to work, adding to it his/her right to choose a vocation, 'taking into account social requirements'. Full employment was 'guaranteed' in the first instance by the nature of socialist planning which enabled the state to foresee labour demand and achieve the 'optimum correlation between consumption and accumulation' (Manevich, 1969, p. 31). In other words, Soviet workers were protected from the cyclical and anarchic fluctuations in supply and demand that caused unemployment in capitalist economies. Second, full employment was supported by the 'steady growth of productive forces' (*Konstitutsiya SSSR...*, 1982, p. 141). Vasilii Selyunin wrote in 1967 (p. 11) that 'under socialism there is no such thing as an overproduction crisis'. Even in the event of industry restructuring, the consequent release of labour would be absorbed by the economy's 'infinite expansion of output'.

Such socioeconomic rationalizations of full employment were reinforced by the 'socialist conception of human rights' (Maltsev, 1974, p. 15). The right to work was presented as 'the basis of the entire system of rights of the Soviet citizen' (*Konstitutsiya SSSR...*, 1982, p. 140). In implementing it, the socialist state enabled individuals to become productive members of society and to develop self-esteem by realizing their creative and intellectual potential (ibid., p. 67). There was no contradiction between the pursuit of economic efficiency and prosperity, and social justice and welfare. On the contrary, equity and efficiency objectives were mutually reinforcing. The more efficiently and productively people worked, the more social benefits they obtained (Maltsev, 1974, p. 13). In the case of full employment, the equity–efficiency balance was reached by protecting workers from lay-offs, while fully utilizing labour in the pursuit of continued economic growth. The principal challenge of STP, then, was to improve worker training and retraining. This would satisfy the constantly growing need for more skilled workers and facilitate their transfer to the non-production (services) sphere. Far from threatening the implementation of the right to work, the mechanization and automation of labour emphasized its importance, while enhancing the worker's job satisfaction and quality of life.

The implementation of full employment was not only seen as achieving important economic and social objectives, but it also served to legitimize the Soviet regime by highlighting the 'fortunate' position of Soviet workers compared to their Western counterparts, as well as the 'superiority' of socialism over capitalism in general (*Konstitutsiya SSSR...*, 1982, pp. 142–3). Whereas unemployment in the USSR had ceased to exist after 1930 (ibid., p. 141), there were some 20 million people out of work in capitalist countries by the early 1980s (ibid., p. 143). In this way, the Soviet Union's persona as the workers' state, characterized by the quantitative maximization of labour, was counterposed by the image of the socialist state as benign paternalist entity.

Brezhnev (1970, p. 3) boasted, in a speech celebrating the 100th anniversary of Lenin's birth, that Soviet society was the 'embodiment in fact of the ideas of proletarian, socialist humanism,' and that one of the 'supreme achievements' of socialism was the fact that 'every Soviet person is assured of his future'.

The impulse to change – negative phenomena in the Soviet economy

Traditional Soviet labour ideology dismissed the possibility that the economic and social objectives of socialism were in any way incompatible. In practice, however, there were serious contradictions. Andropov inherited from Brezhnev a rapidly deteriorating socioeconomic situation, most graphically illustrated by the continuing fall in economic growth rates.[5] The extent of Soviet economic difficulties was summarized by the reformist ecoonomist Abel Aganbegyan in a roundtable discussion in *EKO* on 'perfecting the economic mechanism' (August 1983, pp. 16–49). In particular, he (ibid., p. 19) observed that a whole host of important questions remained 'unresolved': the balancing of economic plans; the transition to planning on the basis of the five-year plan; the vested interest of enterprises in adopting taut production tasks; and the accelerated introduction of scientific achievements in production. He also highlighted the continued petty interference (*melochnaya opeka*) of industrial ministries in production activity, and the unhealthy dominance of producers over consumers.

The problems identified by Aganbegyan reflected the influence of certain negative phenomena, the seriousness of which was to provide the impulse to major changes in Soviet economic policy generally, and labour ideology specifically. Before discussing the evolution of policy and ideological responses, therefore, it would be useful to outline briefly four major problems that confronted Andropov upon his accession as General Secretary in November 1982. They were: (i) the exhaustion of labour resources; (ii) the Soviet Union's technological backwardness; (iii) the decline of labour ethics and socialist norms; and (iv) the problem of irresponsibility.

The exhaustion of labour resources

The problem of labour resources arose out of the origins of the full employment doctrine and its nexus with the problem of labour shortage. The guaranteed right to work, proclaimed by many Soviet and non-Soviet commentators as the outstanding achievement of socialism, developed in response to perceived economic imperatives during the 1930s, in particular, the need to create 'the material basis of communism' (Lane, 1987, p. 13). Following the abandonment of the NEP, Stalin's pursuit of accelerated industrialization effectively determined an 'extensive' economic strategy based on the exhaustive utilization of cheap and abundant human resources. The eradication of unemployment became less an end in itself, than a ready means of supplying additional labour for industrial expansion.

The extensive model of development, based on full employment, determined Soviet economic policy for the next half century. Throughout this period, the Soviet economy was distinguished by an 'output-oriented' approach to growth, in which labour demand was subordinated to planned output targets and production capacity (Malle, 1990, p. 97). The priority given to mobilizing vast labour reserves to sustain Stalin's industrialization programme meant, in a sense, that there could never be 'too much' labour. The result – fulfilment or over-fulfilment of ever more ambitious gross output norms (*val*) – was all-important, while the means, provided they were socialist and not 'exploitative', were secondary (Aganbegyan, 1973, p. 2). Driven by the pursuit of the 'infinite expansion of output', every enterprise had an interest in accumulating excess labour in order to guarantee achievement of its production targets. Overstaffing helped to insulate it from variations in the production plan, problems in the supply of certain inputs, the secondment of personnel for non-primary tasks (such as helping out with the harvest), as well as from everyday concerns such as worker sickness, absenteeism and sub-standard performance. In these circumstances, the enterprise became more resource-utilizer than producer of goods for which real demand (in the market sense) existed. The economic use of resources was discouraged both by the double counting of consumed means of production (adding the costs of inputs to the value of finished production), and by the consideration that the more human and material resources absorbed by the enterprise, the larger were its wage and material incentive funds. As Shmelev and Popov (1990, p. 133) pointed out, quantitative indicators were an incentive to 'overstate outlays of all kinds'.

The emphasis on extensive methods in achieving ever higher production targets created what Janos Kornai (1980, p. 389) described as a 'resource-constrained economy', in which production growth was matched by the steady expansion of employment. Eventually, Kornai posited, the latter would hit 'labour supply constraints' as sources of additional workers dried up, and labour shortage would ensue. However, it was not until Soviet economic growth rates began to decline significantly in the late 1970s that the problem of labour shortage assumed serious dimensions in official consciousness. Deteriorating economic performance directed attention to the workforce's increasing inability to satisfy planner demands and to ways of reversing this trend. By the time Andropov came to power, the discrepancy between the regime's theoretical adherence to a forced growth strategy and the decline in actual economic growth rates had become painfully apparent, while worsening demographic indices heightened awareness about resource constraints in general (Gorbachev, 1988a, pp. 19–20). Policy makers and thinkers began to reappraise more critically than ever before resource allocation and utilization, and the role of planning in the economic mechanism as a whole. The problem of labour shortage[6] became closely associated with other negative phenomena, namely the Soviet Union's technological backwardness, the decline of labour ethics, and the problem of irresponsibility.

The Soviet Union's technological backwardness

The growing constraints on labour resources sharpened the focus on the Soviet Union's technological backwardness in both a relative and an absolute sense. Despite the emphasis in Brezhnevian 'developed socialism' on STP as a means of achieving economic and social goals, the gap between rhetoric and reality had widened by the time Andropov came to power. For all the talk about the organization of 'precise systems of planning' (Kosygin, 1966, p. 3) and 'automated management systems' (Brezhnev, 1976, p. 6), the USSR economy remained highly resource-intensive, particularly in its use of raw materials and energy (Abalkin, 1983b, p. 32). At the same time, the traditional emphasis on new capital construction effectively constrained the modernization of equipment at existing enterprises (Kotlyar, 1983, p. 109).

One consequence of the Soviet Union's technological backwardness was the exceptionally high proportion – 40 per cent – of the workforce engaged in manual labour (Bordukov, 1983, p. 2). According to Andropov (1983, p. 16), the 'large number of physically heavy, unattractive, routine jobs, the slow rate of their mechanization, let alone automatization' was the reason why Marx's 'first law on the basis of collective production, the law of economizing working time,' had not yet been fully implemented. This problem was made more acute in a climate of increased superpower tensions. A joint Party and Government Resolution on STP in the economy noted that the development of science and technology acquired 'particular significance' as 'one of the principal directions of competition between the socialist and capitalist systems' [*Pravda*, 28 August 1983, p. 1].

While the concept of STP was not new, the combination of endogenous (the running down of resources) and exogenous factors (heightened superpower tensions post-detente) in the early 1980s imbued it with a new qualitative significance. Under Brezhnev, Soviet technological backwardness had been arguably a problem of more socioideological than direct economic importance. STP functioned as a major plank in the mythology of 'developed socialism', allegedly homogenizing society by breaking down the barriers between city and country, and between mental and manual labour. After Andropov came to power, the direct causal link between technological backwardness and Soviet economic difficulties became much more pronounced in contemporary speeches and writings. In these circumstances, implementation of STP became a matter of considerably greater urgency, concentrating on the immediate need to use human and material resources more rationally.

The decline of labour ethics and socialist norms

The theme of the Soviet worker's declining labour ethic occupied a central place in analyses of Soviet economic problems on the eve of Andropov's accession. Zaslavskaya (1990, p. 18) thus commented: '(m)oral decay ran extremely deep. The borderlines between good and evil, mercy and cruelty, human feelings and people's alienation from one another, began to disappear from public consciousness.' By the early 1980s, the problem was no longer simply a moral conundrum, but rather an issue with far-reaching economic consequences. The popular aphorism, 'they pretend to pay, we pretend to work', described a situation in which a 'communist attitude towards labour' and the 'Protestant ethic of socialism' (Lane, 1987, p. 12) had given way to the notion of job as welfare.

Criticisms of worker slackness were hardly new. A famous 1976 survey of Leningrad workers revealed that only 30 per cent of those questioned considered they were working at full capacity (Yadov, 1983, p. 58). However, as with the problem of technological backwardness, the decline of the Soviet labour ethic acted as a spur to real policy changes only in the circumstances of the USSR's tightening resource constraints and increased international tensions. The essential difference in the attitudes of the Brezhnev and Andropov administrations towards poor worker discipline and habits was in terms of urgency. Whereas the first came to view it merely as an unfortunate and undesirable phenomenon limited to a relatively small number of miscreants, the latter considered it both more pervasive as well as unaffordable given the Soviet Union's rapidly worsening circumstances.

The problem of irresponsibility

The growing evidence of the decline in the Soviet work ethic highlighted the crucial issue of responsibility. Soviet commentators identified, on the immediate level, two closely related dimensions to this problem: the difficulty in determining who or what exactly was responsible for the level of work performance, and the inadequacy of existing performance criteria.

In the first case, the sheer complexity of vertical and horizontal links in the chain of production and administration made it extremely difficult to assign responsibility for performance on a meaningful or equitable basis. The state's excessive regulation of economic activity, exacerbated by numerous and contradictory production indicators, not only constrained enterprise autonomy but also discouraged the taking of responsibility (Abalkin, 1983a, p. 3). In effect, the Soviet economy was hamstrung by what Vladimir Shlapentokh (1988, p. 4) termed a 'defective mechanism of EP [evaluation of performance]: the incorrect assessment of human work and improper public reaction to bad performance.'

The system pre-Andropov responded to the problem of its defective EP mechanism in two ways. The first, described by the reformist economist Raimundas Karagedov (1983, p. 60), was for responsibility to be 'dissolved' among the various administrative bodies involved in adopting a particular decision. Since work performance could not be measured accurately, the question of responsibility was essentially ignored. The second response was to pretend that the EP mechanism was fundamentally sound and to continue assigning responsibility for work performance on the basis of existing production indicators. The irrationality and inequitability of these criteria meant, however, that the problem of irresponsibility was no nearer resolution. Undisciplined suppliers and carriers of inputs remained unpunished when production foul-ups occurred, while penalties were always imposed on those at the end of the production chain even when they were not to blame (Negoduiko, 1983, p. 2).

The absence of reliable mechanisms for assigning responsibility was exacerbated by three important factors. The first was the overwhelming dominance of the producer in the Soviet socioeconomic system. Consumer satisfaction was of little import in a shortage economy where demand for goods and services invariably greatly exceeded supply. The absolute certainty of markets encouraged an insouciant, irresponsible attitude among producers towards questions of quality of product and timeliness of delivery. This problem manifested itself in economic relationships at many levels: between suppliers and recipients of inputs at the production level; between producers of consumer goods/services and shoppers; and between sellers of labour and the enterprises that relied on them to meet plan targets. The influence of the sellers' market (Kornai, 1992, p. 219) was all- pervasive.

The second factor accentuating the weakening of responsibility was the ineffectualness, and consequent neglect, of coercive means to enforce production discipline. Criminal sanctions were toothless, with courts generally reversing decisions over dismissals and rescinding even more minor penalties (Cheban, 1980, p. 3). In general, the worker's right to sinecured employment and *vyvodilovka* – defined by Connor (1991, p. 147) as 'the adequate, justified wage no matter what the real output' – was considered a far greater priority than improved labour productivity.

Finally, the system was incapable of rewarding good work fairly; it was as difficult to determine who was responsible for good performance as for bad. The power of incentives (or 'positive reward', to adapt Shlapentokh's terminology) was therefore extremely weak and haphazard. Since bad performance was only very rarely punished (and then only at the level of the individual, since 'socialist humanism' could not allow enterprises to go bankrupt thereby forcing people out of work), and 'good work' rewarded on the basis of irrational production indicators, workers and enterprises were neither accountable nor interest-driven.

The Andropov economic prescription – intensification through increased labour productivity

The mutually reinforcing tendencies identified above – the squeeze on labour resources, technological backwardness, declining work ethics, and the absence of responsibility – pointed to the unsustainability of resource-intensive (or 'extensive') methods of economic development. The gap between the ideology of 'developed socialism' and its actual achievements became increasingly apparent. At the June 1983 Plenum, Andropov (*Pravda*, 16 June 1983, p. 2) stressed that 'profound qualitative changes in production forces and the perfection of productive relations corresponding to these changes have become not only urgent but unavoidable'. In this context, he described the country's principal economic task as the 'radical raising of labour productivity', noting its 'particular significance, both in terms of our internal development and internationally'.

The theoretical framework outlined in Chapter 1 is especially applicable to the policy prescriptions of the Andropov period, reflecting the reality that regime proposals to raise labour productivity developed within the overall paradigm of moderate intra-systemic reform. Policy differences centred on questions of implementation, methodology and emphasis – such as the appropriate balance between socialist morality, planning-technocratic and incentive–humanistic strategies – not on fundamental dogma. Economic thought and labour ideology had not yet reached the point where the primacy of the state in economic management or the inviolability of the full employment doctrine could be questioned at the level of principle.

Socialist morality

In an early speech at the Ordzhonikidze Machine Tool Plant in Moscow, Andropov (*Pravda*, 1 February 1983, p. 2) declared that 'we will not be able to make rapid progress without proper discipline – labour, plan and state discipline'. Under his leadership, the regime sought to achieve this broad objective in several ways. At the most basic level, this involved a crackdown on 'parasites' and absentee workers. In January 1983, 'Operation Trawl' was launched, in which the militia raided bathhouses, cinemas and shopping queues, questioning and booking people who were absent from work without justifiable cause (Steele and Abraham, 1983, p. 160). Greater attention was also given to the fight against workplace drunkenness (*EKO* editorial, September 1983, p. 15), and there were calls to sack 'violators of (work) discipline' (Loginov, 1982, p. 2) and impose restrictions on workers who constantly changed their place of work (Novoplyansky, 1983, p. 3).[7]

Notwithstanding the increased role (both ideological and practical) of criminal sanctions and other punitive measures, Andropov's disciplinary campaign against poor labour effort focused principally on the question of performance-related pay and bonuses – a concept that will be discussed later in more detail in the context of incentive–humanistic proposals for raising labour productivity. It is important here, however, to mention briefly steps taken to punish poor productivity through the use of various financial penalties. These included government resolutions on transferring violators of labour discipline to lower-paid work (*Pravda*, 7 August 1983, p. 1), as well as the removal or reduction of production bonuses (*Pravda*, 10 February 1984, p. 1) for workers and enterprise directors who failed to meet contractual obligations and plan targets.

Central to the idea of discipline was the accent on the nexus between work effort and reward, and on the productive content of labour in place of the notion of job as welfare. As expressed by Andropov (1983, p. 16), '[w]ork and only work, its actual results . . . should determine the level of each citizen's well-being.' Such comments constituted a vigorous attack against the practice of *vyvodilovka* and challenged complaisant Brezhnevian notions about the supremacy of so-called equity considerations over efficiency. The changed psychological climate regarding the place of labour in Soviet society was also reflected in a greater emphasis on the duty, rather than right, of citizens to work. Some writers (Korelsky and Rozhno, 1984, p. 2) began to dispense with the pretence that the right to work in the Soviet Union was a privilege, instead defining 'the most humanitarian of aims', not as the guaranteed right to work, but as 'the constitutional obligation of each able-bodied citizen to work conscientiously in their chosen area of socially useful activity'. Under Andropov, the duty to work (and work well) became not simply an abstract moral concept, but assumed a wider import: 'In the circumstances of the increasingly tense international situation caused by aggressive imperialist circles, the unconditional fulfilment of the state plan has become not only the obligation, but also the patriotic duty of each Soviet citizen . . .' (text of Andropov's speech read out at the December 1983 Plenum, *Pravda*, 27 December 1983, p. 1).

Although Andropov attached considerable importance to the restoration and conscientious observance of socialist norms of behaviour, Shlapentokh's (1988, p. 171) description of him as a neo-Stalinist who sought only to tighten control through order and discipline is unfair. This stereotyped image is based on a misconception of the notion of discipline under Andropov, since it applies the term only to the individual's immediate relationship to their work. Hewett (1988, p. 259) rightly pointed out that Andropov understood discipline in a broad, systemic, sense. It is worth recalling that his Ordzhonikidze speech mentioned three types of discipline – labour, plan and state. Only the first of these could really be said to be encompassed by socialist morality. Plan and state discipline, on the other hand, fell much more readily within the ambit of the planning–technocratic approach to labour productivity, to which we now turn.

Planning–technocratic prescriptions

Planning–technocratic proposals designed to enhance labour productivity under Andropov were characterized by a dual emphasis on the 'perfection' (*sovershenstvovanie*) of planning and the 'new person' (*novy chelovek*). His administration highlighted, and sought solutions to, major problems and shortcomings in four key areas: (a) planning discipline; (b) the rational planning and utilization of labour resources; (c) the application of STP; and (d) the development of the 'new type of worker' through education and training.

Planning discipline

Whereas the socialist morality conception of discipline related essentially to every citizen's duty to work more conscientiously, planning discipline was mainly concerned with resolving problems of a more organizational nature. Consistent with this understanding, planning indiscipline was characterized not by alleged 'idleness' or 'bungling' (as in individual cases of indiscipline), but rather by 'departmentalism' (*vedomstvennost*),[8] the instability of production plans, and ministerial interference in the form of constant *korrektirovki* (upward adjustments of original plan targets, frequently combined with reductions of production inputs).

Planning discipline under Andropov focused, in the first instance, on regulating the over-zealous conduct of branch ministries in the formulation and implementation of plans. This period witnessed a concerted ideological assault on the system-oriented bias of the Brezhnev era. The 'perfection' and 'technical substantiation' of norms came to be regarded not only as unrealistic and ineffectual, but actually counterproductive. Much contemporary criticism of excessive planning centred on its adverse impact on the development of incentives, initiative and responsibility at the individual and enterprise level, and so will be discussed later in the context of incentive–humanistic approaches to labour productivity. Within the planning–technocratic paradigm, however, overplanning was equated with the disruption and corruption of the planning process.

The emphasis on the stability of norms gave new impetus to medium-(five-year) and long-term or *perspektivny* (10–15 year) planning. Their rationale was to restore order and confidence in the planning process (Yakovlev and Miryushchenko, 1984, p. 2), rather than the tighter regulation of production operations. Planning in the conditions of *intensifikatsiya* and the modern complex economy should determine the strategic direction of enterprise activity. And this required its simplification and rationalization, particularly in respect of performance criteria.

The rational planning and utilization of labour resources

In his first speech as General Secretary, Andropov (*Pravda*, 24 November 1982, p. 2) called for the 'rational utilization of material and labour resources', noting that 'economization, a thrifty attitude towards national wealth, is a question of the realism of our plans'. The running-down of human (and material) resources concentrated attention on ways of reducing the material- and, especially, labour-intensiveness of the Soviet economy.

In identifying the causes of the Soviet Union's labour shortage, the economist Aleksandr Kotlyar (1983, pp. 108–9) mentioned three factors in addition to the standard demographic explanation (that is, the knock-on effect of the enormous manpower losses suffered during World War II). These were: (i) deficiencies in the planning of capital investments and the location of economic establishments; (ii) the 'imperfection' of the mechanism for releasing workers from enterprises and reallocating them elsewhere; and (iii) deficiencies in the use of workers at existing enterprises.

The first of these factors referred to the widespread practice of establishing new enterprises without considering the availability (or otherwise) of labour resources. The creation of 'new work vacancies', while 'old, physically and morally obsolete, low-efficiency equipment' remained unreplaced, militated against increased production efficiency and exacerbated labour shortages (ibid., p. 109). According to Andropov (*Pravda*, 24 December 1982, p. 2), the solution lay in increased reconstruction and modernization, and a reduction in the number of new establishments. The emphasis on redressing labour imbalances by reducing the surplus in individual workplaces exemplified the intensive approach towards economic and labour management. In concrete terms, this strategy was reflected in a much closer focus on the 'passportization' and 'attestation' (technical justification) of workplaces (Malmygin, 1983, p. 26) and, at the regional level, on ensuring a better correlation between the quantity and structure of workplaces, and 'demographic potential' (Churakov, 1983, p. 94).

Kotlyar's focus on mechanisms to release and reallocate labour was characteristic of the new approach of the Andropov period. Under Brezhnev, the concept of labour balancing had been largely restricted to the shuffling of resources between regions, and to creating additional work for the non-employed so as to increase further the total size of the labour force. Now, however, discussion turned on the question of the more efficient intra-enterprise deployment of labour resources – reflected in proposals to revive the Shchekino method[9] – as well as their broader reallocation in response to the changing structure and priorities of the economy. Thus, the imperative of greater labour productivity became translated into pressure to release administrative

personnel to material production (Andropov, *Pravda*, 16 June 1983, p. 3).
At the same time, the higher priority given to consumer goods production was supported by calls to transfer personnel from material
production to the services sector (Dunaeva, 1983, p. 6) and raise
the prestige of service professions generally (*Pravda* editorial, 19 May
1983, p. 1).

Consistent with the theme of the rational deployment of labour
resources, many commentators sought an expanded role for Job Placement Bureaux (JPBs).[10] Some (for example, Malmygin, 1983, p. 30)
advocated an 'all-Union central service for the coordinated movement
of labour places and labour resources', while others (Ezigaryan, 1983,
p. 59) proposed a comprehensive system in which JPBs would be
responsible for placing released workers within their respective territorial jurisdictions. More controversially, the radical economist Pavel
Bunich (1984, p. 10) proposed a system of retraining released workers
that involved the 'perfection' of rates and periods of payment for workers undergoing new training. This was very similar to ideas first proposed by Yevgenii Manevich in 1965 (pp. 29–30), but ignored under
Brezhnev. In its original form, Manevich's argument was that it was
more rational to spend money on retraining workers than pay them to
perform useless work in their current positions. Although the notion of
a 'training allowance' was not really comparable to Western-style unemployment benefits, it nevertheless signified an important refinement in
the concept of the rational utilization of labour resources. For Bunich
and Manevich, the mechanical (but often irrational) matching of available workers with job vacancies was no longer sufficient; workers should
be placed in jobs that were both socially useful and for which they were
suitable.

Kotlyar's third explanation for the existence of labour shortage – the
deficient use of workers at existing enterprises – was closely linked to
Taylorist and Brezhnevian ideas regarding the 'scientific organization of
labour' (SOL).[11] However, whereas in the Brezhnev years SOL had largely centred on conventional policy prescriptions such as raising the
shift index, under Andropov it advocated reducing the number of
administrative to production line workers (Kurashvili, 1983, p. 55),
and reiterated the need to introduce more convenient shopping hours
for workers in order to minimize absenteeism (*Pravda*, 18 January 1983,
p. 1). The search for the rational use of labour through SOL also led to
renewed interest in proposals such as the Shchekino idea of combining
functions from several positions into one job (*sovmeshchenie*). One
senior bureaucrat (Filev, 1983, p. 66) identified this as a major factor in

the anticipated release of around four million people from industrial ministries during the period of the 11th Five-Year plan (1981–85).

The application of STP

STP was, in many ways, the signature motif of the Andropov administration. Just as the terms, 'discipline' and 'order', came to connote the restoration of socialist values, so STP equated readily with 'modernization' and attempts to change the methods of Soviet economic management. At the June 1983 Plenum, Andropov (*Pravda*, 16 June 1983, p. 2) stated that '[t]he main road towards a qualitative change in productive forces is...the transition to intensive development and the combination in practice of the advantages of our socialist system with the achievements of the scientific–technological revolution.'

STP was pertinent to the objective of maximizing labour and material resources. Specifically, it was seen as making a vital contribution in the development of labour-saving machinery. The excessively high proportion of the workforce in manual labour was intolerable given the Soviet Union's deteriorating demographic indices (Andropov, 1983, pp. 16–17). Andropov (*Pravda*, 16 June 1983, p. 2) consequently called for the 'automatization of production', the 'broadest application of computers and robots', and the introduction of 'flexible technology enabling the rapid and efficient regearing of production to the manufacture of new product items'. This rhetoric was accompanied by recognition of the need for practical measures. An *EKO* editorial (January 1983, p. 13) advised the establishment of 'organizational-economic conditions' that would encourage enterprises to introduce new technology and, conversely, penalize those organizations which continued to produce obsolete technology. Government and Party resolutions relating to various 'economic experiments' (see below), included norms for the introduction of new technology among obligatory production indicators for participating enterprises (*Pravda*, 26 July 1983, p. 1).

Official attitudes towards the ideology and practice of STP under Andropov did not differ greatly from those under Brezhnev. Both administrations assigned to it central importance in the achievement of economic, political and social goals. Brezhnevian ideas of developed socialism continued to find expression in many speeches and writings. Andropov's (1983, p. 17) article in *Kommunist*, for example, stressed the 'social-political significance' of mechanizing and automating production, of the citizen being able to 'realize more fully his political, democratic rights given to working people by the socialist revolution – the rights of the unchallenged masters of their own society and their own state.' Nevertheless, although STP under Andropov retained many Brezhnevian characteristics, there were major differences in approach. In the first place, the application of STP was integrally linked to the new emphasis on intensive methods of economic development and increased labour productivity. Long-term sociopolitical objectives of STP, such as the 'increase of the worker's free time for the harmonious, all-round development of the personality' (Dunaeva, 1983, p. 6), were often relegated to an ideological footnote in the face of more pressing economic concerns.

More crucially still, the pursuit of STP was bound up with proposals to restructure the economic mechanism and reform planning methods. Leonid Abalkin (1983b, p. 34) wrote that the evolution of the role of science into a 'direct productive force' necessitated a 'new approach' to solving questions relating to planning, *khozraschet*, economic stimuli and 'the finance–credit mechanism'. He saw STP as the engine of economic and social progress, but in a radically different way to that envisaged under the conventional interpretation put out by developed socialism. Whereas previously STP served both to justify and reinforce existing economic methods,[12] Abalkin held out little hope for its development, and hence for improved labour productivity, as long as 'modernization' remained divorced from structural change.

Development of the 'new type of worker'

The Andropov administration placed particular priority on the development of the 'human factor' (*chelovecheskii faktor*) in implementing the strategic objectives of increased labour productivity and STP. The human factor in Soviet labour ideology manifested itself in essentially two ways. The first was appreciation of the growing instrumentalism of workers, the role of economic and social incentives, and the need to develop *chuvstvo khozyaina* through the devolution of decision-making powers. These issues will be examined later under the incentive–humanistic contribution towards labour ideology. This section, however, looks at the planning–technocratic approach towards the human factor in production, as embodied in the attempt to create the 'new type of worker' (*rabotnik novogo tipa*) through education and training.

On the occasion of the 113th anniversary of Lenin's birth, Gorbachev (*Pravda*, 23 April 1983, p. 2) defined the 'human factor' in the economy in terms of 'the cultural–technological level, professional skill, creativity and discipline of workers,' and claimed it was integral to improved labour productivity and production quality. The central importance of education and training lay in its positive influence on the human factor, first, by raising the overall skill and education level of workers, and, second, by reorienting education more directly towards the urgent practical requirements of *intensifikatsiya*.

The association between improved education and training on the one hand, and higher labour productivity and economic indices on the other, was underpinned by a number of assumptions. The first, outlined above by Andropov and Gorbachev, posited that the higher the worker's skill and education level, the more likely they were to be committed, disciplined and 'creative' (*tvorcheskii*) in the workplace. Many contemporary commentaries, in some cases supported by empirical evidence (Yadov, 1983, p. 55), asserted that indiscipline, 'parasitism' and labour turnover (*Tekuchest*) were most common among the lower strata of the working population, the unskilled and semi-skilled. Such concerns informed the 1984 Education Reform's provisions on labour education and upbringing in schools, the purposes of which included 'familiarizing students with the bases of modern industrial and agricultural production... [and] forming in them good working habits and knowledge' (*Pravda*, 13 April 1984, p. 3).

The second premise was logistical: sophisticated technology required a highly skilled and educated workforce to operate it effectively. This point was reiterated in the preamble to the Law on Education Reform, which noted that advanced forms of science and technology, production automation, and the need to increase labour productivity and improve production to world standards, required people entering the workforce to have 'the most up-to-date education' and 'a deep knowledge of the scientific–technological and economic bases of production' (*Pravda*, 13 April 1984, pp. 3–4). To this end, the Law outlined comprehensive measures designed to improve the existing system of general education. More significantly, the 1984 Education Reform – passed under Chernenko but introduced by the Andropov administration (*Pravda*, 4 January 1984, pp. 1–2) – represented the most determined attempt yet to deal with the problem of the 'overeducated-undertrained' syndrome (Connor, 1991, p. 84). The development of a comprehensive network of professional–technical schools (*professionalno-tekhnicheskoe uchilishche* – PTU) was directed specifically at increasing the supply of skilled labour relative to the number of university graduates. Better-directed education was seen as a way of compensating for diminishing labour resources (Chizhova, 1983, p. 64), while some observers linked a better-trained, more highly skilled workforce to the success of labour-saving measures such as *sovmeshchenie* (Blyakhman and Zlotnitskaya, 1984, p. 46).

Vocational training and the proper professional orientation of the young also loomed large in proposals to redress regional and sectoral labour imbalances. The Education Reform devoted considerable attention to rural schools as a way of accelerating the social development of the village and resolving demographic problems in the countryside (*Pravda*, 13 April 1984, p. 4). Rural education sought to 'industrialize' agriculture through the creation of a skilled and mobile workforce able to perform more than just primary agricultural tasks. It was also tied to the alleviation of labour surplus problems in Central Asia and the Caucasus, and the supply of sufficient labour to sustain economic development in regions such as Siberia and the Soviet Far East (Kotlyar, 1983, p. 117).

Finally, education and training were associated with the emergence of a more flexible workforce, better able to adapt to changing economic priorities and methods, and to consequent changes in workforce structure. At the most immediate level, this involved vocational training and professional orientation aimed at easing labour shortages in low-prestige professions, for example in the services sector (Chizhova, 1983, p. 65). More critically, given subsequent developments in Soviet labour ideology, some economists saw the function of a 'well-organized system of professional retraining' as catering for those – such as middle-aged workers – most vulnerable to technological rationalization and the obsolescence of certain types of work activity (Bunich, 1984, p. 10).

Such attitudes indicated a slight, but definite shift towards the idea of 'conditionality' in labour. Although the full employment doctrine remained essentially inviolate, the planning–technocratic approach towards 'the new type of worker' made far greater demands on the individual than ever before. In emphasizing that labour had to be 'useful', this approach questioned the validity of employment that satisfied only equity considerations. While education and training were seen as bridging the gap between workers' skill levels and the requirements of modern production, the reverse side of the argument, as yet unspoken, was that the worker could not necessarily count on job security 'no matter what'. He/she would be required to demonstrate a sufficiently high level of work skill and knowledge in order to be guaranteed employment.

The incentive–humanistic approach

Each of the four main strands of the planning–technocratic approach towards raising labour productivity was based on an implicit faith in the primacy and efficacy of central planning. In condemning 'that form of self-management that leads towards anarcho-syndicalism', Andropov (1983, p. 19) reaffirmed democratic centralism as '[t]he proven organizing principle of all life in socialist society', one that allowed the 'free creativity of the masses to be combined successfully with the advantages of a uniform system of scientific leadership, planning and management'.

In the Brezhnev era, the regime's system-bias and planning–technocratic orientation had led to a much greater emphasis on centralism than democratization. Attempts to devolve economic management were pursued at best half-heartedly. So-called 'progressive' or 'advanced' forms of labour organization such as the Shchekino method were effectively sabotaged by the ratchet effect[13] and ministerial *korrektirovki* to production targets (Filev, 1983, p. 67). Under Andropov, however, there was a determined attempt to revive the original Leninist spirit of democratic centralism. One senior economist (Belousov, 1984, pp. 4–5) recalled Lenin's warning about confusing democratic centralism with its perversion, bureaucratic centralism. He observed that Lenin's 'socialist centralization' had envisaged 'broad independence, and creative initiative and activity' for local bodies, enterprises and labour collectives.

The drive to democratize economic management acknowledged, implicitly and sometimes overtly, the existence of tensions between individual, collective and state interests. The traditional claim that the 'abyss between the interests of the state and those of the citizen' typical of capitalism had been 'liquidated' in the Soviet Union (Andropov, 1983, p. 19), was regularly qualified and even contradicted. In this context, an *EKO* editorial (September 1983, p. 9) on ways of strengthening discipline admitted that 'the interests of the worker do not always coincide with those of the collective'.

The emphasis in the Andropov period on *bona fide* Leninist democratic centralism and the reconciliation of individual and societal interests, arose essentially from the need to restore the worker's interest, sense of identification and responsibility in the performance of labour. In response to these imperatives, incentive–humanistic policies fell broadly into two categories: (i) prescriptions which sought to give substance to the idea of *chuvstvo khozyaina* – the citizen as master in work and life; and (ii) instrumentalist proposals based on recognition of the dominance of compensatory over conditioned and condign power.[14]

Chuvstvo khozyaina and the restoration of labour values

The concept of *chuvstvo khozyaina* was susceptible to considerable differences in interpretation and application. According to a *Pravda* editorial (8 December 1982, p. 1) soon after Andropov's accession, it showed itself 'in the worker's intolerance of . . . a profligate attitude towards national wealth, and any kind of negligence, slackness and irresponsibility'. In similar vein, Geidar Aliev (*Pravda*, 18 June 1983, p. 2) saw it as providing the opportunity to 'demonstrate a strict, comradely exactingness and intolerance towards violators of discipline. Let loafers, absentees, rolling-stones and bunglers feel the power of the angry collective!'

The restoration of *chuvstvo khozyaina* had, however, far wider application than merely the moral encouragement of order and discipline in the workplace. It went to the heart of the problem of responsibility and accountability at all levels of Soviet society, challenging in the process the appropriateness of the existing system of economic management to achieve the results demanded of it. In an important article in *Kommunist*, Abalkin (1983b, p. 34) argued that the new circumstances of intensive, qualitative development, required a 'profound restructuring' of the economic mechanism. There was now an 'urgent need to broaden substantively the initiative and independence (of production associations and enterprises, *kolkhozy* and *sovkhozy*), and also to increase their responsibility . . .'. Only through strengthening *khozraschet*[15] could *chuvstvo khozyaina* form in the worker (ibid., p. 38). In this context, Abalkin identified a connection between *chuvstvo khozyaina* and discipline that went substantially further than Aliev's narrow interpretation: 'the strongest and most reliable discipline is that which belongs to a master [*distsiplina khozyaiskaya*] which conveys the attitude of a human being who treats the means of production, work and its fruits, as his own, and who has a vested interest in their conservation and multiplication.' Abalkin and other reform economists looked to achieve this confluence through what Pekka Sutela (1991, p. 103) has termed 'indirect centralisation' or 'dual-track planning' (ibid., p. 151). Karagedov (1983, p. 67), for instance, favoured the 'rational combination of the principles of centralized and decentralized (management)', whereby the centre determined 'objectives and strategic tasks', while everyday operational decisions were devolved to enterprises. In this Leninist model of democratic centralism, the '*khozraschet* mechanism' – enterprises or production associations functioning under conditions of responsibility and accountability – decided questions such as 'creating a vested interest in maximum production efficiency' (ibid., p. 68).

The new emphasis on democratic centralism based on *khozraschet* principles arose from a growing recognition of two fundamental realities: that the sheer size and complexity of the Soviet economy made it impossible for the centre to attempt to control every aspect of production (economic roundtable discussion, *EKO*, no.8, August 1983, pp. 25–6);

and that the existing system of economic relations undermined incentive and responsibility, thereby acting as a brake on growth. On these issues, the views of more radical economists, such as Karagedov and Kurashvili, differed little in broad substance from those of Andropov himself. Scarcely two weeks after Brezhnev's death, the new General Secretary (*Pravda*, 24 November 1982, p. 1) was already indicating the need to 'create such conditions – economic and organizational – that would stimulate high-quality, efficient work, initiative and enterprise', and punish 'poor work, inaction and irresponsibility'. Acknowledging calls for expanded enterprise and farm (collective and state) autonomy, he agreed that 'the time has come to move towards resolving this question practically'. Shortly afterwards, Andropov (1983, pp. 18–19) foreshadowed 'extending the parameters' of enterprise and farm autonomy, a statement of intent followed soon after by the introduction of the so-called 'large-scale economic experiment' involving selected Union and republican ministries and enterprises. Under its provisions, enterprise heads were granted much greater flexibility in organizing production, determining individual salary levels, and in using bonus, production development and sociocultural funds as they saw fit (*Pravda*, 26 July 1983, p. 1). The experiment's importance was signalled by Andropov (*Pravda*, 27 December 1983, p. 2) in his last official communication – the text of his address at the December 1983 Plenum – which stated that its results would 'serve as the basis for the preparation of appropriate proposals for the national economy as a whole.'

The revived interest in democratic centralism and dual-track planning was accompanied by a new emphasis on economic levers in production and the reinvigoration of Leninist notions of full (*polny*) *khozraschet* based on profit and profitability.[16] In implicitly rejecting the definition of *khozraschet* as purely an accounting balance between expenditure and revenue, a *Pravda* article identified its basic principles as profitability, self-financing, autonomy, and 'responsibility in the economic stimulation of final results' (Yakovlev and Miryushchenko, 1984, p. 2). Given the ineffectualness of material incentives which disregarded its role, profit should be the 'basic criterion in evaluating and stimulating the economic-production activity (of enterprises).' The primacy of financial considerations was propounded even more enthusiastically by the radical economist Aleksandr Birman (1983, pp. 46–7). Birman condemned 'planned-loss' branches and production associations as 'unacceptable', and argued that the key task of developing a more efficient economy would be unachievable without the 'active use of all value levers: prices, the system of payment for labour, bonuses and sanctions, finance and credit – in other words, without the application of *polny khozraschet* in all branches of the national economy.'

The drive to give new life to *polny khozraschet* was accompanied by a vigorous assault on the hand-out mentality and dependence psychology prevalent under Brezhnev. There were moves to harden the budget constraint of enterprises, for example, by enforcing wage fund and personnel ceilings (Ezigaryan, 1983, p. 54), and clamping down on the practice of mutual debt amnesties between enterprises (Laptev, 1983, p. 46).[17] Mechanisms for granting funding and credit to enterprises came under much closer scrutiny, and a linkage was established between 'real *khozraschet*' and restrictions on the subsidizing of production development by the centre (*Pravda*, 6 January, 1984, p. 2). Some commentators (Subotsky, 1983, p. 36) called for restrictions on the 'free allocation of resources' to enterprises, and implementation instead of the principle of their 'returnability' (payment). As explained by Kurashvili (1983, pp. 52–3) the intention was to 'exclude irresponsibility in the use of "free" property'.

Ultimately, the hardening of budget constraints depended on the proper delineation and devolution of rights and responsibilities to enterprises. Here, the Andropov administration assigned considerable importance to labour collectives and other so-called primary production bodies. The large-scale economic experiment envisaged, among measures aimed at 'strengthening democratic centralism in the national economy', a greater role for labour collectives in the management of production associations and enterprises (*Pravda*, 26 July 1983, p. 1). The emphasis on 'progressive' or 'advanced' forms of labour organization applying *khozraschet* principles led to renewed interest in the Shchekino method and brigades working on the 'single contract' system.[18] And the former's labour-saving proposals (such as *sovmeshchenie*) acquired particular relevance in the circumstances of *intensifikatsiya* and the necessity of compensating for labour shortage through greater productivity (Grotseskul, 1983, p. 2).

In addition to facilitating the development of *chuvstvo khozyaina* and creating conditions for the stimulation of better discipline, work habits and greater initiative at enterprises, labour collectives also supplied a focus from which a dominant, unifying and mutually reinforcing ethic could emerge. This was the interdependency of rights and responsibilities, the accountability for performance and the restoration of the productive content and meaning of labour. Thus, Gorbachev (*Pravda*, 23 April 1983, p. 2) linked the initiative and enterprise of firms, with their 'economic responsibility before society', while official resolutions stressed the importance of giving participating enterprises 'the real vested interest of the master (*khozyaiskaya zainteresovannost*) in achieving high production efficiency and reinforcing their responsibility for the results of their work' (*Pravda*, 26 July 1983, p. 1).

The purpose of the large-scale experiment and its successors, such as the 'service experiment' (*Pravda*, 10 February 1984, p. 1), was therefore twofold. In emphasizing the importance of stable production, investment and total wage norms, these experiments were intended to simplify economic management by cutting out superfluous and obstructive intermediate levels of administration, namely the branch ministries (Karagedov, 1983, p. 69). But this objective was really only the means to a wider end – the restoration of responsibility and accountability at the individual and enterprise level. Rationalization of planning procedures and devolution of decision-making powers were critical precisely because they were designed to uncover real levels of performance (or non-performance) and remove both obstacles to, and excuses for, poor management and production. Such was the intent of the service experiment in allowing participating enterprises greater involvement in plan formulation as well as implementation (*Pravda*, 10 February 1984, p. 1).

Further to this objective, there were moves to make leaders of labour collectives more personally accountable, limiting their ability to transfer responsibility onto higher levels of administration (Parfenov, 1983, p. 2). A *Pravda* commentator (Chekalin, 1983, p. 2) cited Lenin's injunction that the heads of labour collectives should be held directly responsible for the unprofitability of their enterprises. More generally, Abalkin (*EKO*, August 1983, p. 46) argued that the governing principle in the 'perfection' of the economic mechanism – the democratization of management and the development of *chuvstvo khozyaina* – should be that the person making the decision should also be held accountable for its consequences. Efforts to improve the assigning of responsibility included proposals to extend the existing system of production bonuses and penalties to the bureaucracy (*Pravda*, 10 February 1984), reflecting a growing sentiment that higher planning and economic bodies should answer directly for losses arising from faulty administrative decisions (Laptev, 1983, pp. 47–8).

Thinking on economic policy and labour ideology at this time was by no means uniform, with significant differences in tone, emphasis and substance. Nevertheless, most overt differences concerned the means adopted to achieve these objectives, not the objectives themselves. The Andropov period was remarkable for the degree to which the views of progressive thinkers such as Karagedov, Kurashvili and A. Birman coincided with official thinking on the broad essentials of democratic centralism, dual-track planning and the use of economic levers over administrative methods in stimulating greater productivity. There was considerable consensus among political leaders, academics, enterprise managers and bureaucrats, about the need to 'intensify' the economy. Few doubted that existing management practices were stifling initiative, responsibility and accountability. Consequently, the devolution of rights to enterprises and local soviets, and the overhaul of performance criteria, were themes that entered readily into the orthodoxy of economic thought and labour ideology. Even the narrowest, most ideologically rigid interpretation of *chuvstvo khozyaina* – as an instrument for ensuring labour discipline – implicitly acknowledged the inferiority of administrative to self-regulatory methods based on the reconciliation of individual and societal interests.

The notion of *chuvstvo khozyaina* was a multidimensional concept with very wide appeal, embracing socialist morality, the 'perfection of planning', and structural changes in the system of horizontal and vertical economic links. Despite its eclecticism, however, this concept in all its practical and apparently contradictory manifestations was imbued by the common principle of restoring the productive content and meaning of labour and, with it, the notion of a responsible, efficient and vigorous society. *Chuvstvo khozyaina*, like so many other ideas that found currency during the last decade of the Soviet Union's existence, had been propounded in the Brezhnev era. But the stagnation of those years had divested it of meaning and vitality. While Andropov presided over little that was ideologically new, his administration made a critical contribution to the development of a reformulated labour ideology. By seeking to return to the original, Leninist meaning of democratic centralism, *khozraschet* and self-financing, he was responsible for arguably the most significant shift in Soviet economic thought since the end of the NEP over half a century before.

Before discussing the influence of instrumentalism in Soviet labour ideology, it is important to touch upon the relationship between *chuvstvo khozyaina* and what the sociologist Vladimir Yadov (1983, p.61) called 'moral-psychological' factors affecting the individual in the work environment. The Andropov era witnessed a growing awareness of the dynamics in the relationship between worker and workplace. Although the sociology of labour relations had been debated under Brezhnev,[19] it received new life and impetus after his death. In particular, it began to be widely acknowledged that job satisfaction was a complex, multifaceted phenomenon that did not proceed automatically from the 'worker's ownership of the means of production'. The economists Blyakhman and Zlotnitskaya (1984, p. 39) asserted, in this connection, that '[t]here has been insufficient appreciation of the relationship of workers to work as a thing of social value'. There was now a far more realistic, hard-headed understanding of the nature of labour. Although the duty to work conscientiously remained paramount, much of the self-deluding mythology in official attitudes towards labour so characteristic of the Brezhnev years was jettisoned under his successor. The individual might still 'need' to work for reasons of self-esteem and self-expression (Mchedlov and Rozhnov, 1983, p. 3), but this did not necessarily imply that job satisfaction was guaranteed. Some commentators pointed to the inevitability that at least some work was bound to be boring. As Yadov (1983, p. 60) admitted, 'the economic and social resources of our society do not allow us to guarantee each person, either today or in the near future, choice of employment that accords completely with the creative content of labour at a high level of self-organization and free activity.' Commenting on the reference in Article 40 of the 1977 Soviet Constitution to the right of each citizen to work in the profession of their choice, taking into account society's requirements, he (ibid., pp. 60–1) defined the latter as: 'the development of an enterprising, collectivist, responsible and conscientious attitude towards work, including fulfilling obligations that involve sometimes monotonous...and physically arduous labour.' This disabusing of 'romantic' socialist notions of labour contributed to an environment in which instrumentalist (that is, material) incentives assumed growing importance.

Instrumentalism and the development of labour incentives

The growing instrumentalism of the Soviet worker was already a well-documented socioeconomic phenomenon by the late 1970s, and the latter years of the Brezhnev administration saw various attempts to stimulate labour productivity through the use of economic and social incentives. These efforts, however, were stymied by a number of obstacles: the instability of wage norms, the ratchet effect, the obduracy of the gross output culture, chronic shortages of consumer goods and services, and the twin evils of *vyvodilovka* and *uravnilovka*.[20]

Despite superficial similarities, the approach of the Andropov administration towards the problem of incentives differed markedly from that of his predecessor. In the first place, it recognized that the revitalization of socioeconomic incentives depended on the 'restructuring' (*perestroika*) of the economic mechanism. As long as the economy ran on extensive lines, used irrational and inequitable production indicators, and was dogged by petty ministerial interference in enterprise activity, no system of material rewards could operate successfully. This was implicitly recognised by Andropov (1983, p. 13) when he criticized the backwardness of the existing economic mechanism relative to the requirements arising from the material–technological, social and spiritual development of Soviet society.

Second, the regime responded to the instrumentalist leanings of the Soviet workforce by placing much greater emphasis on the production of consumer goods, as well as on improved services. At the June 1983 Plenum, Andropov (*Pravda*, 16 June 1983, p. 3) devoted much of his address to the general theme of improving living standards, acknowledging in the process the adverse effects of unsatisfied consumer demand on the system of material incentives. The text of his speech at the December Plenum (27 December 1983, p. 1) noted that 'the incomplete satisfaction of the population's demand for goods has spawned negative phenomena, including speculation'. While this latter was 'disgusting', the best way of combating it was to increase production, improve the quality of consumer items, and develop the services sector so as to make up the shortfall in goods and services. In other words, action should be taken to attack the root causes of the problem rather than its symptoms.

The Andropov era was notable for a renewed assault on *uravnilovka* and support for greater wage differentiation. The importance the Andropov administration attached to performance-based pay and bonuses, and to the devolution of wage funds to heads of enterprises and production associations, was clearly at odds with the previous tolerance, even encouragement, of *uravnilovka*. Blyakhman and Zlotnitskaya (1984, p. 47) noted approvingly the likelihood of greater wage differentiation resulting from the increased rights of enterprises to use savings in the total wage fund to pay for individual increments and additional payments. Other commentators, such as Kurashvili (1983, p. 53), proposed that the state should only set the minimum wage: 'the actual salary level should be defined by the enterprises themselves, linked directly to production efficiency, labour productivity and the worker's labour contribution. This assumes the possibility of significant (and productivity-stimulating) differences in the remuneration of similar work....' Greater wage differentiation was motivated both by considerations of economic efficiency and ideological 'correctness'. In the former case, it sought to address the adverse impact of unjustified wages growth on labour productivity (Dunaeva, 1983, p. 7), while at the broadly philosophical or 'moral' level it embodied 'the spirit and substance of Marxist views on socialist distribution', (Andropov, 1983, p. 16) in which the level of each citizen's welfare was directly contingent on their work contribution.

The limits to change – conservative influences on labour ideology under Yurii Andropov

It is inappropriate to exaggerate the degree of transformation in thinking on labour and economic issues during this period. Andropov was certainly no revolutionary and established clear limits on what could be discussed, let alone proposed. The debate over economic reform and labour ideology took place within defined parameters that emphasized the primacy of state ownership and the 'non-exploitative' nature of labour.

In this still generally conservative climate, ideological icons such as the full employment doctrine remained largely sacrosanct. Politburo member Grigorii Romanov (*Pravda*, 6 November 1983, p. 1) asserted that 'Soviet people already can no longer imagine their existence without the guaranteed right to work and an all-embracing system of social security', while the old comparisons continued to be made about the respective quality of life under socialism and capitalism. At the June 1983 Plenum, Andropov (*Pravda*, 16 June 1983, p. 3) reiterated the claim that, unlike socialism, 'imperialism is incapable of coping with the social consequences of a scientific–technological revolution whose depth and scale are without precedent; millions of workers find themselves in unemployment and poverty.'

The limits of reform were signposted by the lexicon of economic and labour ideology, which not only continued to use typical Brezhnevian terms such as *sovershenstvovanie*, but resolutely excluded any mention of 'reform' (*reforma*) as such. Although official and academic adherence to standard Soviet socioeconomic terminology dissimulated significant reformist currents, they nevertheless indicated an underlying assumption that reforms were to be intra-systemic, in other words, they had to take place within the existing socioeconomic framework.

The slowness of the transformation in labour ideology under Andropov was also reflected in the durability of extensive economic prescriptions designed to increase the size of the workforce. There were calls to increase the birth rate and life expectancy (Kvasha, 1983, pp. 78–9), and for pensioners, students, housewives, and other non-employed (*nezanyatye*) groups to be drawn into social production, particularly in the services sphere (see Politburo account of a meeting involving party secretaries of the CPSU and from other socialist countries, *Pravda*, 26 March 1983, p. 1). Similarly, while the 1984 Education Reform was primarily driven by the need to develop a more skilled and flexible workforce imbued with good work habits, a quantitative rationale lay behind proposals to establish direct school–enterprise links (Schroeder, 1987, p. 19) and introduce work experience for later-year secondary school students (*Pravda*, 14 April 1984, p. 3).

Examination of the Andropov period reveals that the development of labour ideology was not matched by concrete achievement. Implementation of reforms was half-hearted at best, and often non-existent. At one of its regular weekly meetings in October 1983, the Politburo made clear its disenchantment with the lack of progress in preparing the large-scale economic experiment, observing there had been 'no tangible restructuring of the style of work of ministries and especially of all-Union industrial associations' (*Pravda*, 10 December 1983, p. 2). The obstructive power of industrial ministries continued during this time, despite the leadership's search for alternative economic institutions and approaches (Whitefield, 1993, pp. 63–4). This power was evident in many areas and at many levels, most notably in the 'habit of wilful planning' (Negoduiko, 1983, p. 2). Even after the large-scale economic experiment began to operate in 1984, ministries constantly issued *korrektirovki* to plans, disregarded distinctions between so-called 'obligatory' and 'voluntary' plan indicators, and continued to regulate practically every aspect of enterprise activity (Hewett, 1988, pp. 264–6; Whitefield, 1993, p. 199).

The non-implementation of reformist policy prescriptions and the perpetuation of ministerial power was facilitated by the collusion of enterprises unwilling (and/or unable) to assume greater responsibility. Considerable anecdotal evidence exists to suggest that 'social passivity was one of the "columns of bureaucratism"' (Ponomarev and Shinkarenko, cited in Whitefield, 1993, p. 169). In a roundtable discussion in *Pravda* (23 November 1983, p. 2) on the large-scale economic experiment, the Ukrainian Republic's Minister of Food Industry (whose ministry was a participant in the experiment) deplored the prevalence of 'parasitical, dependent attitudes': '(Enterprise) directors are used to everything being laid out for them, to acting as purely the executors of plans. This absolves them from initiative and enterprise.'

The passivity and lack of initiative of enterprise leaders stemmed not only from the wish for an easier life, but also from their near-absolute dependence on ministries for information, inputs (even at the end of 1988 only 3 per cent of the trade in the means of production was

wholesale) and markets (Whitefield, 1993, pp. 195–6). In a socioeconomic environment characterized by ministerial monopolism and the
absence of alternative suppliers and customers, enterprises had little
option but to accept the existing rules of the game. This was all the
more so since ministries also controlled other aspects of enterprise
activity such as capital investment and the provision of social services
(ibid., p. 97). Ultimately, as Kurashvili (1983, p. 44) pointed out, there
could be no effective reform to the economic mechanism as long as the
current system of branch management remained unchanged. Until that
occurred, the Soviet economy would continue to be dominated by
the gross output culture that had characterized its development since
the 1930s.

The Andropov conception of Soviet labour ideology

Soviet labour ideology during this period was distinguished by considerable heterogeneity, both in terms of specific proposals and their underlying assumptions which showed the stamp of many different and often
opposing influences. In addition to the obvious legacy of Marxism-
Leninism, political leaders and academic economists were apt to refer
both to the example of other socialist countries and historical precedent.
Thus, Kurashvili (1983, pp. 41, 48) justified 'indirect centralization'
by pointing to the practical experience of Bulgaria and particularly
Hungary.[21] Belousov (1984, p. 17), while acknowledging it would be
wrong to transfer NEP 'mechanically' onto the contemporary socioeconomic environment, nevertheless argued that its 'basic idea – the
close and balanced combination of the autonomy and responsibility of
enterprises – remains valid today.' And Aslund (1991, p. 115) has
remarked on the importance of Kosygin's 1965 reforms in 'inspiring'
Soviet reformers. These diverse geographical, historical and philosophical influences, not to mention functional factors such as the power
of the ministries, created a labour ideology defined by the complex
interplay between socialist morality, planning–technocratic and incentive–humanistic ideas.

Many of the differences in interpreting the essence of labour ideology
under Andropov arise from the relative weight given to each of these
categories. Shlapentokh (1988, pp. 88–9, 108–9) dismissed Andropov as
a 'liberal authoritarian' and 'neo-Stalinist' on the basis of the belief
that regime policy was primarily driven by socialist morality. Steele
and Abraham (1983, p. 173), though more willing to concede Andropov's reformist inclinations, emphasized his determination to 'draw a

contrast with the looseness of his predecessor's rule'. For such writers, Andropov injected dynamism into economic management (Shlapentokh, 1988, p. 82), but did not challenge substantively the operation of the economic mechanism. This argument portrays Andropov as a more energetic version of Brezhnev, rather than as the ideological precursor to Gorbachev.

For others, such as Adam (1993, p. 195), economic debates pre-Gorbachev were dominated by planning–technocratic issues, in particular improvements in planning and performance indicators. Comment and even criticism were permitted here so long as economists did not suggest, directly or indirectly, 'the need for a far-reaching restructuring of the economic mechanism, say, along the principles of the Hungarian economic reform . . . Nothing could appear which challenged the foundations of the socialist economic system.'

Such exclusivist analyses both misunderstand the nature of socialist morality and planning–technocratic policy prescriptions, and underestimate the importance of incentive–humanistic influences on labour ideology. In the first case, 'order' and 'discipline' are wrongly equated with socialist morality. As discussed earlier, Andropov's conception of discipline encompassed socialist morality (labour discipline for the individual), planning–technocratic (planning discipline) and incentive–humanistic ideas (state/bureaucratic discipline as expressed in non-interference in the everyday operational activity of enterprises). Equally, order meant much more than 'orderly' working practices on the factory floor. It also applied to the removal of dysfunctions in the economy, such as the instability of norms, the ratchet effect, weaknesses in the incentive structure, and the absence of responsibility and accountability throughout society.

The emphasis on the regime's planning–technocratic bias is just as misleading. Certainly, political leaders and economists spoke often and at length about 'perfecting' planning and the economic mechanism. But whereas for some 'perfecting' meant fine-tuning, many contemporary observers saw it as involving nothing less than the *perestroika* of economic relations. Although the term *sovershenstvovanie* is redolent of Brezhnevian stagnation, Abalkin and other economists writing for *EKO* used it in quite a radical sense. The constraints of conservative vocabulary did not prevent them from outlining proposals for far-reaching economic reform. It is significant that many of their articles (and Andropov himself) used *sovershenstvovanie* and *perestroika* almost interchangeably to indicate the requirement and solutions for change. In the Andropov era commentators were allowed, and took advantage of, considerable latitude in interpreting labour terminology. And while no-one overtly challenged the primary role of the state in economic management or the full employment doctrine, the Andropov administration's devolutionary and decentralizing proposals nevertheless represented a serious attempt to leaven the overwhelmingly intrusive control of state economic management.

Andropov's short time in office saw a remarkable degree of diversity and intensity in the economic debate. While there were undoubtedly limits, or 'red lines', beyond which one could not go, he succeeded in engendering an environment within which serious economic debate could flourish. Although socialist morality, planning–technocratic and incentive–humanistic prescriptions emphasized different and sometimes apparently incongruous principles, they contributed to the development of an interlinked and integrated labour philosophy. For example, the devolution of the centre's powers in accordance with the original interpretation of democratic centralism, did not arise out of some abstract ideal to 'democratize' society. It was motivated above all by the need to restore accountability and responsibility in economic management and relationships. In doing so, it sought also to rekindle the Soviet work ethic. Similarly, while it did not eschew coercive methods, the Andropov administration believed that discipline at the workplace could only be achieved by developing a genuine *chuvstvo khozyaina* in the worker, thereby creating a sense of common interest between the individual, collective and state. The attainment of these objectives was, in turn, consonant with the good management and order of the economy based on rational planning, efficient utilization of resources and scientific–technological progress. Although it did not have time to implement its vision of economic reform, the Andropov administration attempted at least to reconcile apparently disparate elements into a holistic, comprehensive ideology in which socialist morality, planning–technocratic and incentive–humanistic ideas were intended to be mutually dependent and reinforcing. In the end, it is this multidimensionality and interconnectedness that best defines the Andropov conception of Soviet labour ideology.

The Andropov legacy

The gulf between policy formulation and its implementation under Andropov perhaps explains why many writers have underestimated the importance of this period in the development of Soviet economic thought. The obvious mismatch between theory and practice has even led some writers to question the relevance of ideology. For Whitefield (1993, p. 17), Soviet politics was dominated by functional relationships in which industrial ministries were the 'hegemonic actors', the Communist Party was 'weak', and 'political control at all levels was ineffective'. He argues that social stability 'was not based on force, a relationship between official and mass culture, a social contract, the success of the socialization programme, or a normative commitment to the legitimacy of the ideology; rather, it was organized by the manner in which ministerial power structured social interests, power, and rationality'. Consistent with this hypothesis, Whitefield (ibid., p. 247) identifies the main reason for the Soviet Union's demise as Gorbachev's resolute pursuit of an 'anti-ministerial strategy': 'As societies hold together, so they fall apart; and the Soviet Union fell apart along the lines of the forces which had previously held it together.'

The principal weakness of Whitefield's thesis is that it does not explain why Soviet leaders felt moved to undertake such an obviously risky and difficult course of action. To suggest they did so simply through some quasi-abstract desire to regain political authority explains nothing. Such a theory fails to account for the sharp increase in the intensity of anti-ministerialism from the early 1980s, and the fact that this coincided with the mounting evidence of Soviet economic difficulties.

In fact, the negative socioeconomic phenomena affecting Soviet society had become so acute, and their consequences so damaging, that by the time Andropov became General Secretary the regime no longer felt itself able to postpone action. The idea of *intensifikatsiya* embraced not only the use of so-called intensive economic methods, but also reflected a real sense of urgency in the search for solutions. In these circumstances, labour ideology was crucially significant, for it went to the core of *intensifikatsiya* – the search for greater labour productivity. Contrary to the case under Brezhnev, where ideas generally served ceremonial, propaganda or safety valve purposes, thinking on labour issues in the Andropov era provided the philosophical foundation for, and guide to, concrete policy action.

Although Hewett, Zaslavskaya and others were right in pointing out that Andropov's impact was greatly minimized by his short time in power, he nevertheless left a hugely important legacy. In the first place, the Andropov period saw a major reexamination of the place and function of labour in Soviet society. Under Brezhnev the idea of the Soviet Union as the workers' state in which every able-bodied citizen had a duty to work conscientiously, lost its meaning. Work came to be viewed less as a duty than as a right, a means of 'social protection' and 'social welfare' rather than the instrument of economic and social growth. Soviet society became the ultimate parody of Galbraith's (1987, p. 111) maxim that, '[i]n our own time...the central concern in all public policy is not in getting goods produced; rather it is in providing employment for all who seek to produce them.'

Andropov sought to change this balance by restoring the value and relevance of work performed and, in the process, challenging the traditional dominance in Soviet society of producer over consumer. Although the full employment doctrine remained intact for the time being, the ideological emphasis changed from protection of the rights of the producer to the satisfaction of consumer needs. Labour and employment had to have productive content, and not be limited merely to the individual's occupation of a workplace, performing work of little or no benefit to society. The changes in economic and labour thinking during Andropov's short period in power established an obvious tension between equity and efficiency considerations, challenging the comfortable ideological harmony between them that had been a feature of Brezhnev's 'developed socialism'.

In effect, what took place under Andropov might usefully be called the first stage in the 'economization' of Soviet politics post-Brezhnev. Whitefield (1993, p. 97) uses this term to describe a situation in which the power of the industrial ministries was so great as to confine the state's role to that of mere executor of their economic interests. It seems to me, however, that 'economization' of state and politics refers more pertinently to the impact of the changing equity–efficiency balance on Soviet society: the growing importance of economic performance and, correspondingly, the erosion of traditional equity–first and political–ideological assumptions.

The consequences of the 'economization of politics' on labour ideology were far-reaching, if not readily apparent until some time after Gorbachev's accession. First, reexamination of the use of labour underlined the truth that the phenomenon of labour shortage was illusory or artificial. The real issue was the enormous waste of human and material resources throughout the Soviet economy. It was clear as well that the country suffered severely from the related problems of overemployment and underemployment; there were excessive numbers of people underperforming in production that bore little relation to individual and societal needs. From this, it followed that certain types of labour were obsolescent, and that employment patterns would, sooner rather than later, have to be shaped according to the country's changing socioeconomic priorities. There was now much more pressure for individual workplaces to be economically useful, and not sinecures whose principal *raison d'etre* was the avoidance of unemployment. At the same time, the concept of a 'labour market', although still taboo, grew out of the recognition that considerations of supply and demand increasingly determined both the availability of workers and types of work, and levels of performance.

Second, while the concept of 'rational' (or conditional) full employment was not discussed in earnest until after Gorbachev's advent to power, it was already implicit in the search for economic efficiency and rationalization. In this context, Kotlyar (1983, p. 108) introduced an important refinement to the conventional understanding of full employment under socialism, by defining it as the equivalence on a national scale between the number of work vacancies and job applicants. He stressed that socialist full employment did not exclude the possibility of 'disproportions of a (non-capitalist), non-antagonistic kind', that is, structural and geographical labour imbalances. Kotlyar's comments amounted to more than just a simple restatement of the well-known problem of labour surpluses, in which non-employment in Central Asia and the Caucasus was viewed from either a moralistic (every able-bodied person must work) or labour shortage perspective. In proposing the geographical redistribution of labour as a means of 'softening the surplus' of the able-bodied population in these areas, he (ibid., p. 117) tacitly challenged the conventional wisdom that such people chose not to participate in social production. Later, under Gorbachev, similar thoughts were to translate into an acknowledgement that many of the so-called 'non-employed' (*nezanyatye*) in labour surplus regions were in fact 'unemployed' (*bezrabotnye*).

It was also inevitable that any solution to the problem of the economy's 'material-intensiveness' (read profligate waste and inefficiency) would require a substantial overhaul of the existing system of economic management and relations. First, as Abalkin and others pointed out, contemporary production demanded a socioeconomic mechanism capable of stimulating the profound attitudinal changes towards labour sought by the regime. Second, political leaders, academics and enterprise managers alike, took the view that the power of the branch ministries had to be reduced, if not broken, if reforms were to be implemented successfully. Somewhat paradoxically, the discrepancy between theory and practice acted as a catalyst in the development of a reformulated labour ideology. Bureaucratic interference and obstruction were identified as (in some cases, the) major obstacles to intensification of the economy and improved labour productivity through 'normal', incremental means. Consequently, a 'radical restructuring' would be needed to remove or bypass this obstruction to the implementation of economic reforms and the development of responsibility and accountability in society (Kurashvili, 1983, p. 47). The large-scale experiment introduced in January 1984 testified to this dual and mutually reinforcing agenda: the restoration of labour values on the one hand, and the reduction of the powers of the branch ministries on the other. Despite its very disappointing practical results, Aslund (1991, p. 95) rightly claimed that the experiment at least 'got the reformist ball rolling' by legitimizing 'sharp systemic criticism' and mobilizing reformist economists, organizationally and intellectually.

Ultimately, Andropov's most important achievement was to break the mould of Brezhnevian stagnation and extend the limits of the ideologically possible. While the viewpoint of economists such as Karagedov and Kurashvili diverged considerably in some respects from the ideological mainstream, the fact that they were allowed, even encouraged, to express their arguments in fairly stark terms, suggests in itself the existence of a much more dynamic intellectual environment. What was once radical now became less so, and hence much more acceptable. The significance of Andropov's contribution lay, then, not in specific labour policies that remained largely unfulfilled during his lifetime, but in his creation of a more receptive ideological framework and psychological climate, from which subsequent reforms could and did naturally develop.

3
Soviet Labour Ideology during the Chernenko Interregnum

> The justification of subordination is normally called an ideology.　　　　　　　　Hillel Ticktin (1992, p. 16).

Introduction

Few Soviet leaders have been held in such universal derision and disregard as Konstantin Chernenko. His contribution to the development of the Soviet Union has been dismissed altogether by many commentators, sometimes in abusive terms. Hedrick Smith (1991, p. 76) described him as a 'doddering Brezhnev toady and life-long *apparatchik*,' and claimed he was 'even more of a geriatric embarrassment' than his patron had been. In more restrained vein, Alec Nove (1992, p. 391) summed up Chernenko's brief time as General Secretary as 'the last futile attempt of the older generation, which came politically of age under Stalin, to cling to the old ways'. Even those writers, such as Ilya Zemtsov (1989, p. 2), who have attempted to portray Chernenko in a more sympathetic light – as a man with liberal credentials and humane inclinations – have nonetheless labelled him as 'a nondescript character, a personification of the Party line,' and 'a physically and intellectually feeble leader'.

This short chapter looks at the hiatus in the evolution of labour ideology during the 13 months between Andropov's death in February 1984 and the accession of Gorbachev in March 1985. The argument presented here is in many respects consistent with the view of Chernenko as ideologically conservative and unoriginal. At the same time, however, it challenges claims that he 'continued Brezhnev's immobilism rather than Andropov's active style' (Ellman and Kontorovich,

1992, p. 15), or tried to reverse his predecessor's reforms by unleashing 'a new attack on democracy' (Zaslavskaya, 1990, p. 46).

Notions that Chernenko was merely a second-rate imitator of Leonid Brezhnev and/or a diehard reactionary are not supported by the complex nature of Soviet labour ideology during this period. Far from being uniform, official attitudes towards labour revealed an 'antagonistic'[1] mix of policies in which a Brezhnevian emphasis on 'developed socialism', ideological methods and planning 'improvements', coexisted uneasily with the expansion of typically Andropovian prescriptions such as the devolution of enterprise management. Competing policy prescriptions were neither bound by a unifying political logic nor integrated within a mutually reinforcing labour philosophy, as occurred under Andropov. This disjunction ensured that Chernenko's legacy would be essentially passive: reforms introduced by his predecessor were allowed to develop, while the ineffectualness of his own rule served to emphasize the need for further (and radical) change under Gorbachev.

Continuity and change – conflicting prescriptions in labour ideology under Chernenko

Chernenko had little opportunity, let alone inclination, to depart from the broad policy approaches to labour productivity pursued under Andropov. The shortness of his interregnum (and his ill-health during much of it) ensured that the regime continued to look for solutions along socialist morality, planning–technocratic and incentive–humanistic lines, rather than pursue either more radical conservative or reformist policies. That said, within this paradigm there were important differences of emphasis and nuance that highlighted the relative influence of Brezhnevian developed socialism, notions of socialist justice, collectivism and 'socialist legality', and the regime's commitment to *chuvstvo khozyaina* and enterprise devolution.

Socialist morality

Socialist morality under Chernenko took up many ideas popularized during his predecessor's rule. Soon after he came to power, Chernenko (1984c, p. 2) told workers at a Moscow metallurgical factory that '[i]t is precisely labour, and not the talk of it...that is the tried and true criterion of a human being's political consciousness'. In its timing, venue and content, Chernenko's address closely paralleled Andropov's (*Pravda*, 1 February 1983, p. 2) famous Ordzhonikidze speech in January 1983 (Chapter 2 above). Both speeches were delivered at about the same stage in their respective administrations (just over two and a half months after becoming General Secretary); both were given at prominent factories in key areas of heavy industry; and, finally, both leaders used the occasion to remind Soviet citizens of their responsibility to work conscientiously and productively.

Chernenko appears to have shared much of Andropov's ideological commitment to the concept of performance-based pay and, conversely, opposition to *uravnilovka*. At the All-Union Conference of People's Controllers in October 1984, he (1984d, p. 1) criticized *uravnilovka* as 'a trend which favours the loafer and the bungler and which . . . offends and infringes [the interests] of the good, conscientious worker'. These themes were repeatedly emphasized throughout the Chernenko period. For example, a *Pravda* item based on his article, *'Na uroven trebovanii razvitogo sotsializma'* (Chernenko, 1985a, p. 3), stated that '[t]he strict dependence of wages and incomes on the actual results of labour is an obligatory norm and law of developed socialism'.

Socialist morality under Chernenko revolved around the constant reiteration of the notions of 'organization', 'order', 'discipline', 'socialist legality' and 'social justice'. At the Extraordinary Plenum held following Andropov's death, the new General Secretary (1984a, p. 2) declared the issue of organization and order to be 'one of basic principle'.[2] At the level of specifics, there continued to be injunctions against *tekuchest* and the diversion of workers away from primary labour tasks (*Pravda*, 3 October 1984, p. 1).

Chernenko's position on such issues was in many respects very similar to Andropov's. Nevertheless, there were important differences in approach between them. In the first place, Chernenko's conception of socialist morality was more general in scope. Whereas Andropov focused on socialist morality largely in terms of its direct impact on labour discipline and performance, Chernenko (1985a, p. 3) linked morality in the workplace with that in life as a whole. He argued that 'in order to work better, one must lead a better life'. Chernenko's broader approach towards socialist morality was reflected in his attitude towards drunkenness and alcoholism. After acknowledging the adverse effect of drunkenness on production, he (1984d, p. 1) added more generally that it cast 'a shadow on our way of life' and called for 'more resolute and considered action with the aim of ridding society of this great evil'.

Chernenko's belief that declining moral standards throughout society, and not simply in the workplace, were a prime cause of the Soviet Union's economic difficulties, naturally entailed a different approach in the search for solutions. His perspective on socialist morality emphasized ideological upbringing, education and moral example, instead of 'negative incentives' such as job dismissals and the transfer of slack workers to less well-paid positions. Chernenko overwhelmingly favoured the use of conditioned over condign power (Dembinski, 1991, pp. 76–9) – the inculcation or consolidation of social and political values rather than the threat of criminal and financial sanctions.

The Chernenko regime's 'moral–ideological' approach towards order and discipline centred on the development of a 'genuine spirit of collectivism' (*Pravda* editorial, 14 March 1984, p. 1), defined as 'the conviction of each person in the commonality of their interests with those of the collective and society in general, incorporating the requirement to act for the common good at all times and in everything'. The importance of achieving commonality between individual, collective and state interests remained the same as under Andropov. But the solution to this problem now lay primarily in raising the citizen's ideological–political consciousness. Although he continued his predecessor's attempts to alleviate the underlying economic and social causes of worker alienation (see below under incentive–humanistic prescriptions), Chernenko nevertheless assigned clear priority to elevating the citizen to the moral standards required by the state. To this end, his administration witnessed a marked shift in attitudes towards the role of education and upbringing, labour collectives, and socialist competition.

The main rationale of the 1984 Education Reform proposals introduced during the Andropov period had been the development of the modern, highly educated and skilled worker able to cope with the demands of *intensifikatsiya* and STP. Ideological and political upbringing, though important, had been subordinated to the achievement of more immediate economic goals. Under Chernenko (1984a, p. 2), however, the worker's 'ideological–political growth' assumed intrinsic significance, and no longer became simply a way of achieving superior work performance. 'Whatever our children become,' he (1984b, p. 2) stated, 'they must receive a class upbringing [*klassovaya zakalka*] in the labour collective. In this case, the performance of labour was seen more as the principal means of enhancing an individual's ideological development, than as a paramount strategic objective in itself.

The contrast in the labour ideology of the two administrations was also evident in their different perspectives on the role and operation of labour collectives. Although the 1983 Law on Labour Collectives had been introduced partly as a weapon in the fight for greater work discipline (employing peer pressure), it had given considerable weight as well to the devolution of rights to collectives (*Pravda*, 18 June 1983,

p. 2). In passing this legislation, the Andropov administration tacitly acknowledged the need for the state to take greater account of individual and group self-interest in the workplace. Under Chernenko, however, labour collectives had two closely interrelated objectives, both overwhelmingly infused with the spirit of socialist morality: to foster the all-round ideological education of workers, and to create a morally compelling environment for 'conscientious, highly productive labour' (*Pravda*, 25 November 1984, p. 1). A *Pravda* editorial (24 March 1984, p. 1) exhorted collectives 'to ensure that the highly developed consciousness, discipline and civic maturity of the worker is not restricted to production and social matters. The worker has no right to forget that at home and in private life he is the representative of the labour collective.' At the same time, there was a renewed interest in socialist competition[3] as a means of reviving labour 'activism'. A joint (Party, Government, AUCCTU and Komsomol) Resolution on the results of socialist competition conducted during 1983 (*Pravda*, 18 February 1984, p. 1), identified its 'fuller use' as a means of achieving considerably improved economic results, while Chernenko himself (1984e, p. 2) called for this 'mighty lever' to be used 'in full measure'.

In this changed psychological–ideological climate, the interpretation of 'socialist legality' (*sotsialisticheskaya zakonnost*) reverted to its previous Brezhnevian connotation. Andropov's campaign against official corruption, 'parasitism' (*tuneyadstvo*), *tekuchest* and poor work performance had sought by forcible means to restore the productive content of labour, challenging in the process the idea of job as welfare entitlement. By contrast, the Chernenko conception of 'legality' effectively reestablished the ideological primacy of the 'protection of workers' rights' over the search for greater efficiency and productivity. Complaints about the ineffectualness of coercive means in improving labour discipline (Sadikov, 1983, p. 3) gave way to reminders about the sanctity of workers' rights and complaints about their infringement (Shishkov, 1985, p. 3).

In comparison with Andropov's version, the socialist morality of the Chernenko regime was both more extensive in its ideological vision and less intensive in its practical application. Implicit in this approach was the belief that ideology was the most effective instrument with which to realize the Soviet state's ambitious political and social, as well as economic, agenda – developed socialism. Many of the ideas underpinning Chernenko's brand of socialist morality transcended the struggle to achieve higher labour productivity and superior economic performance. Conviction in the righteousness of its cause also meant that the Chernenko administration rarely saw either the need or the propriety of pursuing tough measures to implement workplace order and discipline. In effect, the intrinsic strength of Marxist-Leninist ideology together with mechanisms for the propagation of its values – improvements in education and the expansion of collective forms of labour – were considered generally sufficient. Although some Western writers (for example, Lewin, 1991, p. 238; Jowitt, 1993, p. 227) have accused Soviet leaders of cynically manipulating ideology, the evidence suggests that many of Chernenko's ideological convictions were heartfelt, if a little simple. Far from wishing to explore Soviet society 'in all its complexities and contradictions', as Zemtsov (1989, p. 137) has claimed, Chernenko pursued an essentially reductionist socialist morality based on an idealized view of human nature, one which led him to underestimate grossly the extent of popular disaffection and indifference.

Planning–technocratic prescriptions

The planning–technocratic approach of the Chernenko administration was encapsulated in the classic Brezhnevian aphorism, 'the economy must be economical' (Chernenko, 1985b, p. 2). Under Chernenko, planning discipline, STP and SOL became subordinated to the immediate task of economizing resources, human and material. 'To produce more with less', he (1985b, p. 1) declared, 'is the simple formula for intensive growth of the economy'.

The Chernenko administration considered a range of planning–technocratic prescriptions to overcoming 'organizational' and 'technological' obstacles in the way of resource economization (ibid., p. 1). In the first instance, there was a particular emphasis on the idea of workplace attestation (or certification): greater use of labour-saving machinery; maintenance and renovation of existing equipment in lieu of new capital construction; the rational deployment of labour resources; and the rationalization of working time, for example, by raising the shift index, *Pravda*, 13 November 1984, p. 1). According to Goskomtrud Chairman Batalin (1984, p. 2), '[t]he systematic elimination of outmoded workplaces' would lead to a reduction in manual labour and improve production standards. The Chernenko administration also revived the previous Brezhnevian emphasis on 'improvements' to planning. These included combining branch and territorial management by means of territorial-production complexes (TPCs) (*Pravda*, 11 June 1984, p. 2);[4] strengthening economic and social links between industry and agriculture through the establishment of *RAPOs* (Efimov, 1984, p. 3);[5] and developing 'detailed' (ibid., p. 2), 'more taut' (Severinov, 1984, p. 2) and even additional performance indicators.

Regime espousal of planning 'improvements' suggested an enduring Brezhnevian influence. On the other hand, the idea of workplace attestation was consistent with the general trend of Soviet labour ideology since Andropov's accession to power: the quest to restore value and relevance to work performed. The importance of this objective was reflected in efforts to alter the structural balance of labour between the so-called 'productive' and 'non-productive' spheres. At the April 1984 Plenum, Chernenko (1984b, p. 1) expressed the Party's aim to establish an 'optimal combination between the number of workers employed in production and those in management', and stressed the importance of creating conditions in which 'people would have an interest in transferring... from the clerk's desk to the lathe'. Restructuring the balance of labour also entailed reducing the size and power of the bureaucracy [6]. Chernenko (1984d, p. 1) spoke of 'simplifying' the administrative apparatus, while the deputy head of Gosplan, Stepan Sitaryan (1984, p. 2), inveighed against the 'petty interference' (*melochnaya opeka*) of ministries and All-Union Industrial Associations (*vsesoyuznye promyshlennye obedineniya – VPOs*) in enterprise activity, including 'the practice of the partial revision of plans'.

As Whitefield (1993, p. 90) has pointed out, such criticisms were by no means new; many Party and government resolutions in the Brezhnev years had sought to deal with the issue of an inflated bureaucratic apparatus and to change the balance of labour back towards material production. Nevertheless, the Chernenko administration's approach here was no mere facsimile of that under Brezhnev. While its planning–technocratic approach contained little that was ideologically daring – there continued to be an overwhelming emphasis on state planning and mechanisms – Chernenko's pronouncements revealed a greater sense of urgency regarding the need to restore the productive content of labour. Major dysfunctions in the Soviet economic system, such as the ongoing problem of supply, might sometimes be glossed over (see, for example, *Pravda* editorial, 20 June 1984, p. 1). But, on the whole, the Chernenko regime exhibited an attitude towards labour closer to the insistent temper of the Andropov period than to the self-satisfaction (and self-deception) prevalent in the later, *zastoi* phase of Brezhnev's rule. This was demonstrated especially in its handling of incentive-humanistic prescriptions to labour productivity.

Incentive–humanistic prescriptions

The incentive–humanistic approach of the Chernenko administration was heavily influenced by the contrasting legacies of the Brezhnev and

Andropov periods. As a consequence, official attitudes towards concepts such as *chuvstvo khozyaina*, the devolution of powers to enterprises, and the role of instrumentalist factors, were riven by logical inconsistencies and ideological tensions.

These were evident, first, in the regime's somewhat contradictory attitude towards *chuvstvo khozyaina*. Chernenko's understanding of this term was both broader and narrower than the interpretations offered during the Andropov period. It was broader in that *chuvstvo khozyaina*, like socialist morality, was presented as a concept of wider political and social, not just economic, application. Whereas Andropov viewed its restoration as a means by which the individual would perceive a real interest in working productively, his successor valued it both as an end in itself and for its symbolic value – a manifestation of the strength of developed socialism. At the same time, the attitude of the Chernenko administration towards the realization of *chuvstvo khozyaina* in the economic domain was far more circumscribed than under Andropov. With few exceptions,[7] this term became generally identified with the moral (or 'comradely' – *tovarishcheskii*) encouragement of order and discipline in the workplace, rather than with reformist ideas of 'indirect centralization', functioning on the basis of a *bona fide* 'khozraschet mechanism' (Karagedov, 1983, p. 68). Viewed in this way, the promotion of *chuvstvo khozyaina* was more reflective of socialist morality than of an incentive–humanistic approach, since it served as an (albeit indirect) disciplinary device rather than as the basis for devolving real decision-making powers to enterprises. In this context, Chernenko (1984d, p. 1) observed that '[o]ur democracy gives everyone the right and imposes on them the obligation to prove themselves actively as master in their country', and cited approvingly the experience of 'advanced *khozraschet* brigades' where 'everyone is both master and controller'.

Notwithstanding his generally conservative conception of *chuvstvo khozyaina*, Chernenko's support for the devolution of decision-making powers to enterprises belies Kux's (1987, pp. 294–7) undifferentiated image of him as a conservative obsessed with the need for continuity and 'the "old way" of the Brezhnev era'. Under his administration, the large-scale economic experiment was expanded to include ministries, industrial associations and enterprises in the machine-building, metallurgical, food and light industries (*Pravda*, 24 August 1984, p. 1).[8] His short interregnum also saw the implementation of the so-called 'service experiment', enacted in the dying days of the Andropov period, as well as the introduction of the Sumy and VAZ experiments in self-financing (*samofinansirovanie*). The 'service experiment' provided for stable wage fund normatives; foreshadowed a substantial role for enterprises in preparing their own economic and social development plans; outlined 'new' forms of labour organization and production stimuli; and devolved decision-making powers on wages to enterprise managers (*Pravda*, 10 February 1984, p. 1). In the Sumy and VAZ experiments, enterprise profits were subject to set deductions, rather than being arbitrarily (and unpredictably) withdrawn by the Ministry of Finance and/or branch ministries; ministries and industrial associations were forbidden to redistribute funds from profitable to unprofitable enterprises; production investments were to be financed principally out of enterprise production development funds, rather than from central allocations; and a tighter correlation was envisaged between labour productivity and salary increases (Aslund, 1991, p. 97).

Although it has been speculated that Chernenko was 'a facade behind which Gorbachev worked' (Hewett, 1988, p. 273), the former's comments on the expansion of the large-scale economic experiment (for example) suggest that he was committed to implementing enterprise devolution. Averring that 'elements of the new economic mechanism' were being 'worked through', Chernenko (1984d, p. 2) underlined the importance of 'setting in motion the powerful levers of personal self-interest and the responsibility of each worker for their labour'. Consistent with this overall strategic direction, the Chernenko regime embraced key elements of devolutionary economic management, such as inter-enterprise (wholesale – *optovy*) trade (see, for example, *Pravda* editorial entitled '*Dogovornaya distsiplina*', 10 July 1984, p. 1) and the use of economic levers. Chernenko (1985a, p. 2) himself called for the application of *khozraschet* and the 'adroit use of prices, profit and other commodity-money levers'. The importance he (ibid., p. 3) attached to effective enterprise devolution was illustrated further in his subsequent complaint that the 'inertia of old, outdated methods of [economic] management' continued to prevail in work organization, pay, the use of social consumption funds, in price formation, and in supply and trade.

Chernenko's progressive leanings were demonstrated also in his approach to instrumentalism. Notwithstanding his faith in ideological methods, he accepted that the Soviet labour ethic could not be restored by 'moral' means alone. As discussed, he shared – at least at the philosophical level – much of Andropov's commitment to performance-based pay and consequent opposition to *uravnilovka*. Schmidt-Hauer's (1987, p. 272) claim that '[t]he promotion of group interests and incentives in the form of wage differentials seemed to (Chernenko) economically rash and politically suspect', is clearly at variance with the evidence of his endorsement of the second stage of the large-scale economic experiment, of so-called '*khozraschet* brigades', and of the operation of economic levers in general. Moreover, Chernenko was publicly cognizant of the intimate relationship between economic and social incentives, drawing attention to the deleterious effect on labour productivity of the population's unsatisfied demand for goods and services (1984e, p. 1). Other political leaders and commentators pursued similar themes by focusing on the need to create a better 'contiguity' between the individual and his/her work environment (Frolov, 1984, pp. 2–3), and by accentuating the importance of sociology as an academic discipline (see Gorbachev's speech at the All-Union Scientific-Practical Conference, *Pravda*, 11 December 1984, p. 2).

In sum, Chernenko subscribed in principle to many of the major elements of the incentive–humanistic approach. While his understanding of *chuvstvo khozyaina* was heavily coloured by his Brezhnevite background, he was more conscious than his long-time patron of considerations of human self-interest as manifested in proprietorial, economic and social aspirations. As a consequence, his attitude towards change was considerably more flexible and multifaceted than has commonly been portrayed.

Chernenko's conception of Soviet labour ideology

Contrary to the conventional summation of this period as one of 'low-key Brezhnevian stagnation' (Connor, 1991, p. 235) and 'immobilism' (Ellman and Kontorovich, 1992, p. 15), official attitudes towards labour revealed political and ideological tensions that were later to find full expression under Gorbachev. On the one hand, a strong Brezhnevian influence was unmistakable in the emphasis on socialist morality realized through predominantly ideological means; in so-called 'improvements' to central planning and the setting of norms; as well as in primitive discipline-oriented conceptions of *chuvstvo khozyaina*. On the other hand, however, Chernenko shared many of Andropov's concerns about the Soviet Union's declining labour productivity and poor overall economic performance. Typically Andropovian prescriptions continued to be advocated. There was considerable pressure to reduce the size of the administrative apparatus; various economic 'experiments' devolving decision-making powers to enterprises were introduced or expanded; and the services sector became the subject of far greater attention than before. Although Chernenko extolled Soviet political, economic and social progress, he was neither as complacent or passive as has generally been suggested. In noting the 'great achievement' of developed socialism, for example, he (1985a, p. 3) warned against treating it as 'some sort of diploma that bears witness to our achievements and automatically guarantees future success'.

Other critics of Chernenko, such as Zaslavskaya (1990, p. 46), have accused him of being an enemy of democracy and of seeking to reverse reforms introduced under Andropov. Yet the evidence to support such claims is flimsy. It is unclear, for example, that attacks during 1983–84 on the work of various economics institutes and journals, including *EKO* to which Zaslavskaya was a key contributor (see Hanson, 1992, pp. 80–3),[9] were part of a conservative ideological backlash. The Party Resolution on the work of the USSR Academy of Sciences' Institute of Economics (*Pravda*, 24 February 1984, p. 1), passed soon after Chernenko's accession, censured its performance in only the most general terms. Calls for the Institute to achieve a 'significantly higher level of ideological–theoretical work' were counterbalanced by exhortations to study the 'consolidation of *khozraschet* relations, strengthening the role of economic levers and stimuli in developing production, and the improvement of price formation and methods of evaluating the results of economic activity, taking into account conclusions from the results of wide-scale experiments.'

The eclectic nature of this Resolution suggests that its objective was primarily planning–technocratic in orientation: to improve the work of economics institutes and make the study of economics questions more 'relevant'. This possibility appears all the more plausible in the light of Gorbachev's (*Pravda*, 11 December 1984, p. 2) subsequent complaint that Soviet economics had not yet supplied a '(properly) developed conception of how to make the transition to a dynamic, highly efficient economy and the creation of a more perfected economic mechanism'.[10] While it is true that fewer 'radical' articles were published during this period, this may simply have reflected official dissatisfaction over the inability of economists to help effect significant improvements in production indices, rather than disapproval of their views. Interestingly, writers such as Karagedov (1984, p. 2 – see note 7) were still able to express fairly frank opinions in the mainstream daily press, while a number of other articles by reformist economists were approved for publication during Chernenko's lifetime (Hewett, 1988, p. 274).

The labour ideology of the Chernenko administration defies ready categorization, since it possessed no binding internal logic or dynamic. The extent of the philosophical equivocation between old and new, past and present, continuity and change, was apparent on several occasions. At the April 1984 Plenum, Chernenko (1984b, p. 1) tempered his enthusiasm for 'new forms and structures of economic activity', with a call for 'the more effective utilization of already existing management institutions, above all the soviets'. According to him, there was 'no need here to create new capacities. The full utilization of existing ones is sufficient'.

This ideological ambivalence cannot be explained by simply agreeing with Zemtsov (1989, p. 163) that Chernenko 'strove for a happy medium between Brezhnev's orientation toward continuity and Andropov's orientation toward change', for this implies a unifying political or ideological sense of purpose that never existed under his administration. Equally, Zemtsov's (ibid., pp. 223–4) distinction between Chernenko the ideologue and Andropov the unfeeling economic rationalist is useful only to the extent that it reveals the former's greater propensity for ideological generalization and distaste for policy detail. Such stereotyping underestimates both the importance of economic considerations in Chernenko's thinking, as well as the seriousness of Andropov's allegiance to the existing Marxist-Leninist ideological paradigm. Given the absence of a convincing image of political or ideological consistency, it may be that the only satisfactory way of encapsulating Soviet labour ideology under Chernenko is to see it as the classic product of an interregnum: an indeterminate phenomenon marked by irreconcilably 'antagonistic' political and ideological pressures.

Paradoxically, the uncertainties in Chernenko's political and ideological outlook constituted his most important contribution to the development of Soviet labour ideology in the post-Brezhnev period. In describing him as a 'a very acceptable caretaker', Hewett (1988, p. 274) concluded that Chernenko 'was somewhat of a pleasant surprise, mainly because of what he did not do'. Despite his close political and ideological relationship with Brezhnev, it appeared that he 'recognized the need for a significantly different approach to managing the economy. At least he seemed sufficiently convinced that he did not get in the way of further discussion and debate...'.

The lack of clear policy direction in the socioeconomic sphere, ill health, and his very short time in office prevented Chernenko from leaving a more substantive legacy, consigning him in the process to ideological and historical oblivion. These same factors also facilitated Gorbachev's task. They enabled him, first, to increase his influence within the Politburo during Chernenko's lifetime (Hewett, 1988, p. 274), and then, after he became General Secretary, to establish and give impetus to his agenda for change. Just as *zastoi* set the stage for Andropov's introduction of wide-ranging socioeconomic reform, so the Chernenko interregnum served to remind everyone of the enormity and urgency of what still needed to be done.

4
Ideological Transformation under Gorbachev: The Moderate Intra-systemic Phase, 1985–87

'If very many cures are suggested for a disease, it means that the disease is incurable.'

Anton Chekhov, *The Cherry Orchard* (in Partington, 1992, p. 196)

General Introduction to Chapters 4 to 6

The transformation of labour ideology during the Gorbachev era was a metaphor for the vast changes wrought by *perestroika* in other spheres of Soviet life. Beginning as the means through which economic recovery was to be effected, the search for labour productivity acted as a major catalyst for fundamental changes in political structures, social expectations and moral–ideological values.

It will be argued here that this process of transformation went through three distinct phases – moderate intra-systemic, radical intra-systemic, and extra-systemic. The moderate intra–systemic stage covers the period from Gorbachev's accession as CPSU General Secretary in March 1985 up to the Law on the State Enterprise in June 1987. During this time, the regime sought to raise labour productivity by enacting incremental reforms within traditional parameters of economic organization and practice. In many respects, this stage represented the logical continuation of the brief Andropov reform period.

The radical intra-systemic phase initiated by the Law on the State Enterprise was characterized by the attempt to bring about structural economic reform, based on a return to original Leninist conceptions of democratic centralism. Although it is tempting to describe this stage of *perestroika* as one of 'systemic reform' (see Zaslavskaya, 1990, pp. 74–5; Colton, 1991, p. 68), what was involved here was not so much a change of system as the attempt, through 'radical reform', to maintain the viability of socialist models of economic management.[1]

The 28th Party Congress in July 1990 marked the beginning of the third, extra-systemic, phase. By now, the regime no longer believed that the problem of labour productivity could be resolved within conventional Soviet socialist paradigms, Stalinist command–administrative or Leninist democratic centralist. Instead, a consensus grew that systemic change via the market provided the only means of arresting the country's accelerating economic decline. The debate no longer revolved around whether to adopt market mechanisms, but rather how quickly and in what form.

Categorizing regime approaches towards labour productivity in this way is, of course, somewhat arbitrary and imperfect. In the first place, there was a considerable overlap in ideas and attitudes between the various phases of *perestroika*. Radical intra-systemic approaches were evident long before the Law on the State Enterprise was introduced, while the transition to a market economy was already being widely advocated during 1988–89. Second, each of these periods revealed important differences in attitudes towards labour ideology within the political leadership, and among academics and bureaucrats. Notwithstanding these caveats, however, the categorizations outlined above supply a useful framework within which to view the development of Soviet labour ideology. The existence of some diversity and overlap does not negate the fact that labour ideology in each of the three phases of *perestroika* exhibited particular characteristics as it underwent incremental, structural, and systemic change.

Soviet labour ideology in the moderate intra-systemic phase of *perestroika*

Soviet labour ideology in the moderate intra-systemic phase of Gorbachev's administration inherited many policy prescriptions pursued under Yurii Andropov. Although Gorbachev was reluctant to acknowledge an ideological debt to his former mentor,[2] the balance between socialist morality, planning–technocratic and incentive–humanistic policies on labour productivity remained largely unchanged during this time. The April 1985 Plenum, far from being a critical moment in the historical development of the Soviet Union (as Gorbachev (1988b, p. 56) was wont to claim), in fact signalled a return to much of the substance and style of the Andropov era after the brief Chernenko interregnum.

Despite the regime's ideological restraint, the moderate intra-systemic period under Gorbachev nevertheless saw the erosion of fundamental labour dogma, such as the full employment doctrine and the individual's 'confidence in tomorrow' (*uverennost v zavtrashnem dne*). This chapter argues that these changes arose, not as anticipated outcomes of deliberate policy, but as the largely unforeseen consequences of chronic systemic weaknesses, aggravated by serious policy mistakes perpetrated in the name of *perestroika*. Labour ideology during this time evolved more by default than design, in reaction to regime prescriptions rather than as the 'logical' result of them. Although Gorbachev appeared to be in control of the reform agenda, the first cracks in the facade were already discernible.

Socialist morality prescriptions

The similarity between Andropov and Gorbachev was most immediately apparent in the area of socialist morality. In contrast to Chernenko's more compliant style, Gorbachev gave fresh impetus to the campaign for labour discipline. Throughout his moderate intra-systemic period, he (for example, 1987a, pp. 215–16) continued to regard its enforcement as an essential instrument of raising labour productivity. There is a striking similarity between Andropov's (*Pravda*, 1 February 1983, p. 2) injunctions to the Ordzhonikidze Machine Tool Plant regarding the primacy of discipline, and Gorbachev's (1987c, p. 200) claim that '[d]iscipline and order are the number one task'.

Like Andropov, Gorbachev (1988b, p. 16) considered the nexus between effort and reward as central to the idea of discipline. His assertion that 'the material and social position of a person must be determined by work and work alone' was virtually identical to Andropov's (1983, p. 16) earlier statement that '[w]ork and only work, its actual results...should determine the level of each citizen's well-being'. Gorbachev also restated Andropov's criticisms of *uravnilovka* and *vyvodilovka*. In his Report to the 27th Party Congress, he (1987b, pp. 225–6) attacked the practice of 'guaranteed' rates of payment that were unrelated to real work contribution; rewarding the good and bad worker equally was an 'unacceptable distortion of the basic principle of social-ism, "from each according to their ability, to each according to their work"'. Finally, Gorbachev (ibid., p. 454) showed a typically Andropo-vian intolerance of 'parasitism' calling for an 'uncompromising battle' to be waged against 'elements who seek to live at the expense of others and of society'.

Gorbachev's approach to discipline and socialist morality nevertheless revealed some important differences in emphasis from that of his mentor. The first of these arose out of his relative longevity as General Secretary, which allowed him much more time to implement policy initiatives such as the government's anti-alcohol campaign. The initial Party Resolution, 'On measures to overcome drunkenness and alcoholism' (*KPSS*..., 1989, pp. 21–7), and subsequent demands for a 'sharp reduction' in the sale of alcoholic beverages (Ryzhkov, 1986, p. 47), were matched by a dramatic fall in actual sales during 1985–86 (Aslund, 1991, pp. 78–9).[3] The campaign's disastrous impact on government revenues (ibid., pp. 190–1) does not alter the fact that the regime showed an impressive ability to implement policy, however misguided.[4] The extent of this 'achievement' is brought into sharper relief if one recalls the very short duration (1–2 months) and failure of 'Operation Trawl', Andropov's most serious attempt to implement discipline.

Another feature of socialist morality under Gorbachev lay in his more developed understanding of the problem of waste. Calls for tough action against workers responsible for damage to public property were complemented by references to 'the expenditure mechanism' (1987a, p. 254). While this did not signify a more forgiving attitude towards 'bunglers' (*brakodely*), it showed an appreciation of the systemic origins of waste. From this, it followed logically that short-term coercive methods needed to be reinforced by more comprehensive, societal prescriptions if the problem of low labour productivity was to be successfully resolved.

These prescriptions were bound, in large part, with the psychological restructuring of society. Gorbachev (1987b, p. 222) acknowledged, for instance, that the mindset of many enterprise leaders had been formed at a time of abundance: 'such riches spoiled them, and led to profligacy'. Now that economic circumstances had changed, it was necessary to 'economize in everything and everywhere – in production and consumption'. Order must be established, in which resource overexpenditure would become unprofitable and thrift rewarded. In essence, Gorbachev (1987a, p. 275) sought to establish a 'counter-expenditure' (*protivozatratny*) economic mechanism. Psychological restructuring also entailed changing social expectations. Workers were warned 'not to count on manna from heaven' (Gorbachev, 1987a, p. 139).

Much of the Gorbachev administration's approach to psychological restructuring was based on the application of incentive–humanistic prescriptions and will therefore be considered later in this chapter. At this stage, however, it is important to identify the peculiarly socialist moralist aspects in the government's struggle to 'activate the human factor'. These centred principally on the continuation of Chernenko's emphasis on moral example, education and upbringing. Thus, the 'Basic Directions of the Economic and Social Development of the USSR for 1986–90 and in the Period up to the Year 2000' (hereafter 'Basic Directions...'), incorporating the 12th Five-Year Plan (*KPSS*..., 1989, p. 253), proclaimed the need to 'restructure anew the economic thinking and psychological mood of people at work, and increase their responsibility for achieving tasks assigned to them'. Gorbachev (1988b, p. 16) told the 20th Komsomol Congress in April 1987 that 'serious economic and educational work is needed to overcome dependent, consumerist attitudes'. Such general exhortations were supplemented by precepts regarding the role of the family in developing human character (*KPSS*..., 1989, p. 126), the Party's responsibility in inculcating workers with 'a spirit of high idealism and devotion to communism' (ibid., p. 135), and the importance of socialist competition (Gorbachev, 1987b, pp. 296–7).

The point has been made earlier that Chernenko's vision of socialist morality transcended the struggle to achieve labour productivity. To a certain extent, the same might be said of Gorbachev. While his immediate priority was undoubtedly to use discipline and the restoration of socialist morality as instruments of economic recovery, he was concerned also to arrest what he perceived to be the moral degradation and consumerization of society. At the January 1987 Plenum, he (1987c, p. 305) complained about the people's lack of interest in social affairs, their scepticism, lack of spirituality, and the excessive importance they attached to considerations of material well-being.

Gorbachev's conception of socialist morality may be characterized as an amalgam of those of his immediate predecessors. Like Andropov, he emphasized a direct connection between indiscipline at the workplace, low labour productivity, and poor economic performance. He also shared his patron's sense of urgency. On the other hand, Gorbachev continued to believe in the usefulness of the moral–ideological, educative methods favoured by Chernenko. Also, Gorbachev's moral agenda was more than instrumentalist. Discipline and socialist morality were not merely means of raising labour productivity; they were valuable objectives in themselves, indicators of a healthy 'developed socialist' society.

Planning–technocratic prescriptions

At the October 1985 Plenum, Gorbachev (1987b, pp. 7–8) described the essence of the Party's current course as 'the achievement of a qualitatively new condition of Soviet society via the acceleration of the country's socioeconomic development'. The theme of 'acceleration', or *uskorenie*, was central to the planning–technocratic approach towards labour productivity during the first two years of the Gorbachev period. *Uskorenie* was founded on the 'acceleration of scientific-technological progress'. Soon after coming to power, Gorbachev (1987a, pp. 251–2) declared that the Party considered STP to be 'the principal direction of its economic strategy, the basic lever for the intensification of the national economy'. He (ibid., p. 197) established a direct causal relationship between the acceleration of STP, increased economic growth rates and the outcome of economic competition with capitalism. Some 18 months later, the priority given to STP had scarcely diminished: 'The principal idea of our [socioeconomic] strategy is to combine the achievements of the scientific–technological revolution with the planned economy, and bring into play the full potential of socialism' (Gorbachev, 1987c, p. 308).

The acceleration of STP went to the heart of what Gorbachev (1987a, p. 197) identified as 'the main criterion of economic development today – the achievement of good end-results together with the most efficient utilization of resources'. STP became the nucleus of regime efforts to raise labour productivity by planning–technocratic means. Its importance was demonstrated in the regime's approach to five major policy questions: (a) the modernization and rationalization of production processes; (b) transformation of the character of labour; (c) the development of superior production standards; (d) creation of 'the new type of worker'; and (e) the rational deployment of labour resources and managing the process of structural adjustment.

The modernization and rationalization of production processes

The acceleration of STP was linked to the modernization of production through the reequipment of existing plant (*perevooruzhenie*). In June 1985, Gorbachev (1987a, pp. 257–8) told a conference on the acceleration of STP that a drastic change in investment and structural policy was needed, based on the technical reequipment of enterprises and the economizing of resources. According to Gorbachev (1987b, p. 204), the key to economic reconstruction and STP was expansion of the machine-building industry. It would, he told the 27th Party Congress, provide the foundations for the move to new resource-saving technologies, greater labour productivity and higher production quality. Gorbachev noted, furthermore, that the growing influx of new-generation technology in the machine-building industry would enable the country to 'economize on the labour of nearly 12 million people' over the coming year.

The labour-saving aspects of STP were especially pertinent at a time of apparent labour scarcity. Although some commentators (for example, Kostakov, 1987, pp. 82, 87) denied that labour shortage had any valid connection with the search for increased productivity, it served at the very least to concentrate the minds of policy makers on the urgency of labour-saving technology. In presenting the 12th Five-Year Plan, Prime Minister Ryzhkov (1986, p. 16) noted that the anticipated growth in national income during 1986 to 1990 would depend on increasing productivity by 20 to 23 per cent over the same period. Without this increase, he asserted, the Soviet economy 'would need an additional 22 million workers', resources it simply did not have.

As important as it was, the economization of human resources was subordinate to the wider issue of the rational use of labour. Here, the political leadership borrowed heavily from the planning–technocratic legacy of Brezhnev and Chernenko. This was evident, first, in the priority given to reducing the utilization of manual labour. The 'Basic Directions...' document (*KPSS*..., 1989, pp. 188–9) juxtaposed the 'full and rational employment of the population' with the intention to lower the proportion of manual labour in material production to 15 to 20 per cent by the year 2000. In this case, the government was motivated less by the exigencies of labour shortage, than by the consideration that the very high percentage of workers engaged in unskilled manual labour did not sit well with the Soviet Union's image as a modern industrial economy. The emphasis on the mechanization of labour was complemented by a vigorous campaign to remove 'superfluous workplaces' (*izlishnie rabochie mesta*) and implement labour attestation. Gorbachev (1987b, p. 429) criticized the creation of job spots that were based on obsolete technology and produced out-of-date goods, and complained that old equipment continued to operate at existing enterprises, while there was 'no-one to man the lathe' at new establishments.

Despite the greater sense of urgency in official pronouncements, the administration's handling of such questions differed little from that of its predecessors. Ryzhkov's (1986, p. 42) presentation of the 'Basic Directions...' document contained more or less pro forma references to 'the systematic attestation of labour places' and 'the scientific organisation of labour'. Likewise, although Gorbachev (1987b, pp. 432–3) described the switch to a two-shift work regime as 'an important initiative', the concept of multiple shifts was already commonplace by the early 1970s. His only refinement – and even this is debatable – was that he linked the attaining of a higher shift index with the regular upgrading of production plant. On the whole, however, he viewed labour attestation and raising the shift index as a means of bringing additional labour to bear in industrial production. The principal rationale behind economizing labour through mechanization became the redeployment of freed resources to second and third shifts to produce more of the same goods. In effect, Gorbachev during this period continued to adhere to the principles of a Stalinist forced growth strategy.

Transformation of the character of labour

The theme of continuity was nowhere more pronounced than in government statements about the impact of STP on the character of labour. Thus, Ryzhkov (1986, p. 42) linked attestation and the scientific organization of labour with the creation of a more healthy working environment and with 'enriching' work content. Automation and mechanization would make the labour of workers, *kolkhozniki* and the intelligentsia 'more productive, creative and attractive' (ibid., p. 19).

Transforming the character of labour through the modernization of production also encompassed expanding the worker's 'constructively used free time' (Kurashvili, 1985, p. 69). The Party Program approved at the 27th Congress claimed that 'new possibilities' would be opened up for shortening the working day and increasing the amount of paid leave (*KPSS* ..., 1989, pp. 123–4). Such sentiments closely paralleled utterances from the Brezhnev era regarding the 'liberating' role of STP, the breaking down of the 'old division of labour', and the conversion of 'a substantial portion' of working time into free time (Rumyantsev and Bunich, 1967, p. 2).

The development of superior production standards

Despite its inherent predilection towards forced growth, the acceleration of STP also generated a new emphasis on production quality. Gorbachev (1987a, p. 264) described this as the 'most objective and universal indicator' of STP and the level of production organization. The new Party Programme called for Soviet output to embody the latest scientific achievements, to 'conform to the highest technical–economic, aesthetic and other consumer standards, and to be competitive in the world market'. Improvement of production quality was linked directly to the satisfaction of consumer requirements and the country's demand for vital goods (*KPSS* ..., 1989, p. 114).

The Gorbachev administration attempted to realize these objectives by introducing, in May 1986, penalties for 'breaches of technological discipline' (*KPSS*..., 1989, pp. 267–8). Workers were to pay compensation for losses incurred through damaged goods, and they could even be temporarily demoted at the discretion of enterprise leaders (ibid., p. 274). At the same time, the government established a 'special organ of supra-departmental control' – *Gospriemka* (*gosudarstvennaya priemka*) – responsible for raising production standards at enterprises (ibid., p. 270). Assessed purely in terms of achieving declared goals, regime efforts to improve production quality failed miserably. There emerged a clear, apparently irreconcilable, contradiction between the pursuit of quality and the prevailing gross output (*val*) culture which gave primacy to quantitative indices (Colton, 1991, p. 71). The imposition of quality standards from above caused confusion in the workplace, shortfalls in production (as government controllers rejected sub-standard goods), and ultimately failed even in its basic aim of raising the qualitative level of production. As a result, the government's campaign soon petered out (Aslund, 1991, pp. 82–3).

In spite of the lack of tangible progress, government efforts to increase production quality nevertheless signalled an important evolution in official attitudes towards labour. This was expressed, primarily, in the challenge to the 'diktat of the producer' – understood here as the indifference of the monopoly producer to consumer needs in circumstances of shortage. Although Gorbachev (1987a, p. 270) had criticized this phenomenon from the outset, his rhetoric remained largely unsupported by concrete action until the introduction of *gospriemka* and other related measures. By imposing quality standards, the government attempted to put an end to the practice of 'production for production's sake' (*proizvodstvo radi proizvodstva* or *rabota na sklad*), emphasizing instead the importance of tailoring output to the consumer. According to Gorbachev (1987b, p. 341), the material position of the labour collective should suffer if its output was not accepted or did not find a market (*sbyt*). More than ever before, labour had to be useful, and usefulness depended on quality.

As Connor (1991, p. 147) has pointed out, *gospriemka* targeted (and disrupted) previously comfortable relations between workers and managers, including the practice of *vyvodilovka*. The move towards the idea of conditionality in labour that took place under Andropov, gained new momentum during the moderate intra-systemic phase of *perestroika*. As early as the 27th Party Congress, Gorbachev (1987b, p. 216) declared that it was no longer tolerable for workers who produced 'worthless output' to live an 'untroubled' existence. By the time of the

June 1987 Party Plenum, the government's attitude had hardened further. In condemning 'production for production's sake' as 'not only wasteful, but also absurd', Gorbachev (1988b, p. 181) indicated his preference for closing down such production.

In looking to develop superior quality standards, the regime was influenced by socialist morality and incentive–humanistic, as well as planning–technocratic, considerations. An example of the first type was the emphasis on 'technological discipline' and the enactment of penalties against 'bunglers'. The incentive–humanistic influence, on the other hand, revealed itself in the idea that poor-quality consumer goods acted as a disincentive to productive labour; the worker would sooner not buy at all than buy sub-standard and/or spoilt items, thereby nullifying the impact of increased wages and bonuses. Generally, however, the regime's treatment of this issue was planning–technocratic, rather than moralistic or instrumental. Soviet leaders saw the promotion of quality as both defining, and contributing to, a developed socialist society founded on STP. Gorbachev (1987c, p. 194) valued saturation of the consumer market with high-quality goods less for their direct incentive value than as 'the main indicator of a full-blooded, prosperous economy'.

Creation of the 'new type of worker'

The heightened production demands arising from the acceleration of STP placed an enormous premium on the development of a committed, highly skilled and flexible workforce. The regime sought to obtain this through a mix of socialist morality, planning–technocratic and incentive–humanistic policies. The stamp of socialist morality was evident in the emphasis on the moral-ideological upbringing of the young (see above). The incentive–humanistic treatment, which will be discussed later, centred on improved material incentives and the notion of *chuvstvo khozyaina* (as in the Andropov period). Here I propose to touch upon the Gorbachev administration's approach to education, training and retraining.

The basic premise informing government policy in this area remained the same as in Gorbachev's speech on the 113th anniversary of Lenin's birth (*Pravda*, 23 April 1983, p. 2): the modern complex economy could not function without a correspondingly sophisticated workforce. Gorbachev (1987b, pp. 228–9) told the 27th Party Congress that the transformation of labour under the impact of STP would make 'considerable demands' on people's educational and vocational training. The administration's position showed the imprint of Brezhnevian rhetoric and practice, for example in the emphasis on the economic importance of computer literacy for students (ibid., p. 229). At the same time, these elements of continuity were counterbalanced by the development of important ideological trends, the most critical of which was the idea of conditionality in labour.

It had long been assumed that the acceleration of STP would naturally be accompanied by the trained workforce needed to sustain it. The possibility that workers might be either unable or unwilling to adapt to new production demands was scarcely considered. Soviet political leaders and propagandists (Ryzhkov, 1986, p. 23; see also *KPSS* ..., 1989, pp. 101–2) contended that STP could have only positive consequences, unlike in the West where it inevitably led to social conflict and mass unemployment. By 1986, however, several prominent reformist economists began to challenge these comfortable assumptions. In an influential article in *Kommunist*, Zaslavskaya (1986, p. 70) observed that STP would necessarily lead to the substitution of 'low-skilled manual labour' by 'highly skilled mechanized and automated labour'. While this process would satisfy people's desire for more interesting work, at the same time 'millions of low-skilled workers would be released from material production'. Such changes would necessitate greater territorial and labour mobility on the part of the individual, as well as the psychological restructuring of historically stable groups of workers. Since this would take time, it was likely in the interim that 'disproportions' between the supply and demand for labour would grow: 'The incomplete satisfaction of the personnel requirements of some branches and territories will be accompanied by difficulties which some population groups will experience in obtaining work'. Zaslavskaya suggested that, in order to minimize these 'disproportions', workers at risk should be identified in advance and retrained in new professions.

Zaslavskaya's article accepted the standard ideological line linking the acceleration of STP with the development of the 'new type of worker'. But she departed radically from orthodox views by, first, refusing to accept that the worker would inevitably adjust to new economic circumstances and, second, by detailing the possible negative consequences of STP. Although Zaslavskaya did not use the still taboo word, 'unemployment' (*bezrabotitsa*), the 'disproportions' she described as being likely to occur during the period of industrial and individual adjustment, accorded with Western conceptions of structural unemployment. Whereas traditional labour ideology deplored manual labour as a brake on STP and a bar to the individual's access to 'creative' and 'interesting' work, Zaslavskaya identified the issue of risk: a person's need to adapt to the changing economic environment, to undergo retraining, in order to remain employed/employable.

The theme of conditionality was even more strongly emphasized by Stanislav Shatalin (1986, p. 63) when he wrote that socialism had yet to create a mechanism of 'socially and economically effective, rational full employment' as opposed to simply full employment (which was achieved in 'the phase of extensive development'). He contended: 'The principles of socialism are not welfare principles, automatically guaranteeing a job to each worker regardless of his/her ability to perform it. The individual must wage a daily struggle to retain an adequate job place'. To assist them in this, Shatalin proposed the creation of a 'hierarchically organized system' to train and retrain workers released from social production as a result of STP, 'structural-technological advances' in the economy, and 'changing requirements for qualifications'.

The novelty of Zaslavskaya and Shatalin's approach lay in their view of education and training as a prophylactic measure against the negative consequences of STP, rather than simply as a catalyst for economic and social progress. Such a perspective, in turn, acknowledged the existence of a real tension between the pursuit of equity and efficiency objectives. Although acceleration of STP was vital to the nation's economic health, Zaslavskaya and Shatalin challenged the validity of automatically linking efficiency dividends with exclusively positive social outcomes. In sharp contradistinction to official platitudes regarding the individual's 'confidence in the future' under socialism (Gorbachev, 1987c, p. 316), they appreciated that many citizens would be adversely affected by economic reform. Moreover, 'honourable, conscientious, but insufficiently educated people' were just as vulnerable as those with an 'indifferent attitude towards work and product quality' (Zaslavskaya, 1986, p. 70). In this context, education, training and retraining fulfilled a critical social role: not in elevating the individual to some higher plane of labour consciousness (as under developed socialism) or enriching the content of labour, but in preventing people from becoming casualties of change.

The rational deployment of labour resources and managing the process of structural adjustment

The principle of labour balancing – the 'closer correlation between the siting of production facilities and available labour and material resources' (Ryzhkov, 1986, p. 31) – continued to be an important regime objective during Gorbachev's moderate intra-systemic period. The approach of Soviet leaders to this challenge encompassed a range of policy prescriptions, not all of them mutually reconcilable. For example, the government's 'Basic Directions . . .' statement (*KPSS* . . . , 1989, p. 235) juxtaposed moving energy-intensive production to fuel-energy sources in Siberia and northern Kazakhstan; the fuller utilization of labour and natural resources in Central Asia, southern Kazakhstan and the Caucasus; the economic development of European areas of the country and the Urals through reequipment and reconstruction, together with a reduction in the number of workers in material production; and the 'broadening' and 'perfection' of territorial-production complexes and industrial units.

Labour balancing was, however, only one facet of the Gorbachev administration's policy towards the rational deployment of labour resources. The deployment of labour was intimately connected to the broader question of structural policy, namely, the reorientation of the economy towards non-material production. This nexus was firmly established by Ryzhkov (1986, p. 16) when he indicated the government's intention to divert nearly all the natural increase in labour resources over the period of the 12th Five-Year Plan (1986–90), to education, health care, and 'other social-cultural branches'. Whereas the role performed by labour balancing was principally reactive – to correct branch and geographical disproportions – structural policy had longer-term, more strategic objectives.

This distinction became increasingly important in the context of the acceleration of STP. In particular, the prospect of labour savings arising out of higher productivity and the phasing out of manual production put the question of how best to deploy freed workers. Traditional labour balancing sought to resolve this problem predominantly by redistributing resources intra-sectorally. This approach was based on the premise that the overall demand for labour remained either constant or was growing. Efficiency dividends arising from the mechanization of production processes were to be used either to increase product volumes at the same enterprise or to cover shortages elsewhere in heavy industry. Labour balancing, like proposals to raise the shift index, was characteristic of an extensive, output-oriented approach to economic development.

Structural policy, on the other hand, derived from the principle that STP would lead to a net overall reduction in labour demand in material production, with some professions becoming obsolete. Vladimir Kostakov (1986a, p. 3) noted in January 1986 that government projections for labour productivity growth up to the year 2000 would mean a 13 to 20 per cent reduction in the number of people employed in material production during that time – between 13 and 19 million people. While some of these would find employment in 'renovated, reconstructed shops outfitted with up-to-date, highly productive equipment', an overall reduction in personnel was unavoidable because, 'in terms of labour results, one person will really replace several current workers'.

Kostakov proposed two sets of solutions to the problem of labour deployment. The first was to increase employment in non-material production, particularly of young people. Accordingly, he suggested that the government's 'Basic Directions...' statement should include a commitment '[t]o develop completely the non-productive sphere' and 'ensure the influx of professionally selected and trained youth' into it. For Kostakov, the effective deployment of labour resources was bound with the wider issue of 'full and rational employment' which, in turn, was 'indissolubly linked with the rapid growth of productivity'. In practical terms, this meant first that labour should be deployed where it was most needed – the services sphere. But Kostakov's approach also implied dispensing with labour that served no useful productive purpose. According to his schema, the rational utilization of some labour resources might best be served by their non-deployment in social production. To this end, he (1986b, pp. 4–5; 1987, p. 87) advocated the expansion of daytime education, and reducing the number of workers through a proportionate increase in the student population. Kostakov argued also for improved maternity leave and pension provisions, and the growth of flexible forms of employment; this, in order to persuade certain population groups – young mothers, pensioners – to withdraw from public employment and ease the overall process of structural adjustment.

Kostakov's ideas were based on a number of assumptions. The first was that the Soviet Union, far from experiencing 'labour shortage', in fact suffered from excessive employment. In a 1987 article, 'Zanyatost: defitsit ili izbytok?', he (p. 82) claimed there was a labour surplus of at least ten million people (out of a total workforce of 130 million). At the same time, there was overemployment among certain population groups – the young, mothers with children, pensioners. Second, so-called equity considerations should not be allowed to hinder the search for economic efficiency: 'he who thinks that growth in productivity is a function of some sort of self-contained interest of production and that people must be made secure from possible harmful effects is profoundly mistaken' (Kostakov, 1986b, p. 5). Third, and consequent to the changing equity–efficiency balance, labour had to be useful, and employment justifiable on efficiency grounds. The theme of conditionality, which had tentatively emerged in the ideological debate under Andropov, was now emphatically brought out into the open. Fourth, there would inevitably be those who would find it difficult to adjust to the new demands for labour efficiency and usefulness. Such people should either be retrained or persuaded to leave the workforce. Finally, those who withdrew (or were removed) from social production needed to be protected through increased pensions, student stipends, and family benefits.

The emergence of the concept of 'rational full employment' marked a critical turning point in the transformation of Soviet labour ideology. Previously, official attitudes had been overwhelmingly driven by the imperative of maximizing labour power through extensive (recruitment of additional human resources) and/or intensive means (raising labour productivity). Very little attention had been focused on the problems of structural adjustment, either at the level of industry or the individual. The regime simply assumed that the more labour power it had at its disposal, the better; there could never be too much of a 'good thing'.

The importance of Kostakov's writings, and those of like-minded thinkers such as Zaslavskaya and Shatalin, was in showing that efficiency and equity objectives were not invariably reconcilable under socialism. Just as in capitalist economies, the acceleration of STP in Soviet society could spawn losers as well as winners. It could no longer be taken for granted that social protection and welfare would ensue automatically from economic progress. Under these circumstances, then, it followed that labour ideology should not be limited only to the promotion of positive economic outcomes – greater productivity, higher growth rates – but should also encompass active measures to minimize the adverse impact of change on the weak or unfortunate.

This is not to say that there was now resigned acceptance of the inevitability of negative phenomena in connection with the acceleration of STP. Even progressive economists retained a basic optimism regarding the Soviet system's capacity to achieve an effective balance between economic and social priorities. Although Zaslavskaya considered the possibility of 'disproportions', she regarded such difficulties as temporary. Far from conceding that unemployment was an unavoidable by-product of STP, she and others (Zaslavskaya, 1986, p. 70; Kostakov, 1986a, p. 3; 1987, p. 86; Shatalin, 1986, p. 63) campaigned vigorously for the introduction and expansion of mechanisms that would assist structural adjustment: improved job placement services, better training and retraining, alternative forms of labour. While the situation was serious and required urgent measures, appropriate and timely action would enable successful transition to a vibrant economy based on STP.

The planning–technocratic approach towards the problem of labour productivity embodied many of the contradictions in Soviet economic thought. On the one hand, regime policy showed the imprint of many classically Brezhnevian prescriptions: the primacy of STP, modernization of production, raising the shift index, labour balancing. Against this, Gorbachev's moderate intra-systemic phase saw a significant expansion in the idea of conditionality in labour, as evinced by the growing emphasis on quality standards, challenges to the 'diktat of the producer' and, most important of all, the emergence of the concept of 'rational full employment' as understood by Kostakov, Shatalin and other reformist economists.

It is tempting to see this dichotomy as indicative of a titanic ideological confrontation between 'old' and 'new', between what Stephen Cohen (1991, p. 65) described as the two main currents of 'conservatism' and 'reformism'.[5] But such a monolithic view underestimates the extent to which 'old' ideas naturally coalesced with, and evolved into, 'new' prescriptions. In focusing on policy conflicts, it underplays the substantial degree of ideological consensus that existed on labour and employment issues. The fact that 'rational full employment' and related ideas were being openly discussed in the CPSU's main theoretical journal, *Kommunist*, indicates that they not only fell within accepted ideological parameters, but even enjoyed a measure of high-level support.

This substantial degree of consensus was apparent, first, in a general commitment to raise labour productivity through the acceleration of STP, rather than relying on the recruitment of additional sources of labour. Second, there was no substantive disagreement on the point that labour had to be useful. The Soviet Union's difficult domestic (declining growth rates) and international circumstances (escalation of the arms race following initiation of the United States' Star Wars programme) clearly demanded not only greater productivity, but also labour that served a definite productive purpose, for example, improved living standards, raising the country's defence capabilities (Gorbachev, 1987c, p. 39). The phenomenon of *rabota na sklad* was widely condemned, and official pronouncements regularly stressed the importance of 'full and effective employment' (Ryzhkov, 1986, p. 12; *KPSS...*, 1989, p. 123). Third, few denied that, for labour to be useful, the resultant output had to be of sufficiently high quality to meet the requirements of the consumer (whether individual, another enterprise, or the state). Fourth, there was general recognition that the acceleration of STP placed greater demands on the quality of the labour force. Consequently, education, training and retraining acquired ever increasing importance. Finally, there were many similarities at the level of specific policy recommendations; thus labour attestation and raising the shift index were propagated not only by alleged conservatives, but also by the likes of Kurashvili (1985, p. 69) and Zaslavskaya (1986, p. 70).

The diversity within the planning–technocratic approach during the moderate intra-systemic phase of the Gorbachev era may be explained principally in terms of emphasis. Political leaders tended to highlight 'mechanistic' solutions – labour attestation, raising the shift index, labour balancing – while reformist economists focused more on the deeper implications of change. The latter group linked much more closely implementation of individual policies with broader changes in labour philosophy. They appreciated that modernization of production processes and the effective deployment of labour resources were not self-contained prescriptions, but rather impacted decisively on fundamental questions such as the full employment doctrine (in its classical form), and the tension between equity and efficiency concerns.

The incentive–humanistic approach

The incentive–humanistic approach towards labour was encapsulated when Gorbachev (1987a, p. 292) declared in a 1985 speech in Dnepropetrovsk: '[t]he central question in the realisation of all our projects is the individual's relationship to work and to the fulfilment of his obligations, his activeness, in short, what is called the human factor.' As in the Andropov period, the regime resorted to two main strategies in its efforts to 'activate the human factor'. The first derived from the principle of *chuvstvo khozyaina*, and aimed to restore the worker's identification with, and responsibility for, labour performance. The chief instrument through which this was to be achieved was the devolution of decision-making powers to enterprises on the basis of democratic centralism. The second incentive–humanistic strategy responded to the growing instrumentalism of the Soviet worker, and centred on the radical improvement of economic and social incentives for productive labour.

Devolution of decision-making powers to enterprises and the revival of democratic centralism

The devolution of greater powers to enterprises on the basis of democratic centralism was a major preoccupation of the Gorbachev administration from the very outset of *perestroika*. The day after Chernenko's death, the new General Secretary (1987a, p. 130) stressed the importance of expanding the rights, autonomy and responsibility of enterprises, and of 'strengthening their vested interest in the end-results of their work'. At the STP conference two months later, he (ibid., p. 269) summarized the basic tenets of democratic centralism as more effective central administration and planning; considerable expansion of the economic autonomy and responsibility of enterprises and production associations; and active utilization of more flexible forms and methods of management, *khozraschet*, commodity–money relations, and economic levers and stimuli generally. Gorbachev claimed that the key to success lay 'in the unity between central and local endeavours, in the diversity and elasticity of socialist methods of management, and in the development of initiative among the masses'.

Under Andropov, discussion of these issues had led to the so-called 'large-scale economic experiment', in which a limited number of Union and republican ministries and enterprises were allowed certain discretionary rights in organizing production, determining salaries, and in utilizing bonus and other enterprise funds. In the moderate intrasystemic phase of *perestroika*, the pressure for economic devolution intensified, with Gorbachev (1987a, p. 158) calling for a bolder advance along the path of expanding enterprise rights and autonomy. Although he described the results of the large-scale experiment as 'not too bad', he concluded that '[t]he stage has been reached where we must move on from the experiment to the creation of an integrated system of management and administration'. In the course of the current five-year plan, all branches of the economy would be transferred to 'new methods of management and administration' (ibid., p. 270).

Gorbachev's more energetic espousal of devolutionary proposals should not mask the reality that his conception of democratic centralism was substantively the same as that outlined in the Andropov era by Abalkin, Karagedov and other reformist economists. This conception arose, in the first place, from recognition that the centre was no longer capable of controlling the minutiae of economic activity. Gorbachev (1987b, p. 337) described the notion of managing the economy from Moscow as 'absurd', adding that the attempt by the heads of branch ministries to do so had been their 'principal error'.

That said, the new emphasis on devolving decision-making powers to enterprises owed more than simply to an appreciation of the futility of over-centralized administration. Gorbachev embraced democratic centralism as the principal means of overcoming the worker's sense of alienation from social production and its outcomes. In affirming the need to 'increase the vested interest of workers in the most effective utilization and multiplication of national wealth', he (ibid., p. 219) declared:

> it would be naive to imagine that *chuvstvo khozyaina* can be taught by words alone. People's attitude towards property is formed primarily by the actual circumstances in which they find themselves; by their opportunities for influencing the organization of production; and by the distribution and utilization of the results of labour.

Gorbachev sought to realize this aim by promoting alternative and flexible forms of labour organization. The moderate intra-systemic phase of his administration saw, consequently, an increasing accent on the brigade as the 'primary cell of the labour collective' (Gorbachev, 1987a, p. 142), revival of the Shchekino method (Gorbachev, 1987b, p. 222), and expansion of non-state forms of labour.

The last of these, in the form of individual labour activity and non-agricultural cooperatives, was especially important. *Perestroika* and the 'need for democratisation' fundamentally altered the meaning of the so-called 'universal character of labour' (Kotlyar, 1991, p. 112). Previously the only really legitimate form of employment had been in social production. Although individual labour activity was legal under Article 17 of the Constitution (*Konstitutsiya . . .* , 1982, p. 72), it was very much an auxiliary form of labour, acceptable only as an adjunct to, not as a substitute for, public employment. Similarly, while cooperative labour *qua* concept was intrinsic to Soviet economic thought, producers' cooperatives, as Gorbachev (1987b, p. 47) lamented, had been liquidated 'prematurely' in the 1950s and 1960s.

At one level, the 1986 Law on Individual Labour Activity appeared merely to confirm and regularize existing labour ideology and practice. In presenting the Law, Goskomtrud Chairman Ivan Gladky (1986, p. 5) stressed that the right of most adults to undertake individual labour activity would be exercised only during the free time away from their primary job in social production. He also maintained that such activity would not lead to an exodus of labour from social production, but instead draw in additional human resources – housewives, invalids, pensioners, students – who would otherwise be unable to work.

Despite its limitations, the Law represented a significant ideological landmark. For one thing, it demonstrated the regime's commitment to give genuine substance to the idea of *chuvstvo khozyaina*. In this context, Otto Latsis (1987, p. 81) listed among the advantages of individual labour activity, 'the direct . . . vested interest of the worker in the results of the enterprise, since here the worker is the "enterprise"...'. The development of non-state forms of labour also signalled regime recognition of the need for ideological flexibility in times of economic difficulty. Developing largely in response to problems in the consumer market, the Law on Individual Labour Activity acknowledged the inadequate performance of the state services sector. From this emerged the formerly seditious thought that public employment did not always provide the most effective medium through which to stimulate productive labour. Gorbachev (1987b, p. 47) admitted the need for 'new forms of assistance to the population in the area of individual labour activity', and proposed the organization of cooperatives in 'various spheres of production and services' (1987c, p. 311). In other words, the poor performance of the state services sector demonstrated the need for other forms of labour to take up the slack. What became of prime importance was not what Shmelev (1987, p. 147) lampooned as 'ideological virginity', but urgent satisfaction of the growing consumer demand for goods and services.

Chuvstvo khozyaina in Gorbachev's conception of democratic centralism was based closely on the nexus between rights and responsibilities. The allocation of greater rights to enterprises was inseparable from the question of their increased responsibility for production outcomes. Gorbachev's views were remarkably similar to those expressed by Andropov soon after he became General Secretary. It will be recalled that the latter (*Pravda*, 24 November 1982, p. 1 – see Chapter 2 this book) canvassed the possibility of expanded enterprise autonomy as a means of 'creating conditions that would stimulate efficiency and initiative and, conversely, punish bad work and irresponsibility'. Similarly, Gorbachev (1987b, p. 219) looked to implement 'the principle according to which enterprises and production associations are fully responsible for operating without loss, while the state bears no responsibility for their obligations... Multiplication of social wealth, as well as losses, should affect the income level of each member of the collective'. In particular, he (ibid., p. 211) targeted loss-making farms as areas of special concern, calling for resistance against 'irresponsibility and parasitic attitudes'.

The logical corollary of the campaign to increase responsibility for economic performance was the removal of obstacles to conscientious and effective labour. This meant minimizing *melochnaya opeka* and reducing the number of, and contradictions in, performance criteria. Gorbachev (1987a, p. 141) associated enterprise independence and responsibility with the 'proper delineation' of the rights and obligations of each level of the bureaucracy. Autonomy could not be achieved if enterprise directors had to 'conform to dozens of petty regulations and detail everything from start to finish'. Bureaucratic interference and the plethora of production indicators not only deterred initiative, but they also enabled enterprises to escape the consequences of poor performance. The regime attempted to redress this situation in several ways. The 1986 Party Programme (*KPSS*..., 1989, pp. 120–1) resolved to reduce the number of centrally determined production indicators. More important still was the significance attached to the operation of economic levers and normatives. For this reflected the regime's concern to determine 'real' performance levels and, on that basis, establish a reliable linkage between work and reward/punishment at the enterprise level. Under Gorbachev there was a renewed and growing emphasis on the use of profit (*pribyl*)[6] as a production indicator (Gorbachev, 1987b, p. 437), on reforming the system of price formation (*tsenoobrazovanie*) (*KPSS*..., 1989, p. 121), and on the development of a proper finance-credit system (ibid., p. 120). Each of these elements was integral to the effective functioning of *polny khozraschet* and self-financing (*samofinansirovanie*). Shmelev (1987, p. 152) noted, in this regard, that profit was the 'basic principle of *khozraschet*' in Leninist thought. But he observed also that it could not serve as the criterion of enterprise economic activity as long as the system of wholesale prices and planned subsidies remained unchanged. Shmelev's views paralleled those of the political leadership. Gorbachev (1987b, pp. 213–14) complained about the 'large-scale' practice whereby losses made by poorly performing enterprises, ministries and regions were covered by those operating profitably: 'This undermines *khozraschet*, encourages dependency, and leads to endless requests for help from the centre.'

Alongside the application of economic levers, the regime attached considerable priority to the fulfilment of contractual obligations by enterprises (Gorbachev, 1987a, p. 197) and the achievement of 'end' (*konechnye*) rather than 'intermediate' (*promezhutochnye*) results (Gorbachev, 1987b, p. 203). Such ideas pointed to the development of a quite different style of labour ethic, in which reward would not be based on work 'according to indicators', 'but on results as judged by the consumer' (Kurashvili, 1985, p. 71). Although official endorsement of 'market relations' was still some years away, the influence of the market was already identifiable in the changing ideological balance between producer priorities and consumer requirements. The growing importance of the nexus between supply and demand engendered a transformation in notions of discipline, responsibility and value. Discipline increasingly became defined as the power exercised by the consumer in deciding whether or not to accept a particular product – the discipline of the market. Responsibility referred to the producer's duty to satisfy the needs of the consumer – individual, enterprise or state. Thus, Latsis (1987, p. 81) mentioned among the advantages of individual labour activity the producer's 'proximity to the consumer, the opportunity of quickly varying the range of products and services'. Finally, value was measured by the extent to which production succeeded in responding to demand. In this schema, the most objective criterion of economic efficiency was, as Aganbegyan (1987, p. 2) later remarked, the 'completeness of the satisfaction of needs' (*polnota udovletvoreniya potrebnostei*).

The devolution of decision-making powers to enterprises and the expansion of legitimate forms of labour were critical elements in the process of marketization in the Soviet Union. In striving to influence the use and performance of labour through predominantly economic methods, the Gorbachev regime implicitly recognized the fundamental weakness of directive approaches towards labour productivity – their unworkability in conditions of the modern complex economy. Instead, a more self-regulating mechanism was needed that would reward effective production and penalize poor work, and provide a psychological environment in which enterprises (and individuals) would naturally aim to raise the productive content of their labour. Gorbachev and others were later to look for this in the market. But, in the meantime, the regime put its faith in the operation of the laws of supply and demand within the framework of democratic centralism and the multiplicity of forms of labour (Gorbachev, 1987a, p. 297; Latsis, 1987, pp. 81–2). In these conditions, there emerged the foundations of competition, and the seeds of what Schumpeter (cited in Kornai, 1992, p. 115) termed 'creative destruction' – the replacement of obsolete production and enterprises by new, healthy organizations.

Instrumentalism and the further development of labour incentives

Gorbachev's (1987a, p. 292) attitude towards instrumentalism was encapsulated in his comment that a new society 'is not built on enthusiasm directly,' but on 'personal vested interest' and *khozraschet*. Like Andropov, Gorbachev was dismayed by the ineffectualness of existing economic and social incentives for labour. Reiterating the need to establish a 'close link between the results of a collective's work and the system of payment for labour', he (ibid., p. 274) admitted that pay levels were unrelated in practice to production efficiency or quality of output. Similarly, in presenting the government's 'Basic Directions...'

statement, Ryzhkov (1986, p. 42) claimed that the growth of *uravnilovka* and the 'gross inadequacies' of labour and salary norms were undermining pay incentives and holding back productivity growth.

During the first two years of his administration, Gorbachev (for example, 1987a, p. 159) restated a number of Andropovian themes: socialist social justice and the notion of performance–based pay; condemnation of *uravnilovka*; and the need to improve social incentives, especially the availability of consumer goods and services. The most important of these themes was the renewed impetus given to the promotion of socialist social justice. Some of its aspects have already been discussed earlier under socialist morality prescriptions to labour productivity. There, the focus was on regime efforts to punish delinquent workers and 'parasites', that is, to strengthen 'negative reward' (Shlapentokh 1988, p. 3). This section examines briefly the other major dimension of socialist social justice in labour – the enhancement of 'positive reward', that is, the encouragement of the good worker, rather than penalization of the bad.

Economic incentives

The Gorbachev administration's emphasis on the 'positive' dimension of social justice was evident in the comprehensive wage restructuring of September 1986. At the Party Plenum a few months later, Gorbachev (1987c, p. 311) proclaimed: 'We have taken a firm course in rejecting *uravnilovka*, in favour of the consistent observance of the socialist principle of distribution according to the quantity and quality of labour.'

The basic principle underlying the wage reform was performance-related pay. However, its interpretation extended beyond mere reiteration of the axiom, 'from each according to their ability, to each according to their work'. There was now a far greater emphasis on pay reflecting different levels of skill as well as effort. The 'Basic Directions ...' statement (*KPSS ...*, 1989, p. 229) called for the improved correlation of pay scales by economic branches and labour categories, 'taking into consideration the complexity and conditions of work carried out'. It also sought to raise the status of engineering work and the 'authority' of experts, designers and production engineers. Although the reform increased wages across the board, the crucial change was the introduction of greater wage differentiation. While the salaries of most wage earners were to go up by 20 to 25 per cent, the decree outlined rises for managerial and professional personnel and clerical workers of 30 to 35 per cent, with even greater increases for specialists involved in technical progress (Chapman, 1991, pp. 180–1). At the same time, the process of differentiation gained further momentum as a result of provisions requiring enterprises to fund salary increases for their personnel. In subjecting wages to the discipline of self-financing, the regime envisaged that enterprises would find the necessary funds for rewarding their best workers through increases in production and/or by cutting staff. Either way, the result would be improved labour productivity.

The bias towards the scientific and engineering professions signified more than just a planning–technocratic faith in the virtues of STP. The wage reform revealed a pronounced meritocratic bent in official attitudes towards labour, somewhat akin to Stolypin's 'wager on the strong' in the 1900s (Teague, 1988, pp. 333–4). A new labour culture was emerging, which accentuated the division between valuable and non- or less valuable labour, and increasingly prized risk and entrepreneurism over the simple (if conscientious) performance of work. The 1986 wage reform, in particular its self-financing provisions, created a new, more demanding ideological environment in which enterprises were under increasing pressure to rationalize their use of personnel. In these circumstances, enterprises started to look at options for releasing so-called 'non-essential' or 'less essential' labour – pensioners, young mothers, students, invalids. Much of the 'labour release' engendered by the wage reform amounted only to intra-enterprise reshuffling and the elimination of unfilled (and unfillable) job positions. But for the first time, the divide between 'primary' and 'secondary' workers began to assume serious proportions. A 1989 article in *Kommunist* (Zakharova *et al.*, pp. 59–60) remarked on the contrast between 'a stable group with good prospects for advancement, good pay and work that involves creativity', and 'a "fluctuating group" with lower pay and few prospects for advancement, whose work consists mainly of carrying out orders, and whose members can come and go without disrupting the production process'. The article's authors argued that self-financing would push women and other 'marginal' groups into the latter category.[7]

Although the full implications of the wage reform were not yet evident in 1986, the government began to suspect that its efforts to stimulate labour productivity in this way could create certain problems of structural adjustment and employment. A future Chairman of Goskomtrud, Vladimir Shcherbakov (1986, p. 2), hinted at this when he indicated that, 'in extreme cases, if there are no jobs at a given enterprise, the job placement bureau will try to find people suitable work, perhaps in other branches, including in the services sphere'.

Such comments signalled tacit acceptance that the former, more or less absolute, concordance between efficiency and equity priorities could no longer be considered automatic. The conception of labour productivity and economic incentives as part of some positive-sum equation, in which everyone bar the morally delinquent stood to gain, was giving way gradually to recognition that the pursuit of economic efficiency entailed certain social costs. Soviet labour ideology was evolving from its previous incarnation as essentially an ideology of production, into a more complex phenomenon characterized by real tensions between economic (increased labour productivity) and social objectives (full employment and social protection in conditions of intensive economic development).

Social incentives

No system of economic incentives, whatever its distributional philosophy, could be effective as long as the imbalance between the measure of production and the measure of consumption continued to worsen. Pay and bonuses could not work if there was nothing to buy (Shmelev, 1987, p. 147). Gorbachev, like Andropov and Chernenko, acknowledged the adverse impact of unsatisfied consumer demand on labour productivity. At the 27th Party Congress, he (1987b, p. 224) condemned the 'residual principle' (*ostatochny printsip*) in the allocation of funds for social development, adding that inattention to matters of popular consumption and leisure could not help but lower the vested interest of workers in labour outcomes.

The regime attempted to address this problem, first, by increasing production of consumer goods and services. Ryzhkov (1986, pp. 27–8) promised that all economic branches would be oriented 'to a greater degree than before' to producing consumer goods and developing the services sphere. In particular, he envisaged the 'relative growth' of group 'B' to group 'A' industry. At the same time, as noted earlier, the entry and expansion of non-state forms of labour in the services sector was officially endorsed as a supplementary means of satisfying the consumer. And the regime sought also to improve the effectiveness of social incentives by restraining consumer demand. This entailed enforcing the principle of the 'surpassing growth' (*operezhayushchii rost*) of labour productivity relative to wage increases (*KPSS . . .*, 1989, p. 195). Quite apart from its social justice aspects, application of this principle had an obvious socioeconomic logic – that of limiting the monetary overhang and thereby preventing further erosion of the incentive effect of wages (Shatalin, 1986, p. 67).

Saturation of the consumer market was seen by the political leadership as a general prerequisite for stimulating productive labour. But the regime was also concerned to change the balance between goods and services purchaseable by the consumer, and those provided free to citizens through social consumption funds at the enterprise. According to Ryzhkov (1986, p. 47), paid services (*platnye uslugi*) comprised only 10 per cent of the total expenditure of the population, a situation that deformed the structure of demand. The government consequently intended to rectify this imbalance by increasing the volume of paid services by 30 to 40 per cent.

The issue of wages versus social consumption funds became accentuated during the Gorbachev era. It highlighted the tension between the socialist principle, 'to each according to their work', and the original communist credo, 'to each according to their needs' (see Taylor, 1991, p. 243). In Shatalin's (1986, pp. 64–5) view, wages expressed 'the economic relations between society, the labour collective and workers in social production', characterized by the nexus between reward and the outcome of labour activity. Social consumption funds, on the other hand, represented 'the essence of the social-production relations between socialist society and its members' and were characterized by the distribution of income 'irrespective of the quality and quantity of labour carried out by the worker'. To confuse the two would only lead to 'social and economic costs'.

The debate over paid versus free services reflected a real tension between efficiency and equity concerns, between the imperative of stimulating greater labour productivity, and the state's preservation of 'the advantages of socialist democracy' (Gorbachev, 1987c, p. 316) – free education and health care, full employment, cheap housing, and heavily subsidized goods. While in theory such a conflict could be resolved by using social consumption funds to guarantee only a 'socially necessary minimum' level of benefit, in practice the excessive compass of these funds restricted the goods and services that could be purchased and, hence, reduced the vested interest of the worker in 'intense and effective labour' (Zaslavskaya, 1986, p. 72).

The effectiveness of social stimuli for productive labour depended also on changing the Soviet Union's commercial and service culture, which Ryzhkov (1986, p. 47) condemned as 'unacceptably low'. Ultimately, the development of such a culture was contingent on the emergence of a consumer-driven market where producers had to compete for business, and where failure to do so successfully could be punished by bankruptcy (Shmelev, 1987, p. 154). Although the Soviet economy was a long way from reaching this stage, the growth of non-state forms of labour and the new emphasis on product quality expanded notions of competition and competitiveness beyond the empty formalism of socialist competition. The development of an economic environment in which the diktat of the producer lost some of its former absolutism constituted perhaps the most significant contribution towards improved social incentives during this period.

The limits to change – the failure of moderate intra-systemic prescriptions

Socialist morality, planning–technocratic and incentive–humanistic prescriptions alike failed in their primary purpose of raising labour productivity.[8] Socialist morality, with its reliance on condign and conditioned power, was a philosophy utterly inappropriate to the political and psychological context of the 1980s. In the first place, criminal and economic sanctions against poor or slack workers were extremely difficult to enforce in circumstances of effective labour shortage. In conditions where the demand for human resources invariably exceeded its supply, dismissed or penalized workers more often than not simply moved to another place of work, thereby exacerbating the problem of *tekuchest* and disrupting production. Equally, 'moral-ideological' methods, based on 'educational–upbringing work' (*vospitatelnaya rabota*), were doomed in a moral climate characterized by 'mass apathy and indifference, thieving, disrespect for honest labour' (Shmelev, 1987, p. 145). Any real unifying vision or sense of purpose among the population had long been displaced by instrumentalist attitudes and general cynicism.

The planning–technocratic approach to labour productivity failed not because acceleration of STP was an inherently unsound concept, but because too much was expected of it, and its wider implications were not properly evaluated. Despite admitting that the economy was now too complex to be micromanaged successfully from the centre, the regime continued to view it through overwhelmingly mechanistic eyes, as an enormous, integral structure whose performance could be improved essentially by sundry fine-tuning adjustments. Furthermore, for much of the first two years of *perestroika*, the Soviet leadership continued to subscribe to the fiction that STP could lead only to good outcomes – more rapid development of the economy, more interesting and satisfying work for the individual. Even if individuals and enterprises were required to change the way in which they worked, it was by and large assumed that this process of adjustment could be achieved relatively easily and painlessly.

By contrast, incentive–humanistic prescriptions were based on a far more developed appreciation of individual humanity, on acceptance of the worker as a social being with particular needs and desires. Nevertheless, in spite of being much more attuned to the social and moral timbre of the times, this approach turned out to be just as unsuccessful. This was principally because the regime's application of incentive–humanistic policies was often half-hearted and inconsistent. There were several reasons for this, of which the most commonly cited was the obstructiveness of the bureaucracy. At the 27th Party Congress, Gorbachev (1987b, p. 265) declared *byurokratizm* to be a 'serious obstacle' to *uskorenie* and the 'radical restructuring of the management mechanism'. More specifically, he (1987c, pp. 319–20) later blamed 'adherence to administrative–bureaucratic methods of management' for the slow development of cooperative forms of labour in the services sector. According to Gorbachev (1987b, p. 219), then, the problem of reform was one of implementation not formulation, of 'departmentalism' (*vedomstvennost*) and 'localism' (*mestnichestvo*) undermining 'realization of the advantages of socialist property'. The solution lay, therefore, in reforming the mechanisms used to translate policy into action, starting with the transformation of the structure, role and attitudes of the bureaucracy.

However, Gorbachev was confronted by the conundrum that the bureaucracy was both the target and the executor of reform. The lack of alternative structures capable of implementing reform meant that, for the time being at least, the fate of incentive–humanistic prescriptions rested precisely with those who had most to lose from change. Although the bureaucracy was by no means as monolithic and 'group egoistic' as some writers (for example, Menshikov, 1991, pp. 97–103) have claimed[9] it nevertheless possessed considerable institutional solidarity and self-interest, particularly in the branch ministries (Whitefield, 1993, pp. 98–109). Moreover, while some senior bureaucrats were able to rise above narrow departmental interests, many lower- and middle-level functionaries were directly threatened by the devolution of decision-making powers to enterprises and the consequent rationalization of administrative structures. Gorbachev (1987a, pp. 141, 287; 1988b, p. 324) himself made this linkage on numerous occasions. In the circumstances, it is hardly surprising that branch ministries endeavoured to justify their 'distended (*razbukhshie*)' (Gorbachev, 1988b, p. 324) staff establishments and, indeed, their very existence, by continuing to interfere in the day-to-day operations of enterprises.

That said, to attribute the failure of incentive–humanistic prescriptions predominantly to institutional factors is to overplay the latter's significance and underestimate the extent of conceptual confusion and ambivalence in official attitudes towards labour. This was evident in a number of areas. For example, while Ryzhkov (1986, p. 47) lamented the tiny impact of paid services on population expenditure, the 1986 Party Programme (*KPSS*..., 1989, p. 124) spoke of social consumption funds playing 'an ever greater role' in education, health, social protection, leisure, etc. On a more general level, rhetoric about the need to build a more consumer-oriented economy was counterbalanced by the continuing importance attached to heavy industry as the 'foundation of the country's economy' (*KPSS*..., 1989, p. 191).

The regime's ideological schizophrenia was demonstrated especially in the debate over non-state forms of labour. On the one hand, it recognized the need for supplementary sources of goods and services to meet the strategic objective of improving people's welfare. On the other hand, however, the emergence of alternative types of labour disturbed its ideological equanimity. Thus, during 1986–87 individual labour activity was officially encouraged, but simultaneously became increasingly condemned for allowing 'unearned incomes' (*netrudovye dokhody*), with individual farms being a particular target (see Shmelev, 1987, p. 147; also Aslund, 1991, pp. 159–60).

The conflict over non-state forms of labour and their income levels went to the core of the equity–efficiency debate. At the same time as the regime was promoting the idea of performance-related pay and condemning *uravnilovka*, it was inveighing against excessive wage differentiation and income growth. Commentators such as Aslund (1991, p. 163) have explained this contradiction in terms of ideological disagreements within the Soviet leadership, arising in particular from the socialist morality aversion to private enterprise of Party Second Secretary Yegor Ligachev. However, even so-called 'reformist' economists such as Zaslavskaya (1986, p. 67) were ideologically ambivalent on this question: 'too great a difference in per capita income (in individual labour activity) compared to social production can lead to the formation of a social stratum which enjoys a disproportionately large share of public wealth compared to the remainder of the workforce.' While proposing favourable conditions for individual labour activity, she insisted at the same time on the necessity of 'strictly accounting for and controlling the incomes' received from such activity, and suggested a system of progressive taxation to this end. Zaslavskaya's objection to 'excessive' wage/income differentiation here was not so much economic – concern about the possible inflationary impact of high wages – as equity-driven. In the light of her well-documented influence on Gorbachev in the area of economic reform (see Aslund, cited in Sutela, 1991, p. 117), this suggests that policy tensions over labour ideology were not so much the product of philosophical differences within the Politburo, but rather reflected the genuine angst of Gorbachev and other 'reformers' regarding an appropriate balance between equity and efficiency priorities.

The theme of the equity–efficiency balance was evident also in relation to 'negative reward'. In one of his early speeches, Gorbachev (1987a, p. 297) emphasized the need for 'a mechanism that impacts materially and morally on the collective – and particularly on the individual directly responsible – which produces output that does not meet society's requirements.' Throughout the moderate intra-systemic phase of *perestroika*, the regime showed itself utterly unable to resolve this problem. In presenting the 'Basic Directions...' statement, Ryzhkov (1986, p. 37) confessed that: 'conditions have not yet been created that would stimulate enterprises and organizations, *kolkhozy* and *sovkhozy*, to use credit rationally, increase profitability, and settle accounts with the state in a timely and complete fashion.'

Much of this failure was attributable to the labour hunger of enterprises which ensured that demand for labour invariably exceeded its supply, thereby nullifying the threat of work sanctions. Likewise, the reluctance of economic ministries to loosen their control over the operational activity of enterprises clearly discouraged (and made less necessary) initiative and the taking of responsibility. But by far the most critical factor was the regime's refusal to take the search for greater labour productivity to its logical conclusion. Tough rhetoric about tightening credit was not matched by committed efforts to 'harden' the budget constraints of enterprises and ministries. On the contrary, the *uskorenie* period was notable for the government's loss of fiscal control.[10] Blaming the bureaucracy was an easy alibi for Gorbachev's unwillingness to take difficult, but consequent, decisions, such as closing unprofitable enterprises and allowing (even short-term) redundancies. His commitment to the concept of *uverennost v zavtrashnem dne* and full employment made such ideas unthinkable at this stage, as his intemperate reaction to Shmelev's famous *Avansy i dolgi* article clearly demonstrated.[11]

The regime's inability to strike an appropriate ideological balance between the pursuit of equity and efficiency objectives, was paralleled by problems in reconciling planning–technocratic prescriptions with the principles of democratic centralism and enterprise autonomy. This lack of success was, again, due less to derelict implementation of policy by the bureaucracy, than to the fundamentally opposing philosophies that underpinned the planning–technocratic and incentive–humanistic approaches to labour productivity. Whereas the former was almost exclusively directive in nature, the latter recognized the profound limitations of administrative methods of management. The logical contradictions between the two approaches were particularly obvious in the contentious area of performance measurement and measurability. For all Gorbachev's pronouncements regarding the need to reduce central instructions and simplify performance criteria, he nevertheless advocated all kinds of centrally determined and bureaucratically monitored qualitative indicators. These included 'effectiveness of resource utilization', 'scale of product renewal' and 'productivity growth on the basis of scientific-technological achievements' (1987a, pp. 269–70); 'quality' and 'end-results' (1987b, p. 203); 'capital-return' (*fondootdacha*) (ibid., p. 431); and 'the strict observance of contractual agreements' (1987c, p. 434).

The regime's ideological hesitancy was equally manifest on the question of price reform. In his Report to the 27th Party Congress, Gorbachev (1987b, p. 214) called for more flexible prices, so that they would reflect not only production costs, but also the level of consumer demand. Accordingly, he announced the government's intention to broaden the use of 'agreed' (*dogovornye*) prices, negotiable between buyer and seller. A few months later, however, he (ibid., p. 444) warned against 'an extremely dangerous tendency': the 'artificial raising of prices' based on 'an expenditure-intensive approach', which concealed 'defects in technology and the organization of production'. In effect, the regime found itself caught between two irreconcilable objectives: enhancing production incentives through the partial decentralization and liberalization of price-formation; and rigorously controlling economic activity on the basis of centrally determined wholesale, retail and purchasing prices. Its indecisive response to this dilemma meant that the implementation of *khozraschet* and self-financing during this period was notional rather than actual. Shmelev (1987, p. 151) rightly pointed out that, unless the legacy of the 'voluntarist pricing decisions' of the late 1920s was abandoned, there could be no 'objective indicators of value' and, consequently, no 'real *khozraschet*'.

The failure of incentive–humanistic prescriptions amply illustrated the difficulties inherent in introducing 'normal' reform into an abnormal system. Such prescriptions were effectively rejected as foreign bodies by a system that, for better or worse, had its own particular logic. Without a change of system, or at least a radical recasting of its structures and governing principles, proposals to restore *chuvstvo khozyaina* and activate the role of labour incentives had very little chance of success.

Conclusion

For much of the first two years of the Gorbachev period, the regime attempted to introduce various incremental reforms while leaving the existing command–administrative system more or less intact. As under Andropov, Soviet labour ideology during this time combined socialist morality, planning–technocratic and incentive–humanistic ideas within a comprehensive approach designed to raise labour productivity. Although Gorbachev's conceptions of democratic centralism, enterprise autonomy, supply and demand principles, were certainly more developed than those of Andropov, they differed little in terms of their philosophical premises.

Some Western commentators have theorized that Gorbachev's ideological unadventurousness during this period was something of a ruse that obscured his real intentions for far-reaching reform. Hough (1991, p. 471) has contended that '[t]here is no reason to assume that the (*uskorenie* and discipline-oriented economic) program represented (Gorbachev's) actual economic thinking at the time.' Similarly, Aslund (1991, p. 28) has argued that Gorbachev, even before he became General Secretary, 'had quite a clear idea of the direction of his political and economic strategy... but he had political reasons for caution.' This line of reasoning implies that Gorbachev envisaged (and was untroubled by) the main directions of the Soviet reform process for much of his administration. The application of such an argument to the case of Soviet labour ideology would explain its development largely as a function of *glasnost* and political liberalization. Thus, the intra-systemic prescriptions of 1985–87 were not really indicative of Gorbachev's own views, but were instead an interim outcome of leadership compromise, circumspection and temporization while political conditions for *bona fide* reform matured. The subsequent transformation of labour ideology becomes explicable, then, as the gradual but steady conversion of covertly expressed reformist thinking into overt policy prescriptions.

Such a reading of events is not entirely inconsistent with Gorbachev's rationalization at the time of what he termed the 'transitional stage' (*perekhodny etap*) of *perestroika*. He regarded measures such as the strengthening of discipline, the anti-alcohol campaign and the fight against 'law-breakers' as contributing to the cleansing of society's moral atmosphere. 'Without these preconditions – political, organizational, economic, legal, ideological', he (1987c, p. 404) argued, the transfer of the economy to 'new methods of administration and management' would not have been possible. Gorbachev was later to describe this first stage as a period of working out the 'conception of *perestroika*' (1988b, p. 19) and as a time of 'analytical reflection and moral assessments' (1990a, p. 230).

Common to both the Hough/Aslund and Gorbachev analyses of this period was the notion of the grand design, of strategic consistency. However, the evidence of the first two years of *perestroika* casts serious doubt on such interpretations. First, Gorbachev's enthusiastic endorsement of many socialist morality and planning–technocratic prescriptions – the campaigns against alcohol and for better product quality – and their zealous implementation, suggests that he was fully committed to making them work. Indeed, in his Memoirs he (1996, p. 217) admits that the regime had hoped to overcome stagnation through the 'planned mobilization of reserve capacities', 'organizational work', and 'evoking consciousness and a more active attitude from the workers'. He himself (ibid., p. 218) had 'placed particular hope on targeted programs for information science and computer technology'. Second, the considerable inconsistency in Gorbachev's attitudes towards dichotomies such as equity versus efficiency, and central control versus devolution, does not support the self-justifying line that the *perekhodny etap* of *perestroika* was marked by the logical maturation of reform ideas. Far from the transformation of labour ideology being a controlled process, the regime found itself often driven by events, in particular the unforeseen consequences of earlier policies. As various approaches towards the problem of labour productivity were attempted and then discredited, and as the wider implications of intra-systemic prescriptions became clear, Gorbachev and others were moved or forced to modify previously strongly held ideological positions. In this way, labour ideology evolved by default, by trial and error. Even at this relatively early stage of the Gorbachev era, there were already clear signs that the regime's control of its ideological agenda – and the practical consequences of change – was becoming increasingly suspect.

5
Ideological Transformation under Gorbachev: The Radical Intra-systemic Phase, 1987–90

> '*Perestroika* is a return to the Leninist forms of economic management that were the basis of the economic system of the 1920s but that were subsequently forgotten and distorted.'
> Nikolai Shmelev and Vladimir Popov (1990, p. 3)

Introduction

The three years between the enactment of the Law on the State Enterprise in June 1987 and the 28th Party Congress in July 1990 were the last great hurrah of Soviet socialism. During this period, the Gorbachev administration looked to revive the economy on the basis of a return to Leninist principles of democratic centralism prior to their 'distortion' under Stalin.[1] Realizing the futility of incremental change that left the command–administrative system unscathed, but unwilling as yet to embrace the market wholeheartedly, Gorbachev resorted to a fundamentalist approach in a last effort to solve the problem of labour productivity within the parameters of Soviet socialism. This phase of *perestroika* may properly be called 'radical intra-systemic', in that the regime sought to retain the essence of the Soviet socialist economic system while introducing important changes to existing operational practice. Although the idea of combining strategic direction of the economy by the centre with increased autonomy for enterprises was not new, the Law on the State Enterprise nevertheless initiated a new orthodoxy in Soviet labour ideology. In reemphasizing democratic centralism as the dominant principle of socialist economic management, the Law signalled the primacy of the incentive–humanistic approach to labour productivity. While socialist morality and planning–technocratic prescriptions were not jettisoned completely, they played an ever decreasing role in influencing official attitudes towards labour.

Labour productivity policies during the radical intra-systemic phase of *perestroika* revolved around two key strategic issues: the tension between central planning and the devolution of economic powers to enterprises, and the equity–efficiency balance. These questions, which had begun to be seriously discussed in 1986 by Shatalin, Zaslavskaya and others, now entered the mainstream of the ideological debate over the nature and performance of labour in Soviet society. Moreover, the viability of Soviet socialist economics and of socialism itself came to be judged according to how successfully these conundrums could be resolved. In this way, the search for labour productivity metamorphosed gradually under Gorbachev into a more general quest for a socioeconomic system capable of creating a society at once productive and humane. Conceptions of socialist social justice and the social contract were transformed, as the principle of the 'universal character of labour' became undermined by the exigencies imposed by the Soviet Union's rapidly deteriorating economic circumstances. In particular, the traditional emphasis on the full-employment doctrine gave way to a new attitude which focused instead on 'rational full employment' and containment of the socioeconomic consequences of labour rationalization.

Towards the end of this period, the failure of attempts to increase labour productivity via NEP-style democratic centralism had become painfully apparent. Not only was falling labour productivity not arrested, but the Soviet Union's economic performance continued to plummet. At the same time, there was a corresponding decline in the regime's ability to fulfil its social welfare obligations. By the time the 28th Party Congress convened in July 1990, Soviet labour ideology had become largely devoid of content and credibility, having degenerated into a set of shifting, *ad hoc* propositions. A radically different economic system, that of the market, now emerged with socialism retaining only a vestigial and temporary presence in the form of the 'socialist market'.

Incentive–humanistic prescriptions towards labour productivity

The incentive–humanistic approach to labour productivity during this period comprised five main elements: (a) dual-track planning, combining central strategic control with increased enterprise autonomy; (b) economic methods of management; (c) democratization of management;

(d) expansion of legitimate forms of labour; and (e) improved socio-economic incentives.

Dual-track planning

In its 1987 'Basic Theses of a Radical Restructuring of Economic Management' (hereafter 'Basic Theses...') (*KPSS...*, 1989, p. 407), the Central Committee declared the Party's principal economic task in the current stage of *perestroika* to be the 'implementation of radical reform, and the creation of an integrated, effective and flexible system of management that will allow the maximum realization of socialism's advantages'. The 'Basic Theses...' (ibid., p. 408) assigned particular importance in this context to the 'sharp expansion' of enterprise autonomy and to focusing the activity of central economic agencies on the 'principal processes defining the strategy, pace and proportions of the development of the economy'.

The idea of dual-track planning contained little that was ideologically new. Not only was it grounded in the Leninist tradition of democratic centralism,[2] but it had also had been regularly promoted by Soviet leaders since the death of Brezhnev in the form of various 'economic experiments' (see Chapters 2 and 3). However, there were two important differences that distinguished the Gorbachev administration's approach to dual-track planning during the radical intra-systemic period. The first concerned the question of ideological balance. Previously, the bias in dual-track planning had been towards central direction rather than the expansion of enterprise autonomy. The conditions under which various economic experiments had been introduced left little doubt that the devolution of decision-making powers to enterprises was subordinate to the wider strategic objective of a more 'rational' planned economy. But, with the passing of the Law on the State Enterprise, the balance of priorities clearly changed in favour of the former. Although the pre-amble to the Law (*Vedomosti...*, 1987, p. 427) spoke of 'deepening' the 'principles of centralization', the legislation's principal theme was the devolution of rights and responsibilities to enterprises. There was now a far greater appreciation that stimulating superior economic perform-ance depended primarily on restoring *chuvstvo khozyaina*, and on instil-ling notions of accountability, responsibility and initiative.

The second particular feature of dual-track planning post-1987 was the regime's adoption of a comprehensive approach to the implementa-tion of enterprise autonomy. Such an approach recognized the futility of devolving rights and responsibilities to enterprises on a limited, piece-meal basis only, as in the economic experiments of the 1980s. Although

Gorbachev (1987a, p. 270) had called for an 'integrated system of management' as early as June 1985, it was not until the Law on the State Enterprise two years later that legislation was finally passed subjecting all enterprises and production associations to *polny* full is *not khozraschet* and self-financing.[3]

Economic methods of management

At the June 1987 Plenum, Gorbachev (1988b, p. 163) identified a major role for economic normatives in coordinating central control with enterprise autonomy, and planning principles with 'commodity–money relations'. In the first place, the transfer to 'normative methods' facilitated a better concordance between the interests of the individual, the collective, and society in general. Furthermore, the 'skilful utilization' of commodity–money relations on the basis of price and credit-finance levers, and the 'planned mastering and management of the market', would lead to an 'effective anti-expenditure mechanism' and 'reinforce socialism in practice'.[4]

The importance of economic methods of management was essentially twofold. First, they were intended to establish the means by which production performance – individual and collective – could be evaluated. Second, they provided a framework within which such performance could be rewarded or punished, that is, an effective system of 'negative' as well as 'positive' incentives. Both these interrelated aspects were illustrated in the regime's handling of *polny khozraschet* and self-financing which, during the radical intra-systemic period, amounted to practically the same thing. Thus, the 'Basic Theses...' document bracketed them to describe a situation in which enterprises, by means of income earned through production, would cover all costs (including wages) and invest in reconstruction, the expansion of production and social development. In asserting that 'the state is not answerable for the obligations of enterprises', the 'Basic Theses...' (*KPSS...*, 1989, p. 410) excluded budget financing 'as a rule', retaining it only for 'the very biggest projects'. In lieu of central allocations, enterprises would be granted 'extensive opportunities for the responsible utilization of bank credit'.

Under *polny khozraschet* and self-financing, it was intended that the previous cumbersome system of multiple and contradictory performance indicators would be replaced by the primacy of profit as 'the generalizing index of the enterprise's economic activity' (*Vedomosti...*, 1987, p. 429). The level of profit was increasingly seen as determining whether an enterprise was working well or poorly.

Moreover, its significance went beyond simply providing the wherewithal that enabled enterprises to achieve production and social development objectives. Profit came to be viewed as the ultimate measure of an enterprise's financial viability and the worth of its production. The importance of making a profit, or at least of avoiding loss, was associated also with the need for greater responsiveness on the part of producers to consumer requirements. In a very real sense, the use of economic methods of management embodied the attempt by the Gorbachev regime to subject production and labour performance to the 'discipline of the market'. The crucial test of the usefulness of labour became consumer satisfaction (or dissatisfaction) with goods produced as a result of such work, as measured by the degree of profit or loss. The greater the demand for, and satisfaction with, enterprise output, the higher would be its profit and the well-being of its workers. Profit, then, served a dual function as both performance indicator and production incentive.

For profit to function effectively in this dual role, however, necessitated changes to the existing system of price-formation. At the 19th Party Conference (June–July 1988), Gorbachev (1989, p. 337) stressed the need for a substantial revision of wholesale, purchasing and retail prices. Price reform, he declared, was essential to establishing 'normal' economic relations, including ensuring accurate evaluation of production costs and performance, equivalence in the exchange of goods and services,[5] stimulating STP and resource savings, normalizing the consumer market, and implementing equitable distribution according to labour performance.

Whereas in market economies prices tend to reflect fairly accurately the level of demand for goods and services, the Soviet Union's centralized system of price determination largely ignored such considerations. This arbitrariness led to severe distortions, as Gorbachev (1988b, pp. 171–2) himself acknowledged. Many goods and services in great demand required massive production subsidies, while for other items the 'level of profitability [*rentabelnost*]' was 'unjustifiably high, in no way reflecting production efficiency'. Gorbachev noted that workers whose output fetched 'unjustifiably' low prices did not have any incentive to increase production, while others who received 'surplus profit' on the back of 'excessive' prices had no incentive to lower costs and increase efficiency. Implicit in the notion of price reform at this time was recognition that *polny khozraschet* and self-financing could not stimulate enterprises to operate effectively as long as profit and income depended on factors beyond their control.

The idea of responsible financial management at the enterprise level was as old as the concept of *khozraschet* itself, and had been preached by every Soviet leader since Lenin. In reality, however, enterprises had always looked to the centre for everything from supply inputs, to financial subsidies, to markets. Since the end of the NEP in the late 1920s, *khozraschet* had been little more than an ideological fiction. In identifying the 'basic defect' of the existing system of enterprise management as the 'weakness of internal stimuli to self-development', Gorbachev (1988b, p. 166) observed that virtually all costs incurred by the enterprise were covered, and that the market (*sbyt*) for its output was 'essentially guaranteed'. The most serious aspect of all this, he concluded, was that workers' incomes were 'weakly linked' to contract fulfilment, product quality and profit. Furthermore, the budget constraints on enterprises remained feeble; when they suffered financial difficulties, the government continued to bail them out. In conditions where the penalty for loss-making production was scarcely worse than the reward for profitable and efficient enterprise management, economic incentives were ineffectual.

Gorbachev attempted to redress these problems, in the first instance, by hardening the budgetary constraints of enterprises in relation to credit. In part, he (1989, p. 530) hoped to achieve this through the creation of a 'diversified [*razvetvlennaya*]' banking system. He (1988b, p. 174) also assigned particular priority to resolving the question of the 'returnability' of state loans, having noted that 'the lines separating [credit] from free [*bezvozmezdnoe*] financing have become eroded'. The tougher approach of the administration on credit was reflected in the Law on the State Enterprise which outlined the basic principles of credit operations as follows: 'the credit is provided, it is directed to a specific purpose, it is granted for a specific time, it is to be repaid, and it is in fact repaid.' The Law also outlined a range of sanctions against enterprises which infringed credit conditions. These included preventing them from obtaining new credits; fines and penalties for late settlements; and allowing creditors to stop the delivery of goods and services to enterprises declared insolvent (*Vedomosti...*, 1987, p. 457).

In Western market economies, the critical hard budget constraint for enterprises is the threat of bankruptcy. Solvency becomes a condition of survival because in most cases the state will not intervene to save a company in difficulty. By contrast, under Soviet socialism such methods of enforcing economic responsibility among enterprises had long been rejected as both unnecessary and 'inhuman'. Although a bankruptcy law was enacted in 1954, there was no known example of it having been used until 1986 at the earliest (see Bleaney, 1988, p. 75; Aslund, 1991, p. 138). A fairly typical attitude was that of Kamenitser and Milner (1967, p. 10) who, when discussing the possibility of liquidation in the wake of the Kosygin economic reform, contended: 'The logic of economical management has and can have nothing in common with the logic of depersonalized and callous mercantilism.' Over the next twenty years, official attitudes towards the closure of enterprises changed very little.

By 1987, however, the regime had begun to recognize that the lack of an ultimate economic sanction – liquidation – effectively negated the implementation of *polny khozraschet* and self-financing. Consequently, in Article 23 of the Law on the State Enterprise, it sought to strengthen 'negative reward' by providing for the termination of enterprise activity in certain circumstances:

> if there is no need for its further operation and it cannot be reorganized . . . when an enterprise has operated at a loss for a long time and is insolvent, when there is no demand for its output, and in the event that measures taken by the enterprise and the higher-level agency to ensure the profitability of operations have brought no results.
>
> (*Vedomosti . . .*, 1987, p. 462)

The measures introduced by the government were admittedly tentative. In discussing how to deal with chronically loss-making enterprises, Gorbachev (1988b, pp. 168–9) spoke of first using 'various' forms of ministerial or bank assistance. Only after these had been exhausted, 'might the question be put about the reorganization or cessation of an enterprise's activity. Naturally, this is an extreme measure.' The regime's ideological conservatism on this issue was confirmed by the absence of a specific mechanism for winding up loss-making operations (Rutland, 1992, p. 211), and the subsequent virtual non-implementation of liquidation provisions.

Nevertheless, Article 23 marked a critical moment in the transformation of Soviet labour ideology. For the first time, serious consideration was given in a major policy document to subjecting enterprises to a market-style financial discipline. While this discipline was both rudimentary and not at all rigorous, it was indicative of a new stringency in official attitudes towards labour. The particular emphasis on notions of solvency, demand and profitability pointed to a heightened intolerance of production for production's sake and of enterprise complacency and indifference. This new mood was captured in Aganbegyan's (1987, p. 2) comment that 'the loss incurred by an enterprise is a direct theft from society and real people. Liquidation of a loss-making enterprise is a blessing for the population'.

Democratization of management

Dual-track planning and economic methods of management were aimed at increasing the responsibility of workers and enterprises for productive labour. In seeking to isolate (and expose) good and bad production performance, the regime hoped to establish a firmer nexus between work and reward/punishment. At the same time, such methods were intended to raise labour productivity by persuading enterprises and workers that their economic fortunes were largely under their own control, and not that of the central economic ministries. The underpinning principle, as under Andropov, was that workers should be infused with a genuine *chuvstvo khozyaina*. According to Gorbachev (1988b, p. 162), 'the workers' interest as masters of production is the strongest interest and the most powerful motive force of the acceleration of socioeconomic and scientific-technological progress.'

Gorbachev (ibid., pp. 162–3) looked to convert the worker into a 'real and active master of public property' in two ways. The first was to give labour collectives and individual workers 'extensive opportunities to dispose of public property' while increasing their responsibility for its 'effective utilization'. This approach was embodied in the Law on the State Enterprise, with its emphasis on the devolution of rights and responsibilities to primary production units. The other method focused more directly on industrial democracy, on 'ensuring the participation of the broad masses of workers in economic management at all levels – from the brigade to the national economy' (ibid., pp. 162–3). To this end, the 'Basic Theses...' (*KPSS...*, 1989, p. 412) recommended that collectives form 'labour collective councils' and elect enterprise leaders on a competitive basis.

Democratization of economic management was intended to strengthen *chuvstvo khozyaina* by giving the individual worker a greater say in the planning and running of production. On a more 'moral-psychological' plane, 'democratization' (*demokratizatsiya*) in general was seen as critical in developing a 'new atmosphere' in the workplace and in society (Gorbachev, 1988b, p. 252). At the February 1988 Plenum, Gorbachev (1989, p. 67) stressed the vital nexus between democratization and the successful incorporation of the human factor in the 'profound transformations of all facets of societal life'. Only through democratization and *glasnost* could an end be put to 'deeply-ingrained apathy', and a 'powerful impetus' given to the 'sociopolitical activeness of workers'.

Democratization of economic management was important less for the regime's limited efforts to introduce industrial democracy (later considerably diluted[6]), than as a barometer of changing official attitudes towards labour. This ideological evolution was embodied above all in the reemergence of the idea of 'free labour and free thought in a free country' (Gorbachev, 1987c, p. 317). The underlying premise here was that democratization and *glasnost* would contribute to a society in which workers would naturally become imbued with *chuvstvo khozyaina*, and hence would work productively without compulsion. Implicit in such a premise was that it was not enough to remove the workers' sense of alienation at the workplace; what was needed was to restore the individual's sense of identity with the state, with socialism, and with society generally. Gorbachev (1990a, p. 113) noted, in this context, that the 'most pernicious distortion' of Leninist conceptions of socialism had been the steady transformation of the individual from 'a higher value and objective of societal development into an instrument for the accomplishment of this or that economic or political task'. Ultimately, the restoration of *chuvstvo khozyaina* through the democratization of economic management was inseparable from the overall project of political and social democratization (Gorbachev, 1989, p. 400).

Expansion of legitimate forms of labour

At the June 1987 Plenum, Gorbachev (1988b, p. 163) directly linked democratization of the economy with the 'active participation, alongside state property, of various forms of cooperation and individual labour activity'. Over the next three years, the development of non-state forms of labour gained considerable momentum, both in terms of ideological legitimacy and practical application. In the former case, diversity in forms of labour became equated with Leninist democratic centralism. By the 19th Party Conference, Gorbachev (1989, p. 395) was already describing an 'efficient and dynamic' socialist economy as being based on 'various forms of public and personal property and of production organization...'. Since the primary objective for Gorbachev and many others was the inculcation of *chuvstvo khozyaina* and the consequent increase in labour productivity, prescriptions that were seen as meeting these strategic objectives gained substantial official endorsement. Thus, the softening of regime resistance to the emergence of non-state forms of labour in 1986–87 steadily evolved, under the pressure of the Soviet Union's accelerating economic decline, into enthusiastic approbation of such forms as ensuring a 'direct linkage between pay and the results of labour' (ibid., p. 395).

This trend was especially evident in Gorbachev's support for leasing and alternative forms of labour organization in the countryside. In emphasizing the need to change people's attitudes towards labour, he (ibid., pp. 521–2) reiterated the motif of greater autonomy and responsibility for producers. To this end, he advocated the universal introduction of *polny khozraschet* and 'self-repayment' (*samookupae-most*);[7] collective contracts and leasing; creation of family farms and other production units operating under conditions of long-term land leasing; and the encouragement of auxiliary farms. Addressing criticisms that long-term leasing was tantamount to private land ownership, he insisted there was nothing anti-socialist in such arrangements. On the contrary, this was 'the most genuine socialism, for it puts the individual to the forefront'. Socialism, Gorbachev argued, must end the individual's alienation from both the means of production and from political life. By allowing the 'fuller realization of the possibilities inherent in socialist property', leasing arrangements ensured society's interests while providing stimuli to productive labour. In the latter context, he (ibid., p. 523) highlighted 'moral' as well as material incentives: 'The individual receives the opportunity to reveal and realize his abilities in real life...'

Non-state forms of labour derived additional ideological legitimacy as a result of the regime's emphasis on developing genuine economic competition. The 'Basic Theses...' (*KPSS...*, 1989, p. 412) had proclaimed the need to enlist this as a 'weapon against monopolism and the diktat of the producer over the consumer.' Gorbachev (1990a, pp. 151–2) claimed that an increase in the numbers of cooperatives and the growth of 'healthy competition' would have a positive impact on the consumer goods and services market, and on price levels. By the time the First Congress of People's Deputies met in May 1989, he (1990a, p. 573) was already tying the fate of economic reform directly to the 'radical renewal of the relations of socialist property'. Each property form should be allowed to 'demonstrate its strength and right to exist in lively and equitable competition', with the only ideological limit being the 'unacceptability of exploitation, the alienation of the worker from the means of production'.

The stimulation of *chuvstvo khozyaina* and the spirit of competition were not abstract ends. They were seen as helping to solve specific socioeconomic problems. Gorbachev (1989, p. 148) noted that cooperatives, by encouraging *chuvstvo khozyaina* and enterprise, could help materially in solving the food problem, in increasing the availability and quality of consumer goods and services, and in improving living standards. He (ibid., p. 522) also saw private cooperatives and leasing as injecting new life into the state sector, in particular by giving a 'second wind' to *kolkhozy* and *sovkhozy* operating on the basis of *khozraschet*. Gorbachev (ibid., p. 151) claimed that cooperative forms of labour in the countryside had 'quite quickly' increased profitability, by liquidating mismanagement, reducing the number of workers, and enabling 'the rational organization of labour and use of material goods'.

Notwithstanding regime recognition of the growing importance of non-state forms of labour, their expansion during the radical intra-systemic period was hindered by numerous obstacles, ideological and practical. The uneven development of the private cooperative movement between 1986–90[8] underlined the regime's conceptual confusion and ambivalence on the critical issues of equity versus efficiency, and central control versus economic devolution. On the first of these questions, the uncertainties and discrimination suffered by non-agricultural cooperatives indicated the intractability of the government's basic dilemma in wanting to stimulate economic enterprise while simultaneously limiting the 'excessive' wages of non-state workers. On the one hand, the regime recognized the critical importance of diverse forms of labour in stimulating *chuvstvo khozyaina*, proper economic competition, a developed consumer goods and services market, a vital economy generally. But it was reluctant to countenance the income differentiation that was a natural by-product of the increased variety in enterprise forms (see Chapman, 1991, p. 190), all the more so when popular resentment against cooperatives and their profits was so great (Aslund, 1991, pp. 172–8).

Nor was this ambivalence simply explicable in terms of a conflict between 'reformist' and 'conservative' elements within the Politburo. Although Aslund (ibid., p. 178) has contended that Gorbachev was personally opposed to the application of tighter controls on cooperative activity, the evidence suggests otherwise. For example, Gorbachev (1989, p. 153) insisted that 'cooperation … must not find itself outside the sphere of state influence' and, to this end, set great store by 'reliable economic instruments' of control – taxation, credit policy, agreements with cooperatives, and state orders (*goszakazy*). In a speech in Kiev in February 1989, he (1990a, p. 333) criticized some cooperatives for being the 'channel of the uncontrolled growth of personal incomes', and affirmed the necessity of finding 'optimal criteria' for evaluating the activity of cooperative members, including 'hard rules which would allow cooperation to develop while at the same time excluding or minimizing the opportunity for evil-doing'. In this context, he mentioned approvingly a recent decision to devolve the taxation of cooperatives to individual republics, a move essentially designed to tighten administrative restrictions on non-state economic activity.

Such pronouncements suggested that, despite increasingly frequent references to the 'market' (*rynok*) and 'competition' (*sostyazanie*), Gorbachev and the Soviet leadership still thought of economic reform substantially within an intra-systemic, planned socialist paradigm. Alternative forms of labour continued to be viewed as adjuncts to social production, and state ownership remained paramount. Thus, while extolling private cooperatives, Gorbachev (1989, p. 154) cautioned that 'the boundaries of cooperation are not limitless'. And although he was prepared to concede juridical parity to cooperative property, he reaffirmed the leading role of state and public ownership in the national economy. These ideological constraints were reinforced in practice by the overwhelming dominance of the public sector. The concentration of economic power in branch ministries effectively ensured that cooperatives and other forms of production could function only by the grace and favour of state instrumentalities. Cooperatives in many cases relied greatly on state enterprises for supply inputs; faced considerable practical difficulties in obtaining credit; and were subjected to harassment and even prohibition by local authorities (Kuznetsova, 1991, pp. 287–8). Consequently, many so-called 'cooperatives'[9] found it necessary to engage in a symbiotic relationship with state enterprises. A 1989 Goskomstat survey showed that nearly 80 per cent of cooperatives were 'set up with the participation of state enterprises and organisations'. According to the survey, cooperatives borrowed up to 60 per cent of their capital and bought more than 60 per cent of their raw materials from state enterprises, to whom they also sold about 70 per cent of their output (Kuznetsova, 1991, p. 285).

The situation regarding private cooperatives typified that of non-state forms of labour in general. On the one hand, the regime understood that the former near-absolute reliance on the public sector was increasingly untenable. 'Social production' no longer provided a sufficient vehicle with which to reverse the process of the worker's growing alienation. The political leadership on the whole acknowledged that the emergence of previously marginal or even taboo forms of labour was critical to stimulating greater labour productivity. At the same time, however, this recognition arose under duress. The Soviet Union's economic difficulties during 1987 to 1990 were so serious that the regime felt it had little option but to allow, even encourage, diversity of ownership and forms of labour. But that did not mean it was comfortable with this choice. The zigzags in government policy towards private cooperatives, not to mention the reluctance to countenance private land ownership as opposed to long-term leasing (see Ryzhkov, 1990a, p. 215), indicate that political leaders, Gorbachev included, retained considerable ideological baggage from the past. The regime's apparent inability to pursue economically consistent policies owed something to political and ideological tensions at the upper echelons of power. However, the decisive factor was the deeply entrenched influence of the Soviet ideological heritage on even reformist political leaders, and their consequent angst when confronted with the imperative of change.

Improved socioeconomic incentives

At the June 1987 Plenum, Gorbachev (1988b, p. 181) declared that labour incentives had to be 'constructed anew'. To this purpose, he outlined several basic principles that were to shape regime policy on wages over the next three years. The first and arguably most significant of these in its long-term impact was the decentralization of wages determination. Gorbachev noted approvingly that the Law on the State Enterprise, by guaranteeing enterprises the right to raise salaries, had sharply increased 'the possibilities of effective stimuli'. Two other key tenets of regime policy on wages were incorporated in his call for performance-based pay, and the removal of maximum limits on wages. According to Gorbachev, the only criterion of a salary's equitability was whether it was earned or unearned.

In devolving wage determination to enterprises, the regime anticipated that the hardening of budget constraints would put an end to the widespread practice of labour hoarding, since superfluous labour would literally become unaffordable. The 'Basic Theses...' (*KPSS...*, 1989, p. 426) mentioned in this context 'strengthening the vested interest of workers in carrying out work in fewer numbers'. It was also assumed that, under the conditions of self-financing, enterprises would naturally allocate their wage fund in the most rational and efficient way: rewarding their best workers well, while penalizing poor performers (see Article 14 of the Law on the State Enterprise, *Vedomosti...*, 1987, pp. 449–51). For Gorbachev (1990a, p. 309), wage devolution naturally entailed greater salary differentiation which was critical to raising labour productivity: 'Let them earn. Just so long as things get moving.' The only proviso was that the state should guarantee the minimum wage. Consistent with this philosophy, the regime pursued a sustained verbal assault on 'levelling tendencies'. Confusing *uravnilovka* with social protection and justice would, Gorbachev (ibid., p. 413) warned, undermine economic reform as a whole.

Many commentators have identified the wages explosion that followed implementation of the Law on the State Enterprise as a major factor in the Soviet Union's collapse. Aslund (1991, p. 187) wrote that an immediate effect of the Law's introduction was the tripling of the annual increase in the population's monetary incomes to 30 billion roubles in 1988, a phenomenon which amounted to the 'singular [sic] most important cause of the economic crisis'. The 'new general laxity towards state enterprises' allowed directors to raise wages without worrying about productivity increases. Aslund (ibid., p. 189) summarized the general effect of the 1987–88 reforms as offering enterprises 'hitherto unknown liberties and no responsibility'.

Soviet leaders were aware of these problems. And, accordingly, official attitudes towards labour incentives revealed important qualifications to the broad ideological positions outlined above. The first of these focused on the runaway growth in wages and the absence of consequent increases in labour productivity. Whereas at the January 1988 Plenum, Gorbachev (1989, p. 33) claimed that the imbalance between wages growth and labour productivity during 1981 to 1984 had been corrected, fifteen months later he (1990a, p. 481) was forced to admit that 'the negative tendencies here... are continuing all the while to gather strength'. Under the pressure of escalating fiscal imbalances, the government sought to renege on its previous stance regarding the limitlessness of personal incomes. Prime Minister Ryzhkov (1990a, p. 221) advocated state regulation of monetary incomes, foreshadowed the introduction of tough new taxation arrangements (ibid., pp. 226–7) and assigned particular importance to 'anti-inflationary levers', including taxes on wage fund growth and on 'excessive profit [*sverkhpribyl*]' (ibid., p. 231).

The pronouncements of Soviet leaders on the general issue of wages growth pointed to a major change in emphasis in the regime's approach towards labour incentives. Previously, the accent had been on removing the various obstacles – the ratchet effect, *uravnilovka*, ministerial interference – that undermined or neutralized the effect of incentives on productive labour. There was an assumption that a reformed system of 'positive' incentives would naturally lead to greater productivity; all that most individual citizens wanted in the new society created by *perestroika* was to be allowed to 'express' themselves. Once this was done, then the health of the economy and of society would begin to revive. This reasoning, incidentally, was central to the idea of greater democratization. By 1989–90, however, it was increasingly apparent that this sanguine approach to incentives was no longer sustainable given the continued softness of enterprise budget constraints. The regime came to realize that positive economic incentives to labour could not lead to superior production performance while systemic weaknesses existed and the threat of negative sanctions remained more theoretical than real. As long as state enterprises retained their monopoly producer position in the absence of genuine economic competition, and could continue to tap into seemingly endless sources of government funding, then they would give their workers pay rises unmatched by corresponding increases in productivity.

The decreasing impact of economic incentives was aggravated by growing shortages in consumer goods and services. Regime policies here were informed by many of the same principles as in the moderate intra-systemic phase of *perestroika*: improving production of consumer items; increasing the ratio of paid to unpaid services; controlling total consumer demand by limiting wages growth; accelerated infrastructural development in the countryside and in particular regions; and the creation of a service culture. However, these issues now acquired far greater urgency than before, with Gorbachev (1989, pp. 331–2) complaining that most state enterprises treated the production of consumer items as secondary. Stressing the importance of a 'modern and powerful industry for producing consumer goods', he insisted this objective concerned not only light industry, but also the defence complex and heavy industry 'whose contribution to the production and delivery of consumer goods must be decisively augmented'.

Defence conversion – the application of military-oriented industry to the production of consumer goods – was important for two reasons. In the first place, as Gorbachev indicated, it was intended to supplement the inadequate performance of Soviet light industry in satisfying the mounting demand for such goods. Second, conversion had symbolic importance, underlining the redirection of the Soviet economy away from its traditional heavy industrial base towards a more consumer-oriented model. While the actual results of conversion over the next few years were poor,[10] the regime's commitment to changing the orientation of Soviet economic development represented a genuine attempt to treat the individual as 'the object of ... social and economic development' rather than just as a 'worker' valuable only by virtue of his/her labour contribution (see Kostakov, 1987, p. 83).

The Gorbachev administration's commitment to the individual *qua* human being was evident also in the importance it attached to radical improvements in the quantity and quality of housing. Although Soviet leaders had long paid lip service to this problem, it was not until the advent of Gorbachev that its resolution became a matter of compelling need. The General Secretary (1990a, p. 567) stressed the importance of fulfilling the government's 1986 pledge (Ryzhkov, 1986, p. 10) to provide each family with its own apartment or house by the year 2000. More specifically, Ryzhkov (1990a, p. 244) announced the intention to increase the volume of new housing during 1991 to 1995 by 40 per cent compared to the previous five-year period. The sense of urgency that characterized the regime's approach to social incentives was manifest in the increasing importance given to the development of paid services as a check to inflation and means of reducing the monetary 'overhang' – the gap between people's incomes and the goods that could be bought with them (Gorbachev, 1989, p. 35).

At one level, Gorbachev and others viewed the monetary overhang as indicating non-observance of the fundamental principle of reward according to performance. But what gave the appeal to social justice particular point was the mounting fiscal and monetary strain on the Soviet economy. As Gorbachev (1990a, p. 562) observed, salary rises unmatched by higher productivity would engender a situation characterized by 'a lot of money and few goods'. The imbalance between incomes and available goods might indicate that the former were, in some cases, 'unearned' and hence morally indefensible. But the real crux of the matter was that this imbalance undermined not only labour incentives, but also the very foundations of the socialist economic system. On the one hand, it exposed the impotence of intra-systemic incentives in stimulating productive labour and economic growth. On the other hand, the gravity of the monetary imbalance was now such that the search for labour productivity acquired a momentum and desperation that took it well beyond the ideological parameters of Soviet socialism, Stalinist or Leninist.

The search for labour productivity and its impact on socialist social justice and the 'social contract'

Regime attempts to raise labour productivity through incentive–humanistic means had crucial implications for conceptions of 'socialist social justice'. This idea had always been integral to Soviet labour ideology. In its plainest form, it was defined by the dictum, 'from each according to their ability, to each according to their work'. However, such an apparently simple summation masked the existence of powerful tensions which became increasingly overt in the deteriorating circumstances of the Soviet economy post-1987.

The most fundamental of these was the equity–efficiency balance – the conflict between the preservation of social guarantees, and the need to stimulate productive labour by positive and negative incentives. This tension was tacitly recognized by Gorbachev (1988b, p. 134) at the June 1987 Plenum:

> We are proud of the high level of social protection for the individual in our country. This is what makes socialism socialism, a system of the workers and for the workers. But the basis of the individual's material and moral position in socialist society must be labour and only labour. Creative, highly productive labour, talent, the real contribution of the individual to the common cause must be given the utmost encouragement. And, correspondingly, passivity, idleness, a low culture of labour, anti-social manifestations must be judged in the appropriate way – socially and economically. It is precisely in this that lies the socialist content of social justice.

At first sight, this definition of socialist social justice appeared nothing more than an articulate reiteration of similar sentiments uttered under Brezhnev. However, taken together with subsequent pronouncements, it pointed to a much fuller understanding than before of the practical consequences of applying the principles of socialist social justice to Soviet labour practice and economic management. Such statements acknowledged, in the first instance, that the idea of socialist social justice had hitherto been honoured more in the breach than in the observance. Gorbachev (1988b, p. 408) frankly admitted that its principles had been 'distorted' and 'deformed' under Brezhnev. This had 'undermined people's faith in it, and [given] rise to social alienation and amoralism in its various guises'.

The theme of a 'deformed' or 'distorted' conception of socialist social justice was a common one in Gorbachev's speeches during 1988–89. He focused, in particular, on the need to resolve three basic problems. The first was the culture of mediocrity that had become identified with socialism. Gorbachev (1989, p. 211) emphasized the importance of dispelling notions about socialism as 'something of minimums – a minimum of material benefits, a minimum of justice, a minimum of democracy'. Regime attempts to counter attitudes of 'equality in misery' and comfortable mediocrity entailed intensifying the struggle against *uravnilovka*, which Gorbachev (1989, pp. 550–1) condemned as 'alien to socialism' and something to be 'resolutely rooted out'.[11] Underpinning this struggle was the increasing priority given to economic differentiation as a basic principle of socialist social justice. So long as appropriate guarantees were maintained for the most vulnerable social groups – pensioners, invalids, students, young mothers – then it was only right that there should be winners and losers in Soviet society, provided of course this outcome reflected the individual's honest labour contribution (Zaslavskaya, 1990, p. 130). Such differentiation was justified also by arguments that the countering of levelling tendencies would enhance, rather than diminish, social protection. Gorbachev (1990a, p. 334) claimed that 'strict observance of the principle of payment for labour' would stimulate productivity, increase public wealth, and enable the allocation of greater funds for the 'resolution of social problems'.

The corollary of greater differentiation was the attack on 'false welfare' notions. The radical intra-systemic period witnessed the regime's espousal of ideas previously canvassed only by reformist economists such as Shatalin (1986, p. 63) and Shmelev (1987, p. 149). In particular, the traditional socialist tenet of *uverennost v zavtrashnem dne* was vigorously assailed. Although Gorbachev (*Pravda*, 22 June 1987, p. 1) had criticized Shmelev (1987, p. 149) for challenging the doctrine of unconditional full employment ('our parasitical certainty of guaranteed work'), by November of the following year he (1990a, p. 112) was voicing very similar sentiments: 'It is . . . very bad, when the individual himself is not at all concerned about his future. Social protection in such circumstances is easily transformed into social antithesis [*protivopolozhnost*]. It weakens stimulus and initiative, and adversely affects people's attitude to labour.' The principal target of Gorbachev's criticisms was what he (1989, p. 549) termed the 'dependence psychology' (*psikhologiya izhdivenchestva*) prevalent among the Soviet population. In particular, he (ibid., p. 571) was concerned to rid 'social consciousness' of its 'faith in the "good tsar"', in the omnipotent centre', an attitude that was 'the worst kind of social dependency'.

The evolution and redefinition of socialist social justice was part of a broader change in official attitudes towards the role of the state in providing the population with a secure, if not necessarily prosperous, existence. In his well-known 1987 article, 'Gorbachev's Social Contract', Hauslohner (1991, p. 35) suggested that Gorbachev was looking to renegotiate the 'implicit social contract' between regime and society, including through a 'significant reallocation' of economic security. This involved 'greater security for those who cannot work...while threatening less security for everyone else.' (ibid., p. 43). In concrete terms, reallocation entailed raising child payments and pensions on the one hand, while at the same time ending 'overfull employment and extraordinary job security'. Although the timing of Hauslohner's article meant that much of his analysis was necessarily predictive rather than conclusive, he nevertheless identified two issues critical in the development of Soviet labour ideology: the growing distinction between the right to work and the right to a given job; and increasing acceptance of the inevitability of some temporary unemployment. The trends suggested by him in 1987 emerged much more clearly in the course of the next few years.

Traditionally the right to work had been understood as the right to a given job in a given place. This association was reinforced by the practical reality that the demand for labour had long greatly exceeded its supply. In conditions of a real, if irrational, labour shortage, individual workers were effectively guaranteed a job position for life. Indeed, the focus on the problem of labour turnover reveals that the regime's main priority was to fix the worker to his/her workplace. Following Andropov's accession, and then during Gorbachev's moderate intra-systemic period, greater attention was given to developing a more flexible worker, capable of adapting to the demands of *intensifikatsiya*. However, in spite of efforts to make full employment less unconditional, the right to work remained for all practical purposes indistinguishable from the right to a given job.

Three closely interrelated factors changed this state of affairs after 1987. The first was the government's commitment to structural economic reform. This, in turn, was linked to a radical reduction in the amount of unskilled manual labour as a proportion of the total workforce. Finally, and most important, the implementation of democratic centralist principles in economic management – notably the devolution of rights and responsibilities to enterprises on the basis of self-financing – meant that the utilization and affordability of labour became the subject of much closer scrutiny. As a result of the confluence of these factors labour release for the first time became a major social as well as economic issue. Ideas previously only tentatively expressed by Kostakov, Zaslavskaya and Shatalin in 1986–87 (see Chapter 4) now entered the mainstream of Soviet labour ideology. Already early in 1988, senior bureaucrats such as Goskomtrud Chairman Gladky (1988, p. 2) were acknowledging publicly that the release of labour arising out of forecast productivity increases would lead to 'emotional turmoil and disappointment'. In these circumstances, 'a serious psychological restructuring [was] necessary and unavoidable'. Igor Zaslavsky (*Nedelya*, 29 February–6 March 1988, p. 8), later to head Moscow's first employment exchange for 60 years, observed that '[e]very job is now becoming a zone of heightened economic responsibility; keeping it requires greater efficiency than before ... people will value their job places more ...'.

The notion of 'rational full employment' had by 1988 become the core of the regime's revised conception of the full employment doctrine. The onus began to shift from the state's absolute obligation to find or keep work for the individual, to the requirement that the latter make him/herself employable in the changing (and more demanding) economic environment. The joint Party, Government and AUCCTU Resolution, 'On ensuring the effective employment of the population ...' (*Izvestiya*, 20 January 1988, p. 1), counterposed assurances that all workers 'should be confident that the right to work is really guaranteed to them', with the injunction that 'each worker, specialist and employee ... should treasure their work; should constantly maintain themselves in the collective through conscientious, highly productive labour; should improve their qualifications and expertise; and should value the social guarantees given by the state'. A Deputy Chairman of Goskomtrud (Buinovsky, 1988, p. 3) declared that the state's approach to the utilization of labour resources was 'to ensure full and effective employment of the population ... but taking into account the social necessity of such labour'. This would require a whole new approach to retraining: 'the individual does not necessarily acquire a profession for life. These days knowledge is renewing itself so rapidly.'

The confirmation of conditionality in the full employment doctrine naturally brought with it consideration of how best to deal with workers who were either unwilling, unable or slow to adapt. Gladky's successor as Chairman of Goskomtrud, Vladimir Shcherbakov (1989, p. 2), told *Izvestiya* in October 1989 that a Goskomtrud working group was developing the 'conception of a law on employment', including a 'legal interpretation' of an unemployed person and 'the notion of unemployment benefit'. Shcherbakov envisaged the creation of additional individual workplaces, the establishment of an employment fund, and examining 'the whole complex of social guarantees for the unemployed from society's point of view'. His remarks reflected the extent to which Soviet labour ideology had evolved since the death of Brezhnev in November 1982. Not only was the regime recasting the full employment doctrine by establishing the concept of conditionality, but it was now openly admitting the existence of unemployment (*bezrabotitsa*), rather than simply non-employment (*nezanyatost*). Official attitudes towards unemployment moved from denial to acceptance of the need for comprehensive measures to alleviate its socioeconomic impact.

Labour release and redeployment: employment policy in the radical intra-systemic period

Notwithstanding the redefinition of socialist social justice and revision of the so-called 'social contract', Soviet labour ideology during 1987 to 1990 remained strongly paternalist in its overall orientation. This was clearly illustrated in the regime's handling of the problem of labour release. At the June 1987 Plenum, Gorbachev (1988b, p. 181) observed that the 'regrouping' (*peregruppirovka*) of the labour force to the service professions would require special attention. The state had an obligation 'to ensure social guarantees for the workers' employment [and] the constitutional right to work'. Thus, he (1990a, p. 407) continued to justify the existence of loss-making *kolkhozy* and *sovkhozy* by referring to the human cost of closing them, and excoriated economists for proposing 'abstract ideas and schemes unconnected with real life. How can one ... destroy human destinies with an economic plough!'

The issue of labour release and redeployment highlighted the regime's difficulties in achieving a workable equity–efficiency balance. As in the moderate intra-systemic phase of *perestroika*, these difficulties were less the result of political–ideological disagreements within the Politburo (though these undoubtedly existed), than the product of Gorbachev's own ideological ambivalence. On the one hand, he recognized the pernicious influence of 'dependence psychology' and a widespread welfare mentality and complacency in Soviet society. But he was also averse – for 'moral' as well as political reasons – to taking tough but necessary remedial action. Gorbachev (1988b, p. 324) continued to believe that the search for greater labour productivity could, and should, be achieved 'in a socialist way'. At the level of specifics, the regime looked to minimize the socioeconomic impact of labour release by emphasizing 'gradualist' over 'shock therapy' solutions. The joint Resolution, 'On ensuring the effective employment of the population...' (*Izvestiya*, 20 January 1988, p. 1), provided for the postponement of labour release 'in exceptional circumstances' in the interests of the 'more organized job placement of released workers'. It also decreed that workers should receive at least two months notice of possible redundancy, during which time they would be informed about opportunities for job placement as well as for retraining in new professions.

The regime was also extremely reluctant to implement the provisions of Article 23 of the Law on the State Enterprise. Well might Gorbachev (1990a, p. 332) condemn 'chronically loss-making enterprises in which... parasitism flourishes and where pay is in no way related to labour input', and assert that continued budgetary support for such enterprises was both 'impossible and ill-advised'. Throughout the radical intra-systemic period, the political leadership behaved as if the mere threat of bankruptcy was sufficient in itself to induce greater economic self-discipline among enterprises. Emphasis was placed on restructuring rather than liquidation, and the soft budget constraints on enterprises became softer, not harder. At the same time as Ryzhkov (1990a, pp. 224–5) was proposing to deal with loss-making farms through 'the application of contemporary forms of management', including leasing, he announced that their current debts would be written off and assumed by the government. Paternalist and conservative attitudes were also evident in the regime's insistence that released workers should be redeployed, in the first instance, at their original enterprise (*Izvestiya*, 20 January 1988, p. 1). Despite rhetoric about the state's responsibility for job placement, enterprises remained the primary instrument both for keeping people in work (Chapman, 1991, pp. 182, 196) and for hiring new workers. One senior bureaucrat (Prostyakov, 1988, p. 2) stated that enterprise managements and job placement agencies should work on the principle, 'first find someone a new job, then dismiss them', while others (Kostin, 1987, p. 2) anticipated that the effects of labour release would be at least partially mitigated by enterprises moving to a multishift work regime, a view formalized in the 1988 Resolution on employment (*Izvestiya*, 20 January 1988, p. 1). There was considerable anecdotal evidence to suggest that much of the 'release of labour' took the form of intra-enterprise shuffling or natural wastage. According to the head of Moscow's labour placement bureau (Demchenko, 1988, p. 2), attempts to redeploy administrative resources to the service professions came to naught as 'released' employees simply flowed 'out of one pool into the other' at their current place of work. Such impressions were confirmed by statistical evidence. Of 1,364,000 people released in industry during 1988, 605,000 were given other jobs at the same enterprise, 220,000 retired, while 209,000 left jobs that remained unfilled (Manykina, 1991, p. 403).

Nevertheless, it became increasingly apparent that such tactics were at best a temporary palliative. There was an obvious need for a comprehensive employment policy, particularly given the regime's emphasis on enterprise self-financing and the challenge to the diktat of the producer.

By 1989, few in the political leadership retained any illusions that short-term unemployment could be avoided altogether. The priority was now to minimize its extent and alleviate its impact. Consequently, the regime embraced a range of prescriptions aimed at (a) restructuring employment; (b) engendering demand for labour; and (c) limiting demand for employment.

Restructuring employment

This arose logically out of the regime's previously declared objective of reorienting the economy towards the production of consumer goods. Initially, the government looked to the services sphere to employ those people – pensioners, invalids, housewives, students – 'whose labour, for various reasons, cannot be used in government enterprises and organizations' (Gorbachev, 1989, p. 149). However, as the process of labour release gathered momentum, the services sector began to be viewed as a receptacle for redundant administrative employees (ibid., p. 336). Similarly, the expansion of alternative forms of labour – cooperatives, leasehold enterprises, individual labour activity – was seen as providing a useful escape valve for workers forced out as a result of production rationalization at state enterprises (Shcherbakov, 1991, p. 37).

For people to capitalize on employment opportunities in new, or previously neglected, areas of economic activity necessitated radical improvements in the system of job placement. In acknowledging this imperative, the 'Basic Theses...' document (*KPSS...*, 1989, p. 427) announced the intention to create a nationwide network of bureaux for 'the placement and retraining of the population'. As a senior Goskomtrud official (Kolosov, 1991, p. 55) admitted, a comprehensive system had yet to be created. The employment service was ill-equipped to conduct vocational training for 'unoccupied people'; it had 'no reserve of temporary jobs'; and was unable to provide workers with financial support during periods of training or between jobs. Furthermore, its activities bore little relation to regional requirements, since they were not based on a 'serious analysis' of the local employment situation and were 'not coordinated with the structural, investment and technical policies for locating production facilities' in regions. The use of job placement bureaux both by enterprises and individuals seeking work remained as limited as ever; in 1989, only 3.2 million out of a total of 18.5 million successful job applicants obtained work in this way.

The notion of a genuinely nationwide system of employment exchanges was predicated on the encouragement of greater labour mobility. Whereas for much of the decade this question had been associated with *tekuchest* and hence viewed in a negative light, by the late Gorbachev era it had become a key component of state employment policy. Maintenance of full employment – defined as the greater availability of jobs nationwide compared to the total number of job-seekers (Zaslavskaya, 1990, p. 91) – was increasingly seen as contingent on creating conditions for enhanced labour mobility. This meant not only providing incentives for workers to move to labour-scarce regions such as Siberia and the Soviet Far East, but also facilitating the general movement of workers throughout the country (Ryzhkov, 1990b, p. 109). Support was expressed for 'a flexible system for the redistribution of personnel' under which people would either avoid 'social losses' arising from change of occupation or residence, or would be compensated for 'temporary loss' (Shirokov, 1989, p. 2). There was consequently growing pressure for the development of a housing market and liberalization of the existing internal passport/*propiska* system which severely restricted where people could live and work. In his report, 'On the economic position of the country and the conception of a transfer to a regulated market economy', Ryzhkov (1990b, p. 109) directly linked labour mobility to the development of a housing market. And although he (ibid., p. 130) was much more guarded on the question of *propiska*, he nevertheless left open the possibility of changing its rules in order to enable the emergence of a fully functioning labour market.

Engendering demand for labour

The most important ideological and practical outcome of the labour release initiated during 1987–88 was the evolution of a labour market in the Soviet Union. While this market was certainly undeveloped and primitive by Western standards, it nevertheless represented a major landmark in the reformulation of Soviet labour ideology. In particular, by focusing attention on the demand for (as well as supply of) labour, the concept of a labour market posed an extremely serious challenge to the Soviet full employment doctrine. For, implicit in the notion of a labour market, no matter how nascent, was the principle that the only true guarantee of an individual's right to employment was the existence of demand for that person's labour. As a result, much of the regime's approach to the problem of labour release and employment was based on both stimulating demand for labour and limiting the demand to work. In the former case, the leadership found itself caught on the horns of a critical dilemma. On the one hand, it was evident that the economy's health could no longer stand the grossly inefficient and wasteful utilization of labour by Soviet enterprises. On the other hand, the rationalization of labour use created a problem of employment, of what to do with those individuals and job positions that were redundant.

One solution lay, of course, in developing a more professional and flexible workforce through improvements in education, training and retraining. The previous stress laid by Zaslavskaya and Shatalin on the prophylactic and alleviative socioeconomic role of education (see Chapter 4) was reinforced during this period. The Resolution, 'On ensuring the effective employment of the population...' (*Izvestiya*, 20 January 1988, p. 1), proclaimed the intention to 'carry out the training and retraining of released workers in necessary professions...'. Goskomtrud Chairman Shcherbakov (1989, p. 2) observed that the most crucial issue was not job placement as such but retraining which aimed to convert redundant labour into workers whose new-found skills would place them in demand.

Another important prescription was the creation of sector- and region-specific job programmes. For example, as discussed earlier, the regime saw the expansion of the services sphere and alternative forms of labour organization as providing useful employment for released administrative employees. There was also growing interest in several hitherto little-considered options. Thus, Gorbachev (*Izvestiya*, 26 April 1990, p. 2) pointed to the potential of the trade sector for absorbing workers released from material production, while Ryzhkov (1990b, p. 112) called for people to be trained in the 'basics of commerce and marketing.' Other ideas included the export of labour abroad (Lisichkin, 1990, p. 2), the use of joint ventures as vehicles for employment (Maslova, 1991, pp. 138–9), and public works projects (community service) to cater for the difficult to employ (Kolosov, 1991, p. 56). The political leadership also continued to propose the establishment of labour-intensive industries in traditional labour-surplus regions as a means of 'soaking up' excess human resources. At the March 1989 Plenum on agricultural reform, Gorbachev (1990a, p. 381) claimed that seasonal non-employment could be significantly minimized by developing auxiliary plants and businesses, and by opening affiliates of industrial enterprises, 'especially for the production of consumer goods'.

Such remarks came during a period (1989–90) when, for the first time, unemployment (or non-employment) became causally linked to social unrest. Previously, the unacceptability of unemployment had lain in its contradiction of the 'humanist' character of socialism and in its reflection of the incomplete, and therefore inefficient, utilization of labour resources. Since unemployment 'did not exist' in the Soviet Union, the country by definition did not suffer from the social consequences that accompanied its incidence in the West. These comfortable assumptions were severely undermined following outbreaks of inter-ethnic fighting in Novy Uzen (Kazakhstan) and the Fergana Valley (Uzbekistan) during 1989, and then later in Dushanbe (Tajikistan) in 1990. Uzbek First Secretary Nishanov (1989, p. 2) noted, in respect of the Fergana Valley disturbances, that 'the lack of any real opportunities for putting their lives in order is evoking among some (young people) dissatisfaction with their situation, heightened excitability and a sharply aggravated feeling of their own inferiority'. The linkage between unemployment/ non-employment and ethnic unrest was supplemented by the perceived connection between the former and a rising crime rate. Addressing the Uzbek Party *aktiv*, Ryzhkov (*Pravda*, 16 June 1989, p. 5) declared that '[a] large number of people without work... offers a nutrient medium that automatically engenders a propensity for unearned income, parasitism and law-breaking'. The conclusion was inescapable: 'some very radical efforts' were needed to increase employment in the republic, given both 'the critical nature of the current situation' and the likelihood of future growth in labour resources.

Notwithstanding the regime's new focus on employment problems in Central Asia, the scope of job creation schemes in fact extended well beyond the usual labour surplus areas. The development of additional opportunities for useful employment became accepted as a nationwide imperative, reflecting the reality that difficulties in job placement could no longer be dismissed as a phenomenon limited to regions such as Central Asia and the Caucasus. Emergent concepts of a Soviet labour market highlighted the growing division between so-called 'primary' and 'secondary' sources of labour. The fears expressed by Zakharova *et al.* (1989, pp. 59–60 – see Chapter 4) were corroborated by growing evidence of job discrimination against women and 'workers of pension age', as well as 'skilled workers to whom placement services were not yet adapted' (Maslova, 1991, p. 136). The regime attempted to relieve these problems by introducing sheltered workshop arrangements. For example, the Resolution, 'On ensuring the effective employment of the population...' (*Izvestiya*, 20 January 1988, p. 1), identified women and youth as priority groups for affirmative action.

The distinction between primary and secondary sources of labour represented a fundamental contradiction of the 'universal character' of socialist labour. As such, it threw up a novel challenge to the Soviet regime for which it was ill-prepared. Formerly, the rationale behind job creation schemes, involving 'flexible work schedules', 'work at home' (*nadomny trud*) and part-time work (*nepolny rabochii den*), had been to induce as many people as possible to work in social production so as to alleviate labour shortage. In the wake of the general shift to enterprise self-financing, however, ostensibly similar prescriptions were intended simply to provide a place of work for those who wished to remain employed. It was no longer the case that the regime necessarily wanted these people to continue working or, to put it differently, to occupy a job slot. The contrast in perspective illustrated the extent to which Soviet labour ideology had moved from its original primary objective of 'putting people to work', to that of finding them employment.

Limiting demand for employment

Whereas traditional Soviet labour ideology had looked to maximize the number of people engaged in public employment, the radical intra-systemic period witnessed attempts to reduce, and not just re-structure, the total workforce. The notion that there was 'excessive employment' (*sverkhzanyatost*) had already been discussed by Kostakov (1987, p. 87) in his article, 'Zanyatost: defitsit ili izbytok?' (see Chapter 4). Kostakov claimed that only one approach had been considered in pursuing the objective of full employment – increasing the number of jobs. Instead, greater consideration should be given to reducing the demand for work. To this end, he advocated increasing student stipends, women's maternity and other household benefits, and pensions, in order to persuade certain population groups not to enter the labour market.

Although Kostakov's suggestion of reducing the total level of employment was initially somewhat ahead of mainstream thinking, the influence of such views was already manifest by 1988. It has already been noted that, as a result of labour release from industry that year, some 220,000 people retired while another 209,000 left jobs and were not replaced. Similar trends were evident in construction and transport (Manykina, 1991, p. 403). Although these numbers represented only a tiny percentage of the Soviet Union's total human resources, they never-theless indicated the changing direction in Soviet labour ideology away from quantitative maximization to leaner employment. As per Kostakov's prescription, the targets of workforce reduction measures were mainly pensioners, workers of pre-pension age, women (particu-larly housewives), the young, and the disabled. In discussing the problems of older workers in adapting to the new economic climate,

Zaslavskaya (1990, p. 92) linked the offer of early retirement to workers of pre-pension age to efforts to soften the impact of administrative cutbacks in government ministries.

An even more striking illustration of the catalysing effect of labour release on ideology was the evolution of thinking on the question of demographic growth. Under Brezhnev, a cornerstone of Soviet labour ideology had been the promotion of a high birthrate and the consequent development of a larger workforce. Even following *intensifikatsiya*, many political leaders and commentators continued to hold such views[12]. However, with the onset of large-scale (by Soviet standards) labour release from 1988 and the consequent problem of finding employment for those released, the realization began to hit home that increased population growth was not necessarily a positive development, particularly in traditional labour surplus regions. Thus, while welcoming the increased birthrate in some areas of the Soviet Union, the demographer Aleksandr Kvasha (1989, p. 2) called for deterrents to population growth and for the introduction of family planning services in the Central Asian republics.

The evolution of demographic policy during the 1980s was symptomatic of the changes in labour ideology during this period. Originally designed as the key to supplying more workers for social production, Soviet demography became steadily more marginalized in the labour debate as the decade went on. Official zeal on this subject gave way to a discreet silence, implying that the regime increasingly looked upon population growth not as a benefit – supplying additional human power to drive economic development – but rather as a burden that set it difficult tasks to solve: extra mouths to feed and extra persons for whom to find employment (Kolosov, 1991, p. 48).

The transformation of the philosophical principles of Soviet labour

Much of this chapter has centred on the regime's handling of relatively concrete issues: prescriptions for increasing labour productivity; the impact of such policies on concepts of socialist social justice; responses to the emergent problems of labour release and employment. It remains to examine the relationship between official attitudes on specific issues, and general philosophical propositions embraced by the Soviet regime regarding the meaning of labour and employment. For example, what constituted 'real work'? What was the purpose of labour? What activities were covered by the term, 'employment'?

The 'universal character' of labour under Soviet socialism had been characterized by several cardinal principles: the universal right to work; the obligation to engage in 'socially useful' labour; non-discriminatory employment practices; the general unacceptability of using labour as a 'commodity', that is, by 'buying'/hiring or 'selling' it; and, ultimately, the nexus between labour and reward according to the axiom, 'from each according to their ability, to each according to their work'. Setting aside the question about whether or not these tenets were realized in practice, the radical intra-systemic period witnessed remarkable developments at the conceptual level.

The most significant change was in redefining 'real work'. Throughout virtually the lifetime of the Soviet state, the individual's performance of labour had been synonymous with his/her engagement in social production. Individual labour activity, although legal, was tolerated only as a tiny adjunct to public employment. It was accorded very minor status, and was viewed either as a means of enlisting additional, secondary, sources of labour unable to cope with the demands of full-time employment, or as a way of topping up the production of consumer goods and services. The non-participation in the public sector of able-bodied individuals of working age was condemned as 'parasitism'.

This monolithic interpretation of labour was closely linked to the essential uniformity of property forms. In practice, the overwhelming preponderance of state property greatly limited the individual's choice of employment. With the expansion of property forms under *perestroika*, however, there was a corresponding increase in the options available for productive work. The absolute imperative of improving the Soviet Union's economic performance forced the regime to be more ideologically flexible. Faced with the inadequate performance of the state sector in meeting the country's socioeconomic (as well as political and strategic) objectives, Soviet leaders sought answers in the diversification of labour forms. Although non-state forms of labour comprised only a small share of total employment[13], by the end of the radical intra-systemic period they had become largely legitimized. Political leaders might still harbour considerable ideological reservations about their operation, but there was already an air of inevitability about their development. The question became no longer one of if, but when and how.

In these circumstances, the notion of legitimate labour evolved from one of employment exclusively in the public sphere, to one based on productive labour in whatever form chosen by the individual (Selyunin, 1988, p. 179). An indication of how far this notion had taken root by the end of the radical intra-systemic period was Ryzhkov's (1990b, p. 108) unequivocal approval of the idea of 'enterprise' (*predprinimatelstvo*), defined as 'enterprising economic activity...based on the utilization of all forms of property'. The political leadership's use of the term, *predprinimatelstvo*, with its highly 'capitalist' connotations, was in itself virtually unprecedented and marked a qualitatively new stage in official thinking on the nature of labour in Soviet society.

The legitimation of non-state forms of labour and the consequent expansion of work options for the individual citizen, in turn undermined two of the pillars of traditional Soviet labour ideology: the unacceptability of 'hired labour' (*naemny trud*), and the universal obligation to work. The first of these dogma derived from the premise that treating labour as a commodity that could be bought and sold like any other was incompatible with a society distinguished by free labour performed by free citizens. The very essence of *chuvstvo khozyaina* was that the citizen was master in both work and life. To sell one's labour was tantamount to selling oneself, of allowing oneself to be exploited as a 'slave' by a 'master'. By 1989, however, conventional assumptions regarding 'free labour' and 'non-exploitation' were coming under increasingly frequent and vigorous challenge. At the First Congress of People's Deputies, the poet Yevgenii Yevtushenko (*Izvestiya*, 3 June 1989, p. 4) proposed that Article 40 of the Constitution be amended to read 'USSR citizens have the right to free labour'. This meant 'the right to purchase means of production from the state' (for example, land); the right of producers to sell the fruits of their labour where they wished and at prices set by them; their right, after paying taxes, to determine wage and development funds; and 'the right to produce not what is forcibly dictated from above but what is dictated by market necessity and people's requirements...'. Implicit in Yevtushenko's position was the belief that free labour meant the individual's specific right to dispose freely of their labour, not some abstract notion based on outmoded conceptions of the 'workers' state'. As long as this basic condition was met, then workers could not be said to be exploited since they were choosing the conditions under which their labour was performed.

The processes of legitimizing *naemny trud* and transforming the concept of free labour, were accompanied by the withdrawal of the universal obligation to work. This ideological outcome had two broad causes. The first arose from the logic of the new conception of free labour. It was a very short step from the individual being able to choose the type and place of labour, to being given the option of deciding whether or not to offer his/her labour in the first place. Arguably labour could not be said to be truly 'free' unless the element of compulsion was removed alto-gether. This point was tacitly recognized by Valerii Kolosov (1991, p. 51) when he observed that the principle of voluntary labour conformed to the Universal Declaration of Human Rights and the ILO's Forced Labour Convention, which outlawed compulsory work in any form[14]. Likewise, Kotlyar (1991, p. 113) sought to explain the change in Soviet employ-ment policy in terms of the shifting legal focus of the universal character of labour, from 'compulsion to a voluntary socioeconomic and moral guarantee of employment'. Such ideological rationalizations were reinforced by the reality that it was becoming much more difficult to guarantee full employment for the whole population, particularly for vulnerable secondary labour groups. In these circumstances, the regime had two, interlinked options: expanding the definition of what consti-tuted work, and legitimizing the non-performance of social labour. Already in early 1988, Zaslavsky (*Nedelya*, 29 February–6 March 1988, p. 8) was arguing in the context of equalizing the status of state and non-state labour, that 'the rearing of children in the family... should be treated as a matter of state importance', while other commentators (Kolosov, 1991, p. 51) called for the definition of the labour force to encompass students.

Such statements represented a kind of sophistry, designed principally to preserve the illusion that the Soviet Union continued to enjoy full or near full employment. But by 1990, the regime was beginning to acknowledge the futility of such ideological sleight-of-hand. An early draft of the 'Principles of Legislation of the USSR and the Union Re-publics on Employment', included an Article headed 'The Unemployed' (*bezrabotnye*), and referred to the individual's right and not duty to work; the only proviso was that a person should have 'legal sources of income'. In commenting on the draft Principles, Kostakov (1991, p. 91) noted the importance of this provision which 'should help to ease the problem of overemployment'. In short, the new emphasis on the voluntariness of labour may be seen at least in part as a manoeuvre to 'justify' the unemployment that had already occurred, or that was inevitable in the near future.

Ideological transformation and the undermining of the state

Soviet labour ideology during the radical intra-systemic period degener-ated steadily from a comprehensive philosophy into an increasingly ragged, shifting set of *ad hoc* propositions. The exceptional pace of change to central tenets of labour ideology – unconditional full employment, the universal obligation to work, the inadmissibility of using labour as a commodity – points to regime expediency and panic in the face of rapidly moving developments. The legitimation and consequent expansion of non-state forms of labour took place principally because the state sector was so manifestly incapable of meeting the regime's socioeconomic and political objectives. Likewise, it was clear that such forms of labour could not function effectively unless restrictions on the movement and choice of labour were removed. The growing use of the term, 'labour market' (*rynok truda*), merely recognized a reality whereby enterprises sought to attract 'good' workers and jettison those seen as less able to cope with the more stringent production demands stemming from self-financing. Finally, the extraordinarily rapid dilution of the full employment doctrine between 1987 and 1990 matched growing evidence of actual unemployment and the seriousness of its socio-economic consequences.

The radical intra-systemic period witnessed the exacerbation of ideological contradictions already apparent in the first two years of the Gorbachev era – the conflicts between equity and efficiency objectives, and between central control and the devolution of responsibility. In the former case, popular perceptions of sharply falling living standards exerted a major influence on regime thinking. At the First Congress of People's Deputies, Gorbachev (1990a, p. 562) rejected the full-scale introduction of the 'mechanisms of the market economy' on the grounds this would 'explode the entire social situation.' Similar sentiments were voiced by Ryzhkov (1990a, pp. 213–14) a few months later, when he warned that attempts to establish 'market relations' nationwide during 1990–91 'could lead to serious economic and social convulsions', involving 'galloping inflation, a declining role for all economic stimuli, a slump in production, mass unemployment, and the worsening of social tension'.

During this period, much of the ideological baggage carried by Gorbachev and other Soviet political leaders was supplemented (and often supplanted) by very real fears of uncontrollable social forces and ructions. Ideology became an almost day-to-day proposition, determined predominantly by judgements as to the political sustainability of a particular course of action. This *ad hoc* approach was evident, for example, in the regime's handling of the miners' strikes that broke out in the summer of 1989.[15] The government offered various short-term palliatives – supplying certain essential consumer items, offering pay increases, etc. – but failed to develop a comprehensive strategy for the coal industry, which would have entailed closing down hopelessly loss-making mines. The most notable change to Soviet labour ideology arising from the confrontation with the miners was legalization of the right to strike in October 1989. But this was simply an attempt to formalize and regularize what had already taken place and, furthermore, was not preventable in any case (Moskoff, 1993, p. 194). Equally, the increasing emphasis on the devolution of decision-making powers to republics, regions, local soviets, and enterprises, reflected as much the centre's loss of ideological and economic control as the attachment of Gorbachev and others to democratization and 'new thinking'. While it would be wrong to discount altogether the sincerity of official commitment to such concepts, many regime policy prescriptions tended either to confirm existing reality or else indicate the centre's concern to divest itself of the burden of delivering socioeconomic benefits as in the past. An example of the latter instance was Gorbachev's (1990a, p. 485) comment that republics, territories and regions were responsible to their populations for ensuring food, living conditions, and 'the state of the consumer goods and services market'.

By the time the 28th Party Congress convened in July 1990, Soviet labour ideology had become largely reactive, devoid of any consistent, unifying vision. The attempt to achieve labour productivity and socioeconomic progress on the basis of a return to Leninist socialist fundamentals, launched with much fanfare at the June 1987 Plenum, lost momentum steadily over the following three years. Although the regime strove to achieve a socialism in tune with modern requirements, it found that the speed of events constantly outpaced its efforts to sustain the relevance and legitimacy of socialist ideology. Moreover, the increasing feverishness of these attempts reinforced the impression of a socialism overwhelmingly driven, even buffeted by pragmatism.

This uncertainty of what Soviet socialism really stood for served to diminish it further in the popular estimation. While admittedly the great majority of the population had long ago abandoned any genuine ideological allegiance, they had nevertheless continued to believe in the regime's ability to deliver socioeconomic benefits, albeit at an often very rudimentary, poor level. But the erosion and often outright negation of 'givens' that had been taken for granted for decades amounted to a crushing indictment both of socialist ideology and the legitimacy of the Soviet state. Just as importantly, the regime's actual loss of control was matched by its awareness of a growing impotence in the face of rapidly escalating socioeconomic challenges. By 1990, most of the political leadership recognized the hopelessness of efforts to achieve superior labour productivity on the basis of either Stalinist or

Leninist socialist economic models. There now appeared only one possible saving resource within the socialist paradigm: that of the socialist market.

In these circumstances it was inevitable that challenges to state authority should become at once more numerous and assume different, ever more volatile forms. The regime's by now evident fragility created new opportunities for dissent and opposition. Thus, Yeltsin was able to launch his political comeback because he represented to many people – and not just to an elite 'pro-capitalist coalition' (Kotz and Weir, 1997, p. 147) – an alternative to the Gorbachev administration's mismanagement of the reform agenda. At the same time, ethnic nationalism grew as regional power elites began to assume greater control over their own republic's affairs. Not only did the centre fail to mount an effective or even committed defence of its authority, but it actively abetted secessionist trends by abdicating socioeconomic responsibilities that had traditionally been its prerogative but which it no longer felt able to sustain. Finally, the loss of economic and ideological control encouraged political liberalization to a degree far beyond what had been originally envisaged. Gorbachev initially saw democratization and *glasnost* as instruments in the campaign to raise labour productivity and create an effective economic system.[16] However, as the Soviet Union's economic crisis worsened, political democracy and its institutions came to assume intrinsic value and a momentum of their own. It was a surprisingly short step for the Gorbachev administration from the limited application of democratic instruments for economic purposes to the uncontrolled maelstrom of political diversity, competition and fractiousness. The liberalization Gorbachev saw as essential to the struggle for superior economic performance created the opportunity for Yeltsin and others to challenge the regime and, specifically, to undermine the CPSU's political and ideological monopoly. Ultimately, it was the tightness of this economic–political nexus which highlighted the reality of diminishing state control and the 'thinness' of regime legitimacy, and exposed the aura of state power and invulnerability for the shams they had become.

6
Ideological Transformation under Gorbachev: The Extra-systemic Phase, 1990–91

'Not only are socialism and the market compatible, but they are indivisible in substance.'

Mikhail Gorbachev (1996, p. 603)

Introduction

The last 18 months of the Soviet Union were a period of extraordinarily rapid and extensive disintegration – political, economic, ideological. These unravelling processes were especially evident in the area of labour ideology which, for over 70 years, had supplied the Soviet state with its dominant ethos. While certain fundamental principles continued to influence policy, the reactive tendencies identified in the previous chapter became ever more pronounced in the climate of desperation that characterized the regime's dying days. Like so many other areas of official thinking, labour ideology underwent constant (and often substantial) modification and dilution in response to rapidly unfolding developments and the changing realities of power. Indeed, so unstable and inconsistent were the regime's attitudes towards labour during this period, that it is no longer appropriate to talk about an 'official' labour ideology as such, but rather about the existence of two opposing trends – the 'disembodiment' of labour ideology, and the 'politicization' of labour issues.

The former trend was evinced in the regime's flexibility in adapting principles to rationalize events. Although such behaviour was hardly novel, the rapidity with which policy changes were effected (and reversed) indicates that ideology became increasingly instrumental and devoid of moral conviction. The regime's concern to arrest the Soviet Union's accelerating economic decline led it further down the path of pragmatism. Specifically, this involved addressing the problems of falling production and labour productivity by going beyond the known parameters of the Soviet socialist system, in other words, by resorting to extra-systemic methods such as the development of 'market relations' (*rynochnye otnosheniya*). In endorsing such methods, the political leadership effectively signalled the final abandonment of Stalinist and Leninist economic (and labour) strategies. Although its understanding and implementation of market principles was often muddled and/or half-hearted, the legitimation of a long-time 'antagonistic' philosophy was in itself a remarkable ideological phenomenon. In espousing the market, the regime signalled the extent of its loss of economic control as well as its inability to stimulate effective labour performance through 'normal' methods, whether socialist morality, planning–technocratic or incentive–humanistic. The market or extra-systemic approach to labour productivity represented the final stage in the collapse of traditional Soviet labour ideology – from its Stalinist 'zenith' through Leninist devolutionary democratic centralism to a constantly shifting pragmatism operating under duress.

The dismantling of Soviet labour ideology was paralleled by its 'politicization'; that is, the growth of overt policy dissensions within the political elite on specific labour issues. Although such differences had long existed, they had generally been subsumed and reconciled behind a more or less unified ideological facade. However, with the expansion of *glasnost* and democratization and exacerbation of the country's economic crisis, the public debate over the nature of labour in Soviet society became much more unconstrained and polychromatic. In these conditions, clear political divisions emerged. In place of an official labour ideology, there were now several strands of dogma that reflected competing vested interests as much as ideological conviction. Labour ideology became transformed from its former incarnation as a general unifying moral ethic into an arena in which were played out the intense power struggles of the late Gorbachev era.

The evolution and definition of 'market' concepts in the Soviet Union

Ideas of the 'market' (*rynok*) in the Soviet context were prevalent long before the extra-systemic phase of *perestroika*. As early as the June 1987 Plenum, Gorbachev (1988b, p. 163) referred to the 'planned mastery and management of the market' as contributing to the creation of 'an effective anti-expenditure mechanism' and the strengthening of socialism (see Chapter 5). The General Secretary (1989, p. 388) also perceived a clear relationship between the market and democratic centralist principles in the economy, based on the 'organic combination of the centre's role in deciding structural questions with the broad autonomy of production units as commodity producers, operating on the principles of *khozraschet* and autonomy in the market'.

The evidence suggests that Gorbachev initially understood *rynok* only in its simplest form: the establishment of basic supply and demand relations. As such, its introduction was seen as a means both of challenging the diktat of the producer and of providing a valid measure of performance. If the consumer – generally the state, but also other enterprises – was unhappy with the product, then it would look for an alternative supplier. The presence of such a threat, in turn, would force producer enterprises to tailor their output to the needs of the market. Subsequently, the concept of *rynok* was applied to the 'consumer market', an association that became stronger as shortages of goods and services worsened in the late Gorbachev era. Gorbachev (1990a, p. 562) told the First Congress of People's Deputies that the most urgent task was to 'arrest the growth of negative tendencies and above all to normalize the situation of the market'. Finally, the term was applied to the 'labour market' (*rynok truda*), a notion that gained currency as the problems of labour release and redeployment came to the fore in the wake of implementation of the Law on the State Enterprise.

Common to all the intra-systemic conceptions of the market was its subordination to the principles of the socialist planned economy. For example, in resorting to the 'laws' of supply and demand, the regime hoped to raise the responsiveness of socialist enterprises to the demands of their main customer – the state. Likewise, the emphasis on satisfying the consumer market arose principally because failure to achieve this objective undermined the legitimacy of Soviet socialism. The emergence of labour market concepts after 1988 was much more about alleviating tensions and contradictions within the system, than about attempting to create a new economic model based on different philosophical tenets.

By early 1990, however, the failure of intra-systemic methods of raising economic performance on the basis of superior labour productivity had become painfully apparent to Gorbachev and many in the political leadership. In his acceptance speech for the Presidency, Gorbachev (1990b, pp. 58–9) confessed that the regime had been, and continued to be, unprepared for the sharp changes necessary to restore the country's socioeconomic health. He recognized, in particular, that economic restructuring 'had turned out to be impossible without the dismantling of the authoritarian-bureaucratic system as a whole', and identified the need to overcome the situation 'in which old and new forms of management – directive and economic – coexist in an antagonistic way, weakening each other.'

Nevertheless, it was not until the 28th Party Congress in July 1990 that the regime set out definitively on the course of marketization. On this occasion, Gorbachev (1990c, pp. 12–13) for the first time formally recognized the need for a change of system in order to achieve a substantial and rapid improvement in living standards. In stating that the 'logic of *perestroika* and the acuteness of the socioeconomic situation' indicated the need for 'fundamental changes in the economic system', he foreshadowed the creation of a new economic model: 'multilayered, with various forms of property and management, and a contemporary market infrastructure.' In this way, he argued, scope would be opened up for people's initiative, along with 'new, powerful stimuli for fruitful labour and the growth of economic efficiency'.

The Andropovian theme of *chuvstvo khozyaina* was central to Gorbachev's market vision. In this context, he (ibid., p. 14) claimed that the existence of diverse forms of property reinforced the democratic bases of society since the workers became 'the real masters of the means of production and the results of labour, with a vested interest in effective work and good end-results'. According to Gorbachev, such a conception of the market was non-exploitative: 'in advancing towards the market, we are not abandoning socialism but rather are moving to a fuller realization of society's possibilities. Therein consists the project of . . . *perestroika*.'

The ideological outcome of the regime's deliberations was the so-called 'socialist' or 'regulated market', a hybrid combining the use of market forces and planning methods. In essence, the socialist market was an attempt to resolve the basic equity–efficiency dilemma that had dogged previous efforts at economic reform. The Party's Programme Statement, *Towards a humane and democratic socialism* (*Materialy XXVIII Sezda . . .*, 1990, pp. 86–7), listed principles such as 'freedom of enterprise' (*svoboda predprinimatelstva*), competition between different property forms and the demonopolization of production, while emphasizing the importance of regulating market relations 'to protect the social rights of citizens'. In noting that the transition to the market was 'not an aim in itself, but the means of resolving social problems', the Programme (ibid., pp. 87–8) envisaged compensating the population for price rises; introducing a 'flexible system of income indexation'; and creating an 'effective mechanism of employment support,' including allowances for 'non-employment' and training.

The debate over the socialist market and other forms of the market

Emergent socialist market concepts supplied a focus for the continuing debate on key issues of economic efficiency and social justice. At a general level, this debate centred on three major questions: the feasibility of applying market principles to the Soviet context; the social and economic costs arising from their implementation; and how quickly to marketize the Soviet economy. The wide spectrum of views on these questions at once affected, and was a mirror of, the transformation of Soviet labour ideology during this final period of *perestroika*. In order best to reflect the complexity and contradictions of the debate, I propose to apply a methodological framework that owes heavily to Anders Aslund's political–functional model (1991, pp. 61–2 – see note 7, Chapter 1). The only differences are relatively minor: in lieu of Aslund's labels – radical reform, half-hearted reform, technocratic rationalization, socialist morality and conservative program – a slightly simpler set of categorizations will be adopted: socialist paternalist, conservative-centrist, reformist pro-market, and radical pro-market.

The socialist paternalist perspective

This perspective was opposed to the whole concept of the socialist market. For diehard conservatives such as Nina Andreeva (1990, p. 5), the implementation of market reforms in any form inevitably led to a reduction in people's social rights. She derided the 'sugarcoated fairy tales about a market economy', and warned instead of incipient unemployment and the 'violation of other principles of social security that go along with socialism'. Andreeva's Stalinist fundamentalism rejected out of hand the possibility that market and planning methods could be combined within a contemporary model of socialism, and instead identified the abandonment of basic socialist principles as the prime cause of the country's political and economic misfortunes.

On a somewhat more abstract level, others regretted what they saw as the emergence of a new grasping materialism in society, and the corresponding decline of more 'human' values. In this context, Yurii Bondarev (1991, p. 3) lamented that out of the 'democratic triad' of liberty, equality and fraternity, only 'orphaned "liberty"' would remain 'amid the elemental forces of . . . an uncontrollable and turbulent market . . .'. Other writers (Shafarevich, 1991, p. 3) highlighted the widening gulf between 'winners' and 'losers': 'The news media are introducing an image of the "hero of our times" – a businessman gambling on the stock exchange, or a parliamentarian busy with foreign trips, or a holder of Western bank accounts. These are the victors today, while the majority of the people have ended up in the camp of the vanquished...'.

According to the socialist paternalists' undifferentiated outlook, there were no significant differences between various species of market. All to a greater or lesser extent were about raising capitalist-style efficiency and inequality at the expense of equity and spiritual priorities. There would always be winners and losers regardless of what type of market was adopted, and however quickly or slowly this was done. The socialist market amounted to ideological trickery, designed to obscure the reality that the population's rights – most notably the right to work – were under assault.

The conservative-centrist position

This category encompasses a broad range of opinion on the socialist market. In particular, it covers many of the views of Gorbachev himself, his Party Deputy, Vladimir Ivashko, as well as those of his two Prime Ministers prior to the August 1991 putsch: Nikolai Ryzhkov and Valentin Pavlov. In essence, the conservative-centrist attitude towards the socialist market was premised on the belief that the equity–efficiency conundrum was soluble; as argued in the Party's Programme Statement, 'market relations' could be combined successfully with a high level of social protection (*Materialy XXVIII Sezda...*, 1990, p. 87). Naturally, the transition to a 'regulated market economy' (Ryzhkov, 1990b, p. 88) would not be easy, and there were obvious social costs to necessary measures such as price reform, tighter credit, and economic restructuring in general (Gorbachev, 1990b, p. 60). The conservative-centrist position identified, in particular, the dangers of possible mass unemployment (Shcherbakov, 1990a, p. 2) as well as of hyperinflation and its impact on general living standards (Pavlov, 1991b, p. 3).

The existence of such perils, however, was not seen as invalidating the concept of the socialist market. What the situation demanded was for the transition to a regulated market economy to be handled carefully and sensitively. Gorbachev sought to achieve this in two ways: by developing appropriate social guarantees to protect the population in the changeover period; and through the methodical, 'step-by-step' introduction of market mechanisms. In the first case, he (1990c, p. 15) proclaimed the need to ensure that, 'in this difficult transitional stage to new forms of management and economic life, (people) will be socially protected and their interests guaranteed', notably through wage indexation, employment security, and benefits for those unable or less able to compete on the labour market. Gorbachev (ibid., pp. 14–15) called also for laws to protect the right to work, and reiterated the state's responsibility 'to support materially those who wish to work but who are temporarily unable to find a suitable job position'.

For Gorbachev and other proponents of the conservative-centrist approach, the workability of the socialist market depended as much on the pace of reform as its content. Much of the debate during the extra-systemic period over the relative balance between equity and efficiency objectives came down to a conflict between 'gradualism' and 'shock therapy'. According to the conservative-centrist view, the successful transition to a regulated market economy could not be made precipitately, risking economic hardship and social convulsions (Ryzhkov, 1990b, pp. 94–5). In the first place, Gorbachev and others believed that the technical difficulties in the way of a rapid changeover to a market-based economy were simply too great. Aside from the consequences of a mass release of employees onto an already more crowded labour market,[1] there were several other major obstacles: the entrenched conservative power of the bureaucracy (Gorbachev, 1990c, p. 12); problems associated with introducing far-reaching price reform in a monopoly production environment (Abalkin, 1991, p. 3), including the very real threat of a hyperinflationary wages-prices spiral (Pavlov, 1991b, p. 3); the absence of an adequate safety net for those unable to adapt to the new economic conditions (Ryzhkov, 1990b, p. 94); and the risk of sharp falls in production as a result of excessively severe finance-credit policies (ibid., p. 94). The regime also feared embarking on action whose consequences were not always clear; the leadership's plan mentality with its emphasis on predicted outcomes remained very strong. In averring that the country and public consciousness were 'in many ways not prepared for an accelerated changeover to market', Ryzhkov (*Pravda*, 30 May 1990, p. 1) declared: 'we cannot experiment to such an extent that we throw 290 million people into the turbulent waters of a market without creating the necessary preconditions.'

The logistical problems of shock therapy and the regime's aversion to the unknown were compounded in the conservative-centrist perception by concerns about rising social tensions at a time of *glasnost*, democratization and declining central authority. Although by the onset of the new decade it was widely recognized that many of the rights embodied in the so-called 'social contract' – such as the unconditional guarantee of employment – had been diluted, this did not mean they could be abandoned altogether. There was a need to revise people's expectations and to 'reeducate' them to accept the new conditions in labour and life. But such a psychological restructuring was not possible overnight. Unless the population could be persuaded to see the necessity of radical but painful changes, then the fate of reform was doomed and the risk of social convulsions would become very great (Yanaev in *Izvestiya*, 28 December 1990, p. 6).

Finally, the conservative-centrist position towards gradualism was influenced by genuine ethical considerations. Although there was a substantial degree of cynicism in regime incantations about social justice, Gorbachev, in particular, retained a commitment to socialist ideals and values.[2] Proposals for income indexation, increased pensions, unemployment benefits, were not just politically or tactically motivated. They also reflected concerns about protection for the weak and a persistent belief that socialism, though tarnished under previous Soviet leaders, nevertheless remained a fundamentally more humane philosophy than capitalism. Consistent with this assumption, Gorbachev's (1990c, p. 8) Report to the 28th Party Congress warned against 'forces pushing us towards a bourgeois system, linking the way out of the current difficult situation to the country's switch to the capitalist path'. The conservative-centrist position considered the socialist market as providing the only effective means of resolving the equity–efficiency dilemma, of enabling both full or near full employment while stimulating more productive labour performance. The market in this context was seen more as a relatively pliant instrument to be directed or at least manipulated by the state, than as a set of forces and pressures shaping government policy. For all their rhetoric about the need for a 'new economic model', Gorbachev and other conservative-centrists remained reluctant to accept a genuine market economy in practice, even while the command–administrative system was collapsing all around them.

The reformist pro-market viewpoint

One of the drawbacks of using political–functional categorizations is that they are sometimes insufficiently flexible to explain the fluctuations in official policy. Many Western commentators (for example, Aslund, 1991, p. 62) have explained such inconsistencies largely as an outcome of tactical manoeuvring between different political factions within the leadership. In fact, as in the radical intra-systemic period, Gorbachev was both plagued by ideological doubts and driven by social and economic forces beyond his control. On the one hand, he recognized the need for a radical overhaul of obsolete political and economic structures, the unsustainability of continuing to subsidize chronically loss-making enterprises, and the importance of developing a new enterprise culture. At the same time, however, he recoiled from the 'inhumanity' of throwing people out of work, and blanched at the sheer practical difficulties of implementing tough economic prescriptions. A natural aversion to the ruthless application of market principles was reinforced in the circumstances of the centre's loss of political control, a disintegrating economy, and declining living standards.

Although Gorbachev's general approach to the socialist market revealed a conservative-centrist bias, many of his pronouncements and actions during the last phase of *perestroika* were influenced by the reformist pro-market views of economists such as Abalkin, Aganbegyan and Zaslavskaya. The first named, in particular, played a significant role as Deputy Prime Minister and Chairman of the government's Reform Commission between July 1989 and January 1991.

The key elements of the reformist pro-market position were outlined as early as October 1989, when Abalkin presented his 'discussion materials' for 'Radical economic reform: immediate and long-term measures'. Abalkin (1989, p. 5) proposed the introduction of a 'complex of large-scale, strong and simultaneous measures to give a powerful impulse to the market' and, at the same time, creating a 'mechanism to regulate this process'. Specific measures included the stage-by-stage lifting of price controls; wage and income indexation; a package of wage, tax and credit reforms; and the introduction of unemployment benefit. Abalkin anticipated that the government would, by 'manoeuvring' prices and incomes, be able to 'support production stimuli'. While some inflation arising from price liberalization was unavoidable, tight fiscal, credit and monetary policies would contain this to an acceptable level. Moreover, what he identified as the preferred, 'moderate-radical' path to a market economy would be smoothed by establishing an effective system of social protection that would 'facilitate the adjustment of workers to the conditions of the market economy'. Although many of his prescriptions differed little from those favoured by the conservative-centrist tendency, the overall thrust of Abalkin's document was clearly towards 'market socialism' rather than a 'socialist market', that is, a mixed economy where market forces predominated. Unlike the conservative-centrists, Abalkin envisaged as the ultimate objective of economic reform the emergence of a full (predominantly non-socialist) market economy. To this purpose, and in marked contrast to more conservative elements in the regime, he sketched out four distinct stages of reform, leading eventually to 'the establishment and development of the new economic system' (1989, p. 7).[3]

Abalkin's views on market socialism remained substantially unchanged over the next 18 months. In an interview he gave soon after his resignation as Deputy Prime Minister, he continued to advocate a steady, 'systematic' approach towards a market economy, offering up a timetable for implementation quite similar (although less detailed) to his original 1989 schedule.[4] He (1991, p. 3) stressed, in particular, the importance of demonopolizing the economy, 'without which economic regulators cannot function', and predicted that a fully fledged market would not be established 'for at least a generation'.

At the time of its original publication, Abalkin's programme represented more a 'radical' than 'reformist' pro-market stance. But, with the radicalization of the economic debate during the extra-systemic period, his views on market socialism became ideologically outflanked by shock therapy prescriptions. From being at the cutting edge of economic reform, Abalkin found himself pushed towards the centre. The extent to which the reformist pro-market position had become unfashionable by early 1991 was indicated by Abalkin's interviewer, who admitted in his introduction that a colleague had advised him not to bother with the interview, because 'new people with new ideas had entered the arena' (see Abalkin, 1991, p. 3). In the end, the frenetic political atmosphere of the last months of the Soviet state and the accompanying ideological polarization, made Abalkin's 'moderate-radical' perspective increasingly marginal to policy thinking and practice.

Radical pro-market views

Notwithstanding their diametrically opposed positions on most questions relating to the market, radical pro-marketeers and socialist paternalists shared at least the conviction that market relations and planning methods were irreconcilable. Already in 1987, Lydia Popkova (1987, p. 239) asserted:

> There is no way to be a little bit pregnant. Either plan or market, directives or competition... Either you opt for the market economy, with its concise and rigorous laws for all and sundry, and with all its pluses (efficiency, for example) and minuses (huge income disparities, unemployment...), or you opt for a planned socialist, collectivized economy – also with all its pluses (for example, the individual's confidence in the future) and minuses (deficits, waste).

Popkova (ibid., p. 240) ridiculed the term 'market socialism' as 'absurd', and invoked Marx and Lenin in support of her contention that socialism and the market were incompatible: 'In a planned economy, the law of value cannot operate to advantage.' Such objections were reinforced by criticisms of the practical consequences of regime attempts to harness market forces to socialist planning. Yevgenii Yasin (1991, pp. 20–1) highlighted the regime's failure to tackle price, finance and credit reform, the burgeoning budget deficit, uncontrolled monetary emission and, most important of all, the weakening of economic stimuli at a time when these needed urgently to be strengthened.

Moreover, from the radical pro-market perspective the substantive weaknesses of the socialist market/market socialism were seriously compounded by its procrastinating approach to problems that demanded early solution. Thus, although the market economy envisaged by Abalkin and other 'moderates' was not incompatible with the model sought by the radical pro-marketeers, the latter argued that the Soviet Union's deteriorating economic circumstances no longer made a gradualist approach to reform feasible. While there were obvious social costs to shock therapy – inflation, unemployment, declining living standards for some – these could only be aggravated by delay and half-measures. Aslund's (1991, p. 221) judgement that, in conditions of steep economic decline, 'gradualism equals a prolongation of economic suffering', reflected that of radical economists such as Yasin, Shatalin and Grigorii Yavlinsky.[5] Not only was shock therapy necessary to stimulate more efficient economic performance, but it also represented the most humane and effective way of improving people's social welfare. As Tatyana Yarygina (1991a, p. 10) from Yavlinsky's Epicentre (Centre for Economic and Political Research) claimed, '[t]here are not, and cannot be, any effective forms of social protection in the context of the collapsing command–administrative system.' In this way, the radical pro-market approach redefined the concept of the equity–efficiency balance. The quicker and more comprehensively production and systemic inefficiencies were eradicated, the earlier and more effectively would solutions be found to acute social problems.

Market concepts and the reformulation of Soviet labour ideology

The debate over the socialist market and the equity–efficiency balance was of crucial importance to the development of Soviet labour ideology during this period. At a time of growing economic crisis and social angst, official attitudes towards this question became centred on resolving the dichotomy between labour and employment; that is, between the search for economic efficiency based on superior labour productivity, and the need to keep people in employment for their own socio-economic protection. Each of the various perspectives on the market identified above contributed to the process of reformulating basic tenets of labour ideology. However, in the circumstances of the Soviet Union's political and economic crisis and the intensifying Gorbachev–Yeltsin power struggle, attitudes towards labour were increasingly dominated by the conservative-centrist and radical pro-market positions, as socialist paternalist and reformist pro-market views became marginalized.

In this section, I propose to focus on contrasting ideological approaches in three critical areas of Soviet labour ideology: (a) the challenge to the diktat of the producer through developing notions of competition and competitiveness; (b) the expansion of labour market ideas; and (c) changing attitudes towards unemployment.

The challenge to the diktat of the producer

Criticisms of the diktat of the producer were common in the earlier phases of *perestroika*. During the extra-systemic period, however, the disastrous condition of the consumer market gave new point to the campaign against poor and complacent producers. This campaign emphasized two fundamental objectives: the orientation of production to consumer needs; and the development of proper economic competition and heightened enterprise competitiveness.

More than ever before, there was a general consensus that work should be measured by its use value to the consumer, rather than by the volume of inputs into it. Ryzhkov (1990b, p. 93) declared that production should be responsive to consumer demand, and complained about the disproportionate output of industrial compared to consumer goods. Even strong advocates of the full employment doctrine nevertheless linked rational employment to 'socially useful activity, judged on whether the resulting output is wanted for industrial or personal consumption' (Kotlyar, 1991, p. 113). There was widespread recognition that elevation of the consumer and the tailoring of production to demand depended on developing competition. Here, however, real differences between the various ideological trends emerged. The socialist paternalists, for example, continued to rely on the existing system, putting their faith in personnel policy and the restoration of discipline at the enterprise level (see Aslund, 1991, pp. 54–7). They understood competition largely as traditional 'socialist competition', and opposed the breaking-up of large industrial enterprises and collective farms into small and medium-sized units (see Ligachev, 1993, pp. 324–6). The conservative-centrist position accepted the necessity and inevitability of economic competition, although it continued to give priority to state enterprises and other collectivist forms of labour organization such as joint-stock companies.[6] For example, in rejecting calls to disband *kolkhozy* and *sovkhozy*, Gorbachev (1990c, pp. 20–1) advocated 'equal opportunities for all forms of management on the land' and stated that competition should take place within essentially socialist parameters – 'the free competition of socialist producers'.

The regime's ambivalent attitude towards competition was illustrated by its vacillation over the issue of enterprise competitiveness and, in particular, the fate of loss-making enterprises. On the one hand, Gorbachev (1990a, p. 332) fulminated against the 'culture of dependency' in Soviet enterprises, claiming that the state could not and would not support them *ad infinitum*. On the other hand, the conservative-centrists shrank from even the thought of carrying out this threat. Gorbachev's deputy General Secretary, Vladimir Ivashko (1990, pp. 23–4), warned that the immediate reduction or cessation of subsidies to planned-loss enterprises would result in mass bankruptcies and unemployment. Revealingly, Ivashko also defended 'planned-loss enterprises' – the use of which term illustrated the extent to which losses continued to be accepted as a normal feature of Soviet enterprise activity – on the basis of the 'specific nature of their production operations'.[7]

Admittedly, the government's 'Basic Guidelines for the Stabilization of the National Economy and the Changeover to a Market Economy' (hereafter 'Basic Guidelines...') (*Vedomosti...*, 1990, pp. 1098–9), made provision for closing 'hopelessly inefficient enterprises'. But this was seen very much as a last resort. The document gave far greater weight to converting loss-making enterprises into joint-stock companies, establishing stabilization funds, and encouraging the issuing of bonds to increase working capital. The overall thrust of the conservative-centrist approach to non-profitability among enterprises remained overwhelmingly paternalist. In observing that 17 per cent of all Soviet enterprises were loss-making, the labour economist Yevgenii Antosenkov (1991, p. 74) commented that '[a]rguments are always found to justify their continued existence and promises are made to introduce modernisation programmes, more effective operation and the like'. He concluded that the long-time failure to make progress in this area demonstrated that the problem of loss-making enterprises was one 'defying solution in a state-controlled system'.

The conservative-centrist approach towards competition might best be described as favouring 'regulated competition'. While diversity in forms of ownership and labour was encouraged, and rouble convertibility and the opening of the Soviet economy to the world market envisaged (*Materialy XXVIII Sezda...*, 1990, p. 87), there was still acute unease at the prospect of economic casualties resulting from free and open competition. Most of the Soviet leadership during this period continued to view competition as some kind of positive-sum game, in which nearly everyone would benefit and only the utterly incompetent or feckless would suffer. Although the term, 'socialist competition', was now obsolescent, its spirit remained strongly in evidence. In place of Schumpeter's 'gale of creative destruction', the spirit of *uravnilovka* continued to manifest itself in the conservative-centrist mistrust of 'surplus profit' (*sverkhpribyl*) and support for profit limits (Ryzhkov, 1990b, p. 97; see also Hanson, 1992, p. 48). Just as no-one should find themselves on the economic scrapheap, so it was important that no-one do 'excessively' well by exploiting 'fortuitous' market conditions and opportunities.

A somewhat more realistic appreciation of the concept of economic competition was shown by Abalkin and other supporters of the reformist pro-market position. His 1989 reform blueprint made the point that market mechanisms could not function effectively without free prices and economic competition (Abalkin, 1989, p. 4). Since this necessitated demonopolization of the economy and removing the virtual economic immunity of state enterprises, Abalkin (ibid., p. 5) proposed the destatization (*razgosudarstvlenie*) of all loss-making enterprises and farms by the beginning of 1991 and 1992 respectively. He (ibid., p. 6) also advocated 'intensification' of foreign economic links and a 'significant increase' in the openness of the Soviet economy. Subsequently, in his post-resignation interview to *Izvestiya*, he (1991, p. 3) reemphasized the crucial nexus between the freeing of prices and the enactment of anti-monopoly legislation to ensure *bona fide* competition.

The crucial difference between the reformist pro-market and conservative-centrist attitudes towards competition, was that the former was more willing to admit that its development would have some adverse socioeconomic consequences. Abalkin (1989, p. 4) observed that '[t]he contradiction between economic efficiency and social justice is an objective [reality]'. Experience had exposed the lack of realism in the classical socialist proposition that the second naturally flowed from the first. Zaslavskaya (1990, pp. 76–7) made a similar point when she wrote that the introduction of self-financing had highlighted loss-making enterprises 'like objects left on the beach when the tide has gone out'. Although acknowledging that declaring such enterprises bankrupt would 'inevitably cause social clashes and tensions', she insisted this had to be done, 'since the viability of profitable enterprises and the liquidation of loss-making ones are two sides of the same coin'. For Zaslavskaya, Abalkin and others, in competition there could not be winners without there also being some losers. Only in this way could the diktat of the producer be seriously challenged, because in the absence of the ultimate 'negative reward' – bankruptcy – , enterprises had no particular incentive to mend their ways.

Despite their acceptance of the need for more drastic measures, the gradualist convictions of the reformist pro-marketeers regarding economic reform precluded a more ruthless approach to loss-making enterprises. They continued to favour restructuring, leasing, the creation of joint-stock companies, rather than outright privatization (*privatizatsiya*). Furthermore, much of the rationale behind a step-by-step timetable for liquidating such enterprises was to give them some breathing space in which to reform their operations. In short, the reformist pro-market position towards the diktat of the producer was still based on the idea of regulated competition, although to a lesser extent than in the case of the conservative-centrists. While acknowledging the imperative of economic efficiency, they were prepared to moderate the quest for this in the name of social protection, equity and harmony.

The radical pro-marketeers were far less constrained. In the first place, they insisted on the rapid introduction of destatization and privatization, as well as active encouragement of private enterprise. In this context, the Shatalin economic programme (Shatalin *et al.*, 1990, p. 3)[8] advocated the development of 'small enterprise' (*melkoe predprinimatelstvo*) in order, among other aims, 'to turn production to the satisfaction of the needs of each specific individual and combat the diktat of the monopolists in the consumer and production markets'. A major theme of the Shatalin programme was the requirement for enterprises to demonstrate their competitiveness and *raison d'etre* (literally speaking). The programme counterposed the granting of new rights and greater economic freedom to enterprises, with the establishment of 'rigorous restrictions', including increased payment for credit, an end to budget subsidies, a sharp fall in government investment, reduction in state purchases and, finally, the entry of foreign competition (ibid., p. 3). Yasin (1991, p. 21), who participated in the preparation of the programme, reiterated the radical pro-market line on enterprise competitiveness in an important article a few months later. 'We must not,' he stated, 'in the transition to a market economy bypass that moment when enterprises...find themselves obliged to seek suppliers and clients...and to study the conjuncture [of supply and demand in the market].' For Yasin and other radical pro-marketeers, the onus was on enterprises to justify their existence by demonstrating their competitiveness in free and open competition with all forms of labour. This essentially *laissez-faire* position differed markedly from that of the conservative-centrists and the reformist pro-marketeers, who continued to assign to the state principal responsibility for providing the means to enable loss-making enterprises to restructure themselves.

This distinction was particularly pronounced on the issues of budget constraints and enterprise bankruptcies. In acknowledging that the hardening of finance and credit policy, along with destatization and demonopolization, would lead to the bankruptcy of 'a significant number of enterprises' and the 'mass release of labour resources', Yasin (ibid., p. 22) nevertheless insisted on the necessity of a tough approach:

> There will be a million demands to strengthen [social] protection, to raise wages, to allocate investment, and these will be the demands of people driven to desperation. We can meet these demands. But then increased inflation would be inevitable, which would deprive those same people of what they have received, and postpone our extrication from the crisis.

The radical pro-marketeers sought to break the diktat of the producer and resolve the equity–efficiency dilemma by drawing a distinction between the security of enterprises and individual social guarantees. They challenged the conventional wisdom that the liquidation of loss-making enterprises would necessarily lead to mass unemployment with all its adverse social and psychological consequences (as in the West). Instead, they suggested that the cost to the individual could be minimized by improvements in training and the job placement system, and by reorienting popular expectations regarding the role of labour and employment in Soviet society. In the final analysis, they viewed the objective of employment as subordinate to that of the productive use of labour; enterprises should not be kept alive unless they served a useful labour, as well as employment, purpose. The objectives of social protection and justice should be met by establishing new welfare mechanisms, not, as in the past, by treating enterprises as dispensers of social largesse. To act otherwise was effectively to sustain the immunity and hence diktat of the producer.

The expansion of labour market ideas

Labour market concepts became fully legitimized during the extra-systemic period. With the exception of the socialist paternalists,[9] all the main ideological tendencies looked to it to influence both the direction and performance of labour, and patterns of employment. The main point of contention, as in the case of the debate over competition and competitiveness, was the extent to which such a market should be regulated.

In fact, even on this point there was considerable consensus. Goskomtrud Chairman Shcherbakov supported the idea of a labour market. Recognizing that it was inseparable from the notion of human resources as commodity and would therefore be seen by many as anti-Marxist, he (1990b, p. 1) nevertheless argued that '[o]nly in the market will the worker receive real freedom of choice and be able to demand full compensation for the value of his labour power'. Restoring the real value of labour through the labour market would change the attitude of employers to its use, simultaneously improving the worker's lot: 'having invested money in a commodity, any proprietor (*khozyain*) will try to use it efficiently' (ibid., p. 2). The conservative-centrist approach to the labour market expanded the idea of 'the new type of worker' (*rabochii novogo tipa*) that had been a feature of Soviet labour ideology earlier in the Gorbachev period (see Chapters 4 and 5). And notions of a post-industrial economy together with the creation of a labour force armed with a new mentality and the latest in education, found increasing favour within the political leadership.

More generally, the emergence and expansion of the labour market intensified the demands made on the individual worker. While proclaiming that the state would not abandon workers to the 'tyranny of fate', Shcherbakov (1990b, p. 1) warned that 'the individual should not wait passively to be offered work, but must undertake retraining, improve his qualifications and master a new profession'. Much the same message was conveyed by Ivashko (1990, p. 26) when he declared that full employment in a market economy could not be maintained 'artificially, by administrative measures'. Instead, workers would bear greater responsibility in their 'relationship to labour', and the value of job positions would increase. The individual's capacity to adjust to the changing demands of the new Soviet labour market became especially important given the regime's pursuit of large-scale economic restructuring. In seeking to redirect the economy away from its traditional emphasis on heavy industry towards the 'satisfaction of consumer needs'

(CPSU Programme Statement in *Materialy XXVIII Sezda...*, 1990, p. 82), the regime changed the conventions governing popular attitudes towards different types of work. In particular, the long-time superior status of industrial over service professions was called into serious question, with even the trade union movement with its heavy industry bias agreeing that the 'social significance' of work in the services sector had been 'underestimated' (Veretennikov, 1991, p. 224).

Perhaps more significant still was the regime's tangible shift away from its traditional fealty to collectivist principles in labour, towards individual or small-group 'entrepreneurism'. While the conservative-centrist position on the labour market continued to give pride of place to social production, entrepreneurial activity, long associated with sharp practice, became fully endorsed during this period. Already at the 28th Party Congress, Gorbachev (1990c, p. 15) was proclaiming that there were no obstacles to creating 'real freedom of enterprise', while the government's 'Basic Guidelines...' (*Vedomosti...*, 1990, p. 1095) predicted that entrepreneurial activity would exert a growing influence in connection with the accelerated development of a 'market infrastructure'.

In these circumstances, conservative-centrist assumptions regarding the demand for various types of labour underwent substantial change. Although the evidence of events such as the miners' strikes of 1989 and 1991 indicated that the old industrial proletariat still retained considerable clout, regime attitudes towards the labour market were increasingly influenced by the ideal of the modern, post-industrial economy with a correspondingly sophisticated workforce. The ideological assault on manual labour initiated in earnest under Andropov and sustained during the early Gorbachev years, developed into a more critical and differentiated outlook on the value of industrial labour generally (see McAuley, 1992, p. 207; Connor, 1991, p. 191). And while this trend was already visible in the 1986 wage reform, with its favouring of white- over blue-collar workers, it assumed ever larger significance as the difficulties in maintaining full employment mounted.

The expansion of labour market concepts during this period also gained further impetus within the framework of regime efforts to check the spread of economic autarky. The fraying of inter-republican and centre-republican economic ties, in addition to its other adverse consequences, was seen as directly aggravating the problem of unemployment. Gorbachev's presidential decree, 'On urgent measures to ensure the stable operation of basic branches of the national economy' (*Izvestiya*, 17 May 1991, p. 2), warned that the 'severing of economic ties' could lead to the closure of 'thousands of enterprises' and leave 'millions' unemployed. The conservative-centrist position attempted to enlist the concept of the labour market in the centre's wider struggle for political and economic dominion over the republics. In the fraught circumstances of the last months of the Soviet state, labour market ideas became not only important in themselves, but also as a means of promoting the Union and resisting the centrifugal forces pulling it apart. The notion of a labour market became another element in the general conception of the 'all-Union market', that is, the maintenance of existing inter-republican arrangements and structures. Since a *bona fide* labour market naturally depended on freedom of movement throughout the territory of the Union, support for its existence and expansion implied rejecting the autarkic inclinations of various republics and regions.

The conservative-centrists' approach to the labour market reflected their attitude towards the market as a whole. While there was now greater recognition of the practical difficulties in regulating the labour market, this did not translate into an acceptance that it should be left largely to its own devices. Just as the conservative-centrists perceived a need for the state to cushion the harshness of market forces, so they supported an interventionist approach to the solution of labour market problems. This embraced in the first instance prescriptions inherited from the Brezhnev era, such as the location of labour-intensive industries in labour surplus areas. However, contrary to the case before *perestroika*, the conservative-centrists acknowledged that the matching of labour resources to production requirements would need to be achieved through primarily economic methods. In particular, the 'liberating' of labour necessitated a freer, more flexible labour market characterized by increased mobility. Although this had become a significant issue in the wake of the Law on the State Enterprise, its importance grew as the Soviet Union's political and economic fabric was torn apart during 1990–91. Without such mobility there could be no prospect of resolving production difficulties in labour shortage regions or of containing worsening unemployment in labour surplus areas. The conservative-centrists understood, furthermore, that success in stimulating labour mobility was contingent on developing a proper housing market. People could hardly be persuaded to shift their place of residence without a guarantee of at least equal (or better) housing (*Vedomosti...*, 1990, p. 1115).

A proper labour market also necessitated a nationwide system of employment exchanges. Even if housing was available in a labour shortage region, and the worker willing to move, how was he/she to know about the existence of job opportunities? In focusing on the problem of 'temporary non-employment' (*vremennoe nezanyatie*) in the transition to market, Ryzhkov (1990b, p. 108) stressed the urgency of 'energetic action in the area of job placement, ensuring a speedy response to structural advances in the national economy'. Article 18 of the 1991 Employment Law provided for the establishment of a 'state employment service ... to pursue an employment policy for the population and to ensure corresponding guarantees to citizens' (*Vedomosti ...*, 1991, p. 187). As envisaged by the regime, the functions of the new employment exchanges were not to be restricted simply to matching workers with vacancies. Instead, they were intended to encompass the training and retraining of workers, particularly those whose jobs had become redundant and whose present level of working experience meant they stood little chance of reemployment. The introduction of such exchanges reflected a continuing conviction that the prime responsibility for ensuring the population's employment fell to the state, rather than the individual. Although there were calls for the latter to show greater professional and geographical flexibility (Shcherbakov, 1990b, p. 1), the conservative-centrists' ideological commitment to the full employment doctrine ensured that such considerations remained secondary to the most urgent imperative: the establishment of a social safety net in the transition to a socialist market economy.

The conservative-centrist influence was evident also in the regime's paternalist attitude towards population groups less able to compete on the open labour market. Article 6 of the 1991 Employment Law provided for 'additional employment guarantees for citizens in need of social protection and experiencing difficulties in finding work'. Among measures foreshadowed were the creation of additional jobs, 'specialized' enterprises, and 'special' training programmes, as well as the introduction of job quotas for target groups – young people, single parents with many children, pensioners and workers of pre-pension age, war veterans, invalids, ex-convicts, and 'persons who have been out of work for a prolonged period' (*Vedomosti ...*, 1991, p. 183).

In typifying the regime's approach to labour market concepts as predominantly 'conservative-centrist', it is important to remember that this categorization is both relative and time-specific. Compared to the more radical viewpoints expressed during the extra-systemic period, the outlook of the conservative-centrists was unadventurous, clinging as it did to much of the paternalist baggage of the old social contract. That said, regime attitudes towards the labour market were already considerably more progressive than those prevailing during the previous, radical intra-systemic period. The commodification of labour, the removal of the universal obligation to work, recognition of the reality of primary and secondary labour markets – all these were highly radical policy positions even as late as 1989. For example, Abalkin's original blueprint for 'radical economic reform' which contained many ideas well in advance of reformist (let alone establishment) positions, opposed the notion of hired labour. While affirming the need to recognize the labour market under socialism, he (1989, p. 4) observed that it would be 'economically restricted by a system of various social guarantees, by the state's guarantee of workers' rights, as by the broad application of forms of collective property, which are characterized by relations of membership and co-ownership, *not hiring* [author's italics]'. Yet only a few months later, Abalkin's position on the commodification of labour had been discarded by all but the socialist paternalists.

The reformist pro-market position on the labour market differed very little from that of the conservative-centrists on the main substantive issues – the commodification of labour, the emphasis on labour mobility and flexibility, the development of a nationwide network of employment exchanges, the enhancement of education, training and retraining. Just as significantly, the reformist pro-marketeers shared much of the conservative-centrists' interventionist outlook on the regulating of labour market processes. The importance they attached to the full employment doctrine (albeit in a modified form), led them logically to emphasize the state's responsibility for manipulating the labour market in order to achieve this objective as far as possible. Zaslavskaya (1990, p. 91) linked the attainment of a 'dynamic balance between the number of jobs in the economy as a whole and the size of the labour force', with a gradualist approach towards worker redundancies. In this connection, she continued to advocate such traditional planning–technocratic prescriptions as the elimination of unfilled job vacancies and increasing the shift index. Although reformist pro-marketeers did not underestimate the requirement for the individual to demonstrate flexibility in the new Soviet labour market, their overall approach on such questions remained highly paternalistic. Ultimately, it was up to the state to help individuals to adapt to the changing economic environment, for example, through education and subsidies for job creation (Kotlyar, 1991, p. 111).

The stance of radical pro-marketeers towards labour market concepts was effectively determined by their preference for shock therapy over gradualist approaches to the development of a market economy. Yet, in important respects, they differed little from the conservative-centrists and reformist pro-marketeers. They believed that the state had a responsibility to create a framework and facilities by which the individual would be given every opportunity to compete successfully in the labour market. The Yavlinsky 500-day programme (Yavlinsky *et al.*, 1991, pp. 102–3) outlined, for example, a two-stage process of labour market development. In the first, 'transitional' stage, the main aim of state employment policy would be 'strengthening the new local, economic and social conditions of using labour resources'. The second stage would be characterized by 'stabilization' of the labour market, a job placement network system, training and retraining programmes, and a comprehensive social security system.

A key assumption informing the radical pro-market view was that the more developed the labour market the 'lower the level of exploitation'. In Yavlinsky's (Yavlinsky *et al.*, 1991, p. 101) conception, the emergence of a proper labour market necessitated allowing citizens the freedom to work 'voluntarily,' migrate freely within and without the USSR, and choose a workplace 'not depending on its territorial situation, ownership form, or working conditions' – in other words, the liberalization of *propiska*. The main distinguishing trait of the radical pro-market approach towards the labour market was therefore more one of emphasis than policy substance. While there was general consensus regarding the necessity for changes in both government policy and individual labour consciousness, the radical pro-marketeers assigned much greater importance to changing the latter. Their professed support for the 'right to work' was tempered by redefinition of the meaning of this term. The Shatalin programme (Shatalin *et al.*, 1990, p. 3) observed that 'the regulation of employment must be ensured, not by the fixing of the worker to a specific job position, but by the creation of conditions for the constant growth of qualifications and professional expertise'.

Implicit in the radical pro-market attitude was the idea that the state's regulatory responsibilities were essentially limited to creating favourable conditions for the population's employment. Once this was achieved, it was then up to a person to make the best use of available infrastructure and facilities. The logical corollary of allocating greater responsibility to the individual was that the state had no obligation to maintain loss-making enterprises for purely employment (social) rather than labour (economic) reasons. Although the Shatalin programme (ibid., p. 3) admitted that the shutdown or restructuring of many enterprises would require 'temporary lay-offs and retraining for a large number of people', the net result would be the formation of a 'new, more efficient employment structure'. At the same time, the radical pro-market emphasis on individual self-reliance and initiative entailed divesting enterprises from the burden of continuing to employ workers whose labour contribution was no longer considered useful. The 500-day programme (Yavlinsky *et al.*, 1991, pp. 101–2) counterposed the right of workers to a free choice of profession (including the right not to be employed at all), with 'the freedom of all employers ... to hire and fire workers' under certain conditions.[10] Freedom in the supply of labour should be matched by the 'freedom in demand for the labour force'. The efficiency-driven approach of Shatalin and Yavlinsky rejected the conservative-centrist and reformist pro-market assumption that solid 'social guarantees' should be established prior to the liquidation of loss-making enterprises and the displacement of large numbers of workers onto the labour market. On the contrary, the latter phenomenon underlined the urgency of a new employment structure that met society's needs.

Changing attitudes towards unemployment

Just as the legitimization and expansion of labour market concepts symbolized the demise of traditional socialist assumptions regarding the 'non-exploitative' nature of labour, so the removal of the universal obligation to work marked the end of the Soviet full employment doctrine. Following its earlier concession that unemployment existed in the USSR, the leadership had begun the search for practical solutions. Nevertheless, the course of the debate over unemployment during the extrasystemic period threw up significant ideological divisions, both at the level of concrete policy and of the general principles governing Soviet labour ideology. Differences centred on two critical issues: (a) what constituted unemployment; and (b) to what extent (if any) was it an acceptable or 'normal' feature of an effectively functioning economy.

Definitional questions

There was a significant divergence here between conservative-centrist and reformist pro-market positions on the one hand, and those of the socialist paternalists and radical pro-marketeers on the other. Although the former group no longer denied absolutely the existence of actual unemployment (*bezrabotitsa*), their pronouncements during this period considerably narrowed its definitional compass. Shcherbakov (1991, p. 37) argued, for example, against identifying unemployment with the 'negative consequences of the lack of preparation for large-scale labour redistribution ...'. For him, unemployment was 'a lever to sustain a high level of profitability... applied in a capitalist economy to limit the growth of wages and to control inflationary processes'. As such, it contradicted 'the humanistic concept of labour and the social character of socialist property'. Earlier, in outlining government measures for social protection in the transition to a market economy, he (1990b, p. 1) had insisted that '[t]he question is not about legitimizing unemployment. Instances in which people temporarily do not have permanent jobs are to be regarded as extraordinary.'

The predilection of conservative-centrists to differentiate between 'non-employment' (*nezanyatost*) and unemployment was evident also at the level of specific policy. An example of this was the Party's Programme Statement from the 28th Congress (*Materialy XXVIII Sezda...*, 1990, p. 88), which envisioned the introduction of benefits 'for the period of temporary non-employment'. Unemployment continued to be seen as a future threat with alien characteristics, in contrast to non-employment which was a current problem. And there was a clear distinction to be made between 'temporary non-employment' which was the natural, but manageable by-product of economic restructuring (Pavlov, 1991a, p. 2), and 'unemployment' which was equated with the uncontrollable mass unemployment characteristic of Western capitalist economies. This difference was not just of semantic interest. The issue of whether unemployment was to be considered a permanent or temporary reality became bound up with the choice between shock therapy and gradualist approaches to marketization. Conservative-centrist opposition to large-scale privatization and the liquidation of loss-making enterprises (Pavlov, 1991a, p. 2) stemmed from a commitment to prove that non-employment was a relatively short-term and soluble problem, and that unemployment was entirely avoidable in the Soviet Union.

Much the same distinction was made by reformist pro-marketeers such as Abalkin. In his 1989 reform programme, he (p. 6) noted the likelihood of some 'temporary unemployment' in connection with the development of the 'moderate-radical' model of market relations. This contrasted with the prospect of 'mass unemployment' that would be a consequence of adopting a 'radical' variant of the transition to a market economy (p. 5). The dichotomy between gradualism/temporary non-employment and shock therapy/long-term mass unemployment, was also present in Zaslavskaya's (1990, p. 91) comparison between 'absolute' and 'structural' unemployment. The former referred to the 'overall balance between jobs and workers', while the latter meant 'the partial balance between them within sectors, professions and regions'.

Zaslavskaya (ibid., pp. 90–1) viewed the achievement of 'absolute' employment – 'by no means simple' but possible if gradualist methods were adopted – as answering Western correspondents who 'constantly ask how we can reconcile high rates of technological progress with retaining the constitutional right of all Soviet citizens to work, i.e., the absence of unemployment'.

By contrast, socialist paternalists and radical pro-marketeers, notwithstanding their diametrically opposed ideological viewpoints, made little distinction between non-employment and unemployment. Neither subscribed to the ideological rationalizations that marked the conservative-centrist and reformist pro-market positions. And both associated increased unemployment with the changeover to a market economy, although they drew very different conclusions from this fact. Thus, at the 28th Party Congress, Yegor Ligachev (*Pravda*, 11 July 1990, p. 5) attempted to resist Gorbachev's shift towards the socialist market by raising the spectre of 'mass unemployment', adding: 'let whoever is pushing the country towards free market relations be the first of the Soviet unemployed.' From the opposite ideological perspective, Yavlinsky's Epicentre (Yavlinsky, Zadornov and Mikhailov, 1991, p. 3) forecast that by the end of 1991 'mass unemployment' would become a 'fact' and would grow further. In a jibe at the 'denial' mentality of the conservative-centrists, it declared that '[c]ombating [unemployment] with incantations like "we will not permit an economic slump" is senseless, since it stems from objective causes'.

The 'acceptability' of unemployment

Opinions on this question exerted a strong influence on, and were strongly influenced by, the definitional debate over unemployment. The conservative-centrist and reformist pro-market bias towards using the term, 'temporary non-employment', reflected their abhorrence of both the idea and actual consequences of 'capitalist-style' unemployment. At the same time, the definitional distinctions they made placed them in something of an ideological *embarras*; the more the regime talked of non-employment, the less acceptable became the notion of unemployment.[11] In addition to such general considerations, they were also profoundly troubled by a number of specific unemployment-related issues. For example, although Article 1 of the 1991 Employment Law decriminalized 'voluntary non-employment' (*Vedomosti...*, 1991, p. 180), non-performance of labour continued to be associated by many with 'parasitic' behaviour (*Izvestiya*, 11 October 1990, p. 2).

The regime found itself caught between ideological pressures and practical difficulties. On the one hand, the Soviet Union had been founded as a workers' state, in which the allocation of socioeconomic benefits was intended to be directly proportional to the amount of labour performed. The notion of not working, then, was unthinkable from both a moral and functional standpoint: a citizen without work could not possibly find the means to live unless they were engaged in some nefarious activity. On the other hand, the search for economic efficiency and labour productivity had led, by stages, to the realization that there were vast numbers of the population engaged in production activity for which there was no demand but who, equally, could not simply be left to their own devices.

As in the radical intra-systemic period, a number of proposals were put forward to lessen the impact of equity–efficiency contradictions on the full employment doctrine. These centred principally on various ideas for reducing employment demand: early retirement provisions; improvements in pensions, maternity benefits and student stipends; geographically selective demographic prescriptions. However, it is striking that these suggestions were invariably put forward by academics rather than by political leaders themselves. Although figures such as Zaslavskaya were close to Gorbachev, the general absence of official pronouncements on such matters pointed to both a deep ideological angst within the leadership as well as fears that too abrupt and overt an abandonment of full employment principles would exacerbate political and social tensions.

The formalization of the right not to work should be seen in this light. Although it was painted in the context of the 'freeing' of labour, the decriminalization of non-work was a measure imposed by the force of circumstances and, specifically, the need to relieve the growing pressures on the new Soviet labour market. At the same time, however, the historical, ideological and psychological baggage accumulated by Soviet leaders over a period of 70 years could hardly be expected to disappear overnight. It remained axiomatic that labour was the major, if no longer the sole, legitimate source of wealth. Such moral-ideological factors in the debate over the 'acceptability' of unemployment were given further impetus in the Soviet Union's deteriorating economic and social conditions. Put simply, the regime did not have the resources to sustain adequate levels of unemployment insurance and benefits in the event of the mass release of human resources onto the labour market (*Izvestiya*, 11 October 1990, p. 2). Financial considerations made it critical that 'unemployment' and the 'unemployed' be defined as narrowly as possible, and that the conditions under which benefits were given out be extremely stringent. The conservative-centrist and reformist pro-market emphasis on 'temporary non-employment' was not only ideologically and politically driven; it also represented an attempt at financial damage-control. When Prime Minister Pavlov (1991b, p. 2) declared the payment of 'direct unemployment benefits' to be an 'extreme measure', he was in effect heavily diluting the social contract between state and people. The regime sought to preserve the illusion that adequate social welfare mechanisms were in place, while simultaneously restricting the number of citizens who might test the worth of such 'social guarantees'. Its disingenuous approach was well illustrated by the ungenerous and restrictive provisions of the 1991 Employment Law regarding the payment of benefits.[12]

On top of ideological and financial objections to the legitimization of unemployment, the regime was also worried about popular reaction to a sudden rise in levels of joblessness. These concerns acquired particular point given the lack of an adequate safety net for the unemployed, the 'successful' implementation of the full employment doctrine over many decades (Kryuchkov's speech to the 28th Party Congress, *Pravda*, 5 July 1990, p. 3), and the fact that the provision of social welfare in the Soviet Union was so closely tied to the workplace. For conservative-centrists such as Pavlov, the perceived social unacceptability of unemployment lay at the heart of their opposition to shock therapy and radical economic reform. This nexus between unemployment and social instability was reinforced by events such as the miners' strikes in 1989 and 1991; Simon Clarke and Peter Fairbrother (in Clarke *et al.*, 1993, p. 140) have rightly emphasized the impact of the 1989 strikes in paralysing the government's reform programme.

Notwithstanding their common aversion to shock therapy, the reformist pro-marketeers were on the whole more flexible than the conservative-centrists in their attitude towards the theory and practice of unemployment. In the first place, they avoided pejorative language in respect of the non-employed. Reformist pro-marketeers such as Abalkin (1989, p. 6) and Zaslavskaya (1990, pp. 112–13) focused more on the need for retraining and psychological readjustment than on any alleged moral dereliction on the part of the individual. They also displayed a generally more sophisticated understanding of the nature of unemployment in Soviet society and the broader issues relating to it. While Zaslavskaya (ibid., p. 189) stressed that the success of *perestroika* depended on it being achieved 'at the lowest possible social cost', she acknowledged that the fear of political and social tensions could become

'a very serious brake on the far-reaching development of this process'.
Although the reformist pro-marketeers shared the conservative-centrist
abhorrence of Western-style unemployment, unlike the former they did
not allow this sentiment to stymie their overall project of structural
economic reform. For example, closure of loss-making enterprises was
desirable so long as 'special measures' were taken to help released workers
find other jobs (ibid., p. 77). In this, their approach was more one of
containment than avoidance of the issue of unemployment.

The belief of the radical pro-marketeers that unemployment was
both an unavoidable and long-term phenomenon, led them to accept
it as a reality of life, albeit an unpleasant one (Yavlinsky, Zadornov and
Mikhailov, 1991, p. 3). This view derived from a number of assumptions.
In the first place, the radical pro-marketeers believed that some unemployment was the natural price for reversing decades of economic
mismanagement and inefficiency under command–administrative socialism. The fault lay 'not with the market, but with its absence'
(Shatalin *et al.*, 1990, p. 3). Moreover, the longer reform was delayed
and the more half-hearted its realization, the more serious would be its
economic and social costs, such as structural unemployment (Bronshtein, 1990, p. 2). Leading radicals such as Yavlinsky and Yasin (1991,
p. 22) acknowledged the importance of taking social tensions into
account, but argued these would only be aggravated and prolonged by
gradualist methods of reform.

More specifically, the radical pro-marketeers focused on the dilemma
between inflation and unemployment, of assessing which of these two
evils was more affordable, economically, socially and politically. Here
they diverged from the other main ideological currents which tended
to bracket these phenomena together as automatic outcomes of shock
therapy. Yarygina (1991b, p. 6) linked the growth of strong inflationary
pressures, such as monetary emission, to the traditional 'impermissibil-
ity' of unemployment in popular and official consciousness. Now, however, this approach was no longer sustainable as declining production
volumes led to higher unemployment across all sectors of industry.
Shatalin, Yavlinsky and others sought solutions in largely monetarist
economic policies, centring on tight fiscal and monetary controls. Without such constraints, they claimed, there could never be a proper
balance between the pursuit of efficiency and equity objectives. A full
employment policy based on the maintenance of grossly inefficient
production and the insouciant diktat of the producer was unacceptable
on moral and socioeconomic grounds. On the other hand, the unemployment resulting from the implementation of tough economic

reforms was entirely justified if it led to the rationalization of production, the development of a new enterprise culture and thence to a general rise in the population's living standards (Shatalin *et al.*, 1990, p. 3). The search for greater economic efficiency should not be allowed to be sabotaged by spurious appeals to 'social justice', particularly since without the former there could be no real social guarantees for the population (Yarygina, 1991a, p. 10). A satisfactory equity–efficiency balance could be achieved so long as economic rationalization was tempered by the introduction of effective protective mechanisms for those who might be left by the wayside, including unemployment benefits, public works programmes, the allocation of land (Shatalin *et al.*, 1990, p. 3), and new pension programs (*Izvestiya*, 24 June 1991, p. 2).

Ultimately, what the radical pro-marketeers sought was to disentangle the fusion/confusion between the economic and social functions of distributive relations – highlighted by Shatalin in 1986 (pp. 64–5 – see Chapter 4) – as a result of which neither the interests of economic efficiency nor social justice were served. In the more liberal/anarchic political and ideological environment of the extra-systemic period, Shatalin's thinking provided the philosophical basis for completely different conceptions of paternalism and the welfare state, whereby social guarantees were freed from their intimate association with public employment and the workplace. Everyone, irrespective of their working status (and performance), deserved at least a minimum standard of living. But it was not the function of employment to make up for the absence of a comprehensive system of social welfare, which, however, remained a fundamental policy priority of the state.

Ideological transformation and the collapse of the state

The first two, intra-systemic, phases of *perestroika* had witnessed a rough consensus in official attitudes towards labour, despite important differences at the level of policy detail and general philosophy. In sharp contrast, Soviet labour ideology during the final 18 months of the Gorbachev era was highly fragmented. Encouragement of pluralism in its many guises – political, economic, ideological, intellectual – acted to bring previously covert policy and philosophical differences out into the open. In an ever more unregulated and unstable political environment, there was little pretence at regime solidarity, as the Gorbachev administration found itself buffeted by opposing forces and specific pressures as intense as any experienced by Western capitalist democracies in periods of crisis. In these circumstances, Soviet labour ideology moved from its former dependence on fundamental positions of principle – the universal obligation to work, the non-commodification of labour, the full employment doctrine – towards a fluid condition where little was sacred, and where the dominant theme was one of political and tactical expediency. The *ad hoc* tendencies identified in the previous chapter only strengthened during this period as the regime became progressively more desperate in the face of the USSR's by now obvious political and economic disintegration. The extra-systemic period began with the political leadership attempting to sustain socialist principles in the economy through the device of the socialist market, but the breakneck pace of events left behind and nullified regime efforts to establish an ideological framework and vision.

Although the Gorbachev administration embraced the idea of a market economy, its understanding of this concept was limited to an idealized conception of the socialist market in which government regulation would blend naturally with market forces. The predominant conservative-centrist tendency during this period showed little grasp of the enormous contradictions and practical difficulties involved in implementing socialist market ideas in the Soviet context. In circumstances where the command–administrative system had become the object of widespread disregard, but where market infrastructure was rudimentary, the synthesis imagined by the regime was the stuff of fantasy. In reality, a quite different outcome emerged, in which the contradictions between central control and devolution, and between plan and market, discredited regime ideology and weakened state power without stimulating a new enterprise culture or raising labour productivity.

Official conceptions of labour became hostage to the struggle for political power and influence – between the centre and the republics, and within the centre itself. Across the ideological spectrum, from socialist paternalist to radical pro-market, there was a general move to respond to, and harness, popular pressures. The country's rapidly worsening economic and social circumstances inevitably led all the main ideological currents to advertise their solicitude for popular welfare, contrasting it simultaneously to the ineptitude and/or inhumanity of their opponents. An illuminating example of this trend was provided by the leaders of the August 1991 putsch who, in their 'Appeal to the Soviet People', sought to justify their actions in part by claiming that '[a]n offensive against the rights of the working people is under way. The rights to work, education, health care, housing and recreation have been called into question' (*Izvestiya*, 20 August 1991, p. 1).

Throughout the extra-systemic period, the conservative-centrist mainstream periodically undermined its broadly pro-market positions on competition, self-financing, the hardening of budget constraints, price reform, etc., by caving in to specific political pressures. This was demonstrated most vividly in the authorities' craven reaction to the exercise of industrial muscle, especially when this took the form of strike action. Confronted with the imperative of resuming production as quickly as possible, the political leadership often made concessions that were not only ideologically inconsistent but also financially irresponsible.[13] In an increasingly fraught psychological climate, principle became whatever appeared to meet the short-term requirements of a given situation (strike, demonstration, or simply intensive lobbying by special interest groups). With the sacrifice or at least erosion of key dogma, Soviet labour ideology became an ideology of improvisation, whose chief *raison d'etre* was to rationalize, *post facto*, reactive government actions rather than function as the bedrock of considered policy. Apparently sacred and immutable tenets became, by the end, largely articles of political convenience. From being an ideology of stability and certitude, it became one of transience and uncertainty.[14]

Gorbachev's ideological indecisiveness was reinforced in the declining economic and social conditions of the USSR. Growing poverty,[15] worsening consumer shortages, panic buying, currency runs, all these pointed to a society in crisis and lacking any confidence in its political leaders. Gorbachev rightly surmised that things could not continue as they were. He also recognized the necessity of far-reaching, 'radical', economic reform. But, faced with the problem of implementing such reforms in a climate of political and social breakdown, he opted for what appeared the safest approach: 'stabilization' before tough economic medicine, gradualism instead of shock therapy. In this way, he hoped to buy time in which to regain a measure of popular confidence, and contain to manageable levels the political, economic and social consequences of marketization. In terms of labour ideology and practice, this involved favouring continued soft budget constraints for enterprises while preaching the need to develop a proper finance-credit system. It meant allowing enterprises to retain vast numbers of unproductive workers, operating inefficient and wasteful plant within a broken-down economic system; this, while reiterating the need for enterprises to streamline and rationalize their operations, and calling for a 'rigorous' attitude towards loss-making enterprises (Ryzhkov, 1990b, p. 95). At the level of the individual, the dominant conservative-centrist tendency in the Gorbachev administration ensured that 'social justice', in the form of employment protection, was given priority over the pursuit of labour productivity as expressed in the release, retraining and redeployment of redundant personnel. For all its talk about the need for heightened demands on the individual, the regime remained unprepared to put this to the ultimate test, that of unemployment. The vast majority of workers continued to enjoy employment protection little worse than in the pre-*perestroika* period.

The Gorbachev regime did not set out initially to legitimize the commodification of labour through expansion of the labour market, remove the universal obligation to work, and allow for a measure of 'temporary non-employment'. These ideas developed essentially in response to events. They merely confirmed existing political and economic realities, serving in the process to gloss over inadequacies in the regime's handling of major socioeconomic issues. Although the Gorbachev administration sought to present its conversion to market principles as a rational and considered position, logically arrived at, its embracing of extra-systemic solutions was tantamount to an admission of ideological bankruptcy. Far from being the product of reformist zeal, the resort to socialist market ideas was the last in a series of ideological compromises made under increasing duress – the final stage in the demise of traditional Soviet labour ideology – as the Gorbachev administration explored every possibility for staving off the country's socioeconomic ruination.

The Soviet leadership little imagined, as David Lane warned in 1988 (p. 237), that 'adoption of a Western-style labor market would undermine public ownership and planning, the present forms of social integration, and the legitimacy of the leading role of the Communist party'. However, the issue of labour productivity not only went to the heart of such seminal questions of socialism as the balance between equity and efficiency priorities, and between central control and local autonomy. It exposed for all to see the limitations of Soviet socialist economic models and the fragility of a regime whose condign, conditioned and compensatory powers (to adapt Dembinski's (1991, pp. 76–9) terminology) were in public and terminal decline during the extra-systemic period.

The most critical impact of regime policies aimed at raising labour productivity was that they stripped away the mystique and substance of state power. Although Gorbachev (1988a, pp. 18–25) was right in pointing out that the legacy left by *zastoi* was unsustainable in the long term, the attempted remedies initiated by Andropov and developed by Gorbachev had the effect of accelerating the disintegration of the Soviet

Union. Well-intentioned reform prescriptions not only failed to fulfil their purpose, but in failing they exposed for all to see (and very painfully for many citizens) the thinness of state legitimacy and the extent of the system's rottenness and unreformability. The increasingly *ad hoc* and reactive nature of labour ideology during the last decade of the Soviet era was eloquent testimony to the fact that the state, having already abandoned hope of instilling in the population visions of 'marching towards communism', had now also lost the ability to command substantial popular compliance. The regime's weakening hold on power, formerly achieved through the exercise of state authority, was further undermined by its inability to find and consolidate other forms of legitimation, for example, by offering the people positive outcomes from economic reforms. By the late 1980s, it was already apparent that the Soviet people neither feared, trusted, nor shared common purpose with the regime. In conditions of precipitous economic decline, falling living standards and mounting ethnic unrest, demystification and delegitimization translated readily and rapidly into the dismantling of the Soviet state. In the end, the 'disembodiment' of labour ideology – reflected in the total victory of short-term pragmatic and populist considerations over fundamental dogma – represented the demolition of the Soviet state's dominant ethos and practical foundation, symbolizing in the process the decline and fall of the system itself.

7
Labour and Legitimacy in Post-Soviet Russia

'Politics is not the art of the possible. It consists in choosing between the disastrous and the unpalatable.'

John Kenneth Galbraith, letter to President Kennedy (in Partington, 1992, p. 297)

Introduction

The dissolution of the USSR in December 1991 appeared to open the way to the rapid introduction of a Western-style market. Already in the last months of the Soviet Union, the imminent accession of Yeltsin presaged the emergence of a new economic culture characterized by financial stabilization, large-scale privatization, and economic liberalization. In the specific context of labour, a significant hardening of enterprise budget constraints was promised, and there were widespread expectations that loss-making firms would be punished by bankruptcy and their workers laid off in large numbers.

Eight years on, it is obvious that local and foreign observers alike greatly underestimated the durability of ingrained attitudes from the Soviet era and their continuing influence on government policy. While there have certainly been far-reaching changes to Russia's socioeconomic environment, the ambitious market agenda of the first Yeltsin government headed by Prime Minister Yegor Gaidar remains largely unrealized. As in the Gorbachev era, much of the transformation that has occurred in recent years has been of a character largely unanticipated by policymakers and thinkers. Periods of financial stabilization have alternated with times of rampant hyperinflation and a plummeting rouble. Notwithstanding the mass nominal privatization of Russian enterprises, the state continues to dominate the economy. And although some Russian enterprises have embraced the opportunities afforded by economic liberalization, Soviet notions of paternalism and a welfare/dependence (*izhdivenchestvo*) mentality remain formidable obstacles to a new enterprise culture based on competitiveness, self-reliance and initiative. This final chapter is by way of an epilogue, picking up some of the themes discussed in earlier chapters and pursuing them in their post-Soviet context. Although the centrality of labour as the dominant ethos and practical basis of the state has not been preserved in Yeltsin's Russia, many of the problems that supplied the original rationale for change in the last decade of the Soviet Union have yet to be resolved: labour productivity is very low, most enterprises have been slow to respond to market forces, and economic actors, high and low, cling desperately to the umbilical cord of the state. The concept of a discrete labour ideology may have become anachronistic, but labour-related issues promise to be a lasting focus for bitter political debate and difference.

This chapter examines four closely interrelated questions. The first is the Yeltsin administration's quest to establish a new market economic system and accompanying ideology in the ruins left from the Gorbachev period. What were the fundamental principles shaping the original reformers' vision of the Russian market, and to what extent have these been realized? The second question relates to the continuing issue of labour productivity and its place in the emergent post-Soviet transition economy, examined here through the critical dichotomies of macroeconomic stabilization versus structural policy, and shock therapy versus gradualism. How has the regime attempted to address the problem of continuing poor economic performance? Indeed, given the circumstances of Russia's steady deindustrialization, does the issue of labour productivity even retain its former relevance? The third section in this chapter looks at the evolution of economic attitudes at all levels of society – within government, among enterprise directors, and in the workforce. To what degree, if any, have classical free market notions of competition, economic responsibility, self-reliance and the 'creative destruction' of enterprises become part of the lexicon and practice of post-Soviet economic behaviour? What sort of ethos – unifying or otherwise – has emerged in place of the old Soviet labour ideology? Finally, I consider the implications of economic and ideological change for the continuing legitimacy of the Yeltsin administration and political stability in Russia generally. It has been argued earlier that the Soviet leadership's search for labour productivity contributed critically to the demystification and delegitimization of the USSR state system. Do the ongoing economic problems of post-Soviet Russia foreshadow a similar fate for the Yeltsin administration, or indeed, more widely for political democracy and notions of popular legitimacy in Russia?

The Yeltsin vision – a 'market economy' for post-Soviet Russia

Attempting to encapsulate the Yeltsin administration's conception of the market is no easy task. First, the fact that different elite groups and interests have held sway at various times over the past eight years has meant there has been little consistency of vision, purpose or means. The original post-Soviet Gaidar government – in which Anatolii Chubais and Boris Fyodorov played prominent roles – set an ambitious and comprehensive ('Western') market agenda which none of its successors has even attempted to match. The contradictory statements of key figures such as President Yeltsin and long-time Prime Minister Viktor Chernomyrdin have, more often than not, pointed to no particular post-Soviet market paradigm, but reflected instead the ebb and flow of the political struggle between competing personalities and factions, as well as the almost Pavlovian policy impact of certain events (such as the Duma elections of December 1993 and December 1995 in which the nationalists and communists scored major successes). The subordination of economic principle to political imperatives has ensured that the Yeltsin administration's understanding of terms like 'market' and 'market economy' has been sensitive to time and political context to a much greater degree than is normally the case in a functioning Western economy. The difficulty in identifying a 'Yeltsin vision of the market' is further exacerbated by the general trends of 'deideologization' and political opportunism discussed in the previous chapter. Just as in Soviet times, ideological conviction or understanding has become for many far less important than saying the right things at the appropriate moment – what James Millar (1995, p. 13) calls 'chameleonism'. In terms of the market, this has often translated into 'in-principle' endorsement of its tenets, while selectively interpreting, diluting or blocking their application. These elements – policy confusion and inconsistency, political opportunism and 'deideologization' – have been critical in shaping the implementation of the main planks of the liberal market agenda in the post-Soviet era: (a) financial stabilization; (b) mass privatization; and (c) economic liberalization.

Financial stabilization

Arguably the most urgent task facing the Yeltsin administration in January 1992 was to reintroduce some sort of order after the financial chaos of the Gorbachev years. In the first place, this meant reducing the massive burden of state subsidies to inefficient enterprises, as well as making cuts to expenditure in such resource-hungry areas as the military–industrial complex and agriculture. The government also set out to tighten monetary controls by clamping down on emission[1] and thereby restrain hyperinflation.

Moreover, the Gaidar reformers hoped that in achieving these objectives they would encourage the emergence of a new enterprise culture based on self-reliance, economic accountability, and entrepreneurial initiative. Anders Aslund (1995, pp. 186–7), who served as an advisor to the Russian government during 1992–93, identified as one of the main challenges of reform the 'asocial behavior' of state enterprise managers in conditions where they 'enjoyed the freedom of a market economy coupled with the irresponsibility of a command economy'. By cutting subsidies to unviable but resource-hungry enterprises, and enhancing the value of money through emission controls, the reformers looked to force firms to be more responsive to consumer demand, if necessary through restructuring and/or downsizing their operations. Those which would not, or could not, adapt should be subject to the laws of Schumpeterian 'creative destruction' via the bankruptcy process.

The record of the post-Soviet period shows that successive Yeltsin governments have failed to achieve lasting success in any of these areas. Notwithstanding much talk about reducing state subsidies to industry and agriculture,[2] financial constraints on enterprises in these sectors continue to be both burdensome and highly arbitrary. In the first place, it remains axiomatic that state funds are provided to firms not according to their economic viability (or need), but on the basis of political clout. Networking and influence (*blat*) are as important as in Soviet times, with the 'winners' generally being those 'who have secured the protection of the authorities and know how to wangle money from the government' (Yeltsin, *Rossiiskaya gazeta*, 25 February 1994, pp. 1–2). Second, as Peter Rutland (1997, p. 32) has pointed out, many enterprises have been able to compensate for the diminution in budgetary funds through access to all kinds of special dispensations, including tax breaks, emergency credits, off-budget funding sources. Third, even the most unviable Russian enterprises have been able to survive by running up massive arrears (to banks, other enterprises and to their own workers),[3] in the knowledge that the state will, sooner or later, cancel these as bad debts. The Russian government's reluctance to punish such practices by implementing bankruptcy procedures (see below) has effectively enabled enterprises to soften the financial constraints under which they operate. The Soviet waste mechanism (*zatratny mekhanizm*) remains alive and kicking, and there is little indication that Russia has moved away from 'energy-wasting production processes' (Yasin, 1994, p. 2). Implementation of the reform agenda has also been hugely complicated by the failure to control money supply. While Russia enjoyed a period of relative monetary stability from late 1994 to August 1998, this followed three years of uncontrolled emission, hyperinflation and a sharply falling rouble. During this earlier period, the Central Bank under Chairman Vladimir Gerashchenko made liberal use of the printing presses to cover the growing indebtedness and insolvency of Russia's industrial enterprises, thereby undercutting the liberal reformers' programme (see Fyodorov, 1993a, p. 10). The financial crash of 17 August 1998 and Gerashchenko's reinstatement as Central Bank Chairman served only to emphasize the fragility of Russia's financial foundations and the constant threat of further significant monetary emissions (interview with Gerashchenko in *Rossiiskaya gazeta*, 15 September 1998, pp. 1–2). The first few months following the crash witnessed a major devaluation of the rouble and a sharp increase in inflation,[4] and the risk of a return to hyperinflation remains ever-present.

Mass privatization

The large-scale privatization of Russian enterprises has been seen by some commentators (for example, Aslund, 1995, p. 223) as the most signal success of the Yeltsin era. Initially confined to small enterprises, by 1996 privatization had spread to an estimated 77.2 per cent of medium- and large-size enterprises, accounting for 88.3 per cent of Russia's total industrial output (Blasi *et al.*, 1997, pp. 25–6). Although the size of Russia's shadow economy makes it difficult to measure the total value of the non-state sector, most estimates put this at well over half of national GDP. On paper at least, Russia has met one of the principal criteria for a modern market economy.

However, the 'achievement' of mass privatization is much more tenuous when assessed against the aims of the first, 'purest', government privatization programme in 1992. These included, *inter alia*, the formation of 'a stratum of private proprietors interested in the creation of a social market economy'; increasing the efficiency of enterprises; improving the social safety net using the proceeds from privatization; creating 'a competitive environment' and encouraging demonopolization; and attracting foreign investment (Aslund, 1995, p. 241). Measured against these objectives, the government's performance has been dismal.

In the first place, much of Russia's privatization has been of a largely nominal character, impinging little on the practical reality that the government retains a much closer connection with enterprise activity than is the case in mainstream Western capitalist economies. While the state may no longer directly hold all the 'commanding heights of industry' (to use Lenin's phrase), the essential point is that those who now possess these do so by the grace, favour and collusion of the state. In Igor Birman's (1996, p. 742) memorable phrase, what has occurred in Russia is 'privatisation of the *nomenklatura*, by the *nomenklatura*, for the *nomenklatura*'. Although a stratum of private proprietors has emerged, membership of it has been dominated by a small coterie of oligarchs – men such as Berezovsky, Alekperov, Khodorkovsky and Gusinsky – heading financial–industrial groups (FIGs) whose monopolistic behaviour and crony capitalism run directly counter to the spirit of a 'social market economy'.

Nor has privatization appeared to have made much difference to the efficiency of enterprises. The intimacy of state involvement in '*nomenklatura* privatization' and FIG economic activity has served to reinforce rather than diminish the former Soviet culture of dependency. The general expectation – largely justified by experience – is that the state in most cases will bail out a privatized enterprise in much the same way as it would a state-owned firm. Hopes that private ownership would, *ipso facto*, increase enterprise efficiency have proved to be pious, principally because the FIGs are in effect quasi-state entities whose form of paternalism often permits firms to remain unresponsive to market forces and the imperatives of accountability, responsibility and good management practice. As Rutland (1997, p. 32) has observed, privatization 'has not stimulated the economic restructuring it was initially intended to achieve'. Like in Soviet times, there is still no proper system of incentives – positive or 'negative' – to reward economic activity. Success and failure are influenced far more by extraneous political factors than the level of labour or enterprise performance.

Economic liberalization

When the first Gaidar government introduced the comprehensive price liberalization of 2 January 1992 (*Izvestiya*, 2 January 1992, p. 1), it appeared to signal the urgency of the government's commitment to a market economy. As Gaidar (*Rossiiskaya gazeta*, 11 January 1992, p. 3) argued, the 'large-scale freeing-up of prices' was intended to introduce the distributive mechanism of the market in place of the former state bureaucratic allocation of resources. In retrospect, however, it is clear that far from being a harbinger of radical reforms to come, this initial freeing of prices in fact represented the high-water mark of the Yeltsin administration's political will in implementing its liberalization agenda. The subsequent backdown over energy prices in April 1992[5] turned out to be only the first of many defeats for the radical reform programme, and the declared goal of an open market economy based on free and fair competition has remained a theoretical construct rather than practical reality.

It is certainly true that the freeing of prices has opened up new possibilities for economic activity and stimulated a much more developed consumer market, whereby most Russians now enjoy far greater access to a wide range of consumer goods. That said, at no time in the past eight years has the Russian economy even remotely resembled a functioning liberal market model. First, as noted earlier, the state continues to play a preeminent role in decision-making at the micro- as well as macroeconomic level. The freeing of economic activity from political interference, seen by Aslund (1995, p. 3) as a prerequisite of a market economy, remains a distant prospect in Russia.[6] Second, the 'oligarchic capitalism' (Nemtsov, *Kommersant-Daily*, 27 August 1998, p. 3) of present-day Russia, operating through collusion and networking, is directly antithetical to notions of competition, transparency and fair dealing. Just like the old Soviet *nomenklatura*, the oligarchs have jealously guarded their privileges and monopolies against outsiders, allowing external economic influences and interests only under very tightly controlled conditions.

This is reflected in a generally unwelcoming attitude towards foreign investment and in support of trade protectionism. For all the rhetoric about attracting foreign commercial participation in the Russian economy, attitudes towards this question have evolved at a glacial pace. Many enterprises are only willing to consider foreign involvement on a strictly limited basis – accepting financial inputs from abroad, but allowing their business partner(s) little or no say in the running of the venture. More often, they have refused even to entertain this notional risk, preferring to rely on government and other internal sources for finance (Blasi *et al.*, 1997, pp. 179–81). The resulting very low levels of foreign direct investment have made for a relatively closed economy, whose insularity has been reinforced by a deeply ingrained protectionist mentality towards international trade. This latter has principally been characterized by an enduring belief that the state has a duty to intervene on behalf of Russian companies by ensuring that foreign competition is kept to 'manageable' levels: 'only enough to stimulate . . . activity, not inhibit it' (Yeltsin, *Rossiiskaya gazeta*, 24 February 1996, p. 2). In its more paranoid-xenophobic guise, this involves introducing tariff and non-tariff restrictions to stop 'unscrupulous competition from abroad,'; eliminating 'all special dispensations for foreign capital'; and placing restrictions on 'attempts to establish foreign control' over 'national-security' sectors of the economy, including the defence industry, mineral resources, telecommunications, trade, finance and electricity (Glaziev, 1996, p. 5).

The extent of the Yeltsin administration's failure to prosecute its economic liberalization agenda is reflected in the continuing difficulties in the way of small-scale economic activity in Russia. Notwithstanding numerous government 'initiatives' designed to encourage small business, the growth of this sector has been severely hampered by criminal activity, a plethora of taxes, minimal government assistance, and prohibitive interest rates. In March 1998, then First Vice-Prime Minister Boris Nemtsov (1998, p. 8) admitted that its contribution to national GDP was a measly 10 to 12 per cent, compared to 50 to 75 per cent in 'countries with developed market systems'. The situation in the countryside is arguably even worse, with the number of small private farms declining from 1994 (Wegren and Durgin, 1995, p. 54). It is hard to escape the conclusion that small enterprises in Russia have developed, 'not thanks to state support...but in spite of it' (Latynina, 1996, p. 3).

The 'competition' and 'liberalization' that has been tolerated in post-Soviet Russia has been far more typical of the late Soviet socialist system than of an open market economy. For example, some sources estimate that more than 50 per cent of the country's capital resources are being used in the shadow economy (Verda, 1997, p. 6), while a 1996 Alliance-Menatep report claimed that the shadow economy's share of GDP had climbed to 40 per cent from 12 per cent in 1989 (*Segodnya*, 18 April 1996, p. 3). If anything, economic trends in Russia have been towards 'de-liberalization', with the volume of barter trade between enterprises reaching a post-Soviet high of 80 per cent in the second half of 1998 (interview with Gerashchenko, *Rossiiskaya gazeta*, 15 September 1998, p. 2).

In sum, then, the liberalization agenda of the Gaidar radical reformers has barely been implemented. Although some consumer goods prices have been freed, the indications are that, if anything, the Russian economy is becoming increasingly illiberal. Growing regionalization has led some governors and local administrations to set artificial price levels;[7] Russia's capital markets remain dysfunctional, particularly following the August 1998 financial crash; barter trade is on the increase;

the FIGs continue to be hugely influential, despite being badly hit by the crash; the small business sector is as puny and fragile as ever; foreign involvement in the Russian economy is tightly controlled; domestic political and economic pressures militate against trade liberalization for the foreseeable future; and the prospects of genuine competition and transparency in the post-Soviet economy appear remote. Overall, when the Yeltsin administration's record on financial stabilization and privatization is taken into account, very little of the original radical economic reform programme has been implemented. Notwithstanding Gaidar's (interview in *Trud*, 28 March 1997, p. 5) claim that Russia had achieved 'a market economy', albeit one with some 'prominent socialist "birthmarks"', it is Yeltsin's earlier (*Rossiiskaya gazeta*, 25 February 1994, p. 2) description of the post-Soviet economy as 'a combination of new but still weak market mechanisms and old command levers' which rings truer at the time of writing (1999).

The search for labour productivity in post-Soviet Russia

The search for labour productivity under Yeltsin has assumed less overt forms than during the last decade of the USSR. Unlike Andropov and Gorbachev, he did not identify it as a specific objective of his adminis-tration. The most pressing priorities for the new Russian president were to reintroduce order out of the Soviet economic chaos and to establish some form of market economy. Nevertheless, the problems of low labour productivity and, more generally, poor economic performance have impinged critically on regime attitudes and policies under Yeltsin. These have been highlighted especially in the major economic policy debates of the post-Soviet period, namely over (a) the appropriate balance between macroeconomic stabilization on the one hand, and structural policy and economic restructuring on the other; (b) the pace and style of reform, centring on the pros and cons of 'shock therapy' versus 'gradualism'; and (c) the political and social price, and associated risks, of economic reform.

Macroeconomic stabilization versus structural policy

The first Gaidar government's emphasis on macroeconomic stabiliza-tion derived essentially from the conviction that controlling inflation was a *sine qua non* of any normally functioning economy (market or otherwise). As then Finance Minister Boris Fyodorov (1993b, p. 4) put it: 'When there is uncontrolled inflation, there can be no normal development of production and no increase in the standard of living... inflation destroys savings, investments and long-term credit, and leads to capital flight, a technological lag and a sharp stratification of society into a handful of super-rich and an impoverished majority.' The Gaidar reformers argued that the choice between an anti-inflationary policy and government support for Russian industry was a false dichotomy, since the latter could only recover once inflation was checked (interview with Chubais, *Literaturnaya gazeta*, 24 May 1995, p. 1). This conclusion naturally led them to their attempts, reviewed earlier, to reduce government financial support for industry and agriculture and impose tight controls on monetary emission.

For the Gaidarists the country's economic situation in January 1992 had deteriorated to such an extent that the issue of individual labour productivity had lost much of its importance as a discrete problem. The challenge for the state was no longer to get the individual worker (or even enterprise) to work 'harder' – through socialist morality, planning–technocratic or incentive–humanistic means – but rather to establish a macroeconomic market climate in which those whose work was useful and productive would naturally survive and prosper, while those who failed to adapt would wither on the vine and eventually become extinct. The 'impartial' market would be the judge of the value or otherwise of labour. Efficiency was measured not by whether more could be produced with less, but by the correlation of output to effective (that is, paying) demand. In this paradigm the issue of the individual worker's productivity was scarcely pertinent.

Such a purist, absolutist view of the market mechanism ran directly counter to the spirit of traditional Soviet labour ideology. True, the idea that labour should be 'useful' was certainly not new; as we have seen, there was much criticism in the Soviet era of the practice of 'production for production's sake'. What was radically different, however, was the *laissez-faire* notion that the worth or otherwise of labour would be determined by the market alone, with little regard for either the 'human factor' of Gorbachev's *perestroika*, or the 'objective' value of and need for an enterprise's production.

Aslund (1995, p. 173) has encapsulated the opposition to the government's macroeconomic stabilization policies as the failure of the 'Russian intellectual paradigm' to shed its 'Marxist prejudices', such as an 'irrational devotion to production' and 'disbelief in market allocation'. However, the nature of public opposition has by no means been as intransigent or uniform as his unnuanced view would suggest. At one end of the spectrum, there are proponents of so-called 'structural policy' who retain an unrealistic view of the intrinsic 'competitiveness' of much of Russia's industry. Critics such as the nationalist economist Sergei Glaziev (1994, p. 2) have frequently inveighed against the 'rapidly progressing deindustrialization of the national economy' and the 'snowballing destruction of scientific and industrial potential', partly because they cling to the traditional Soviet bias that material production represents the 'real' economy, but also out of national *amour-propre*. For them, the massive decline of Russian industry (and agriculture) in the post-Soviet era has not simply been an economic problem, but a national disgrace that threatens to reduce Russia to a 'raw-materials appendage of the developed countries' (see report on Volsky's 13–point programme in *Izvestiya*, 30 September 1992, p. 2).

But not all criticism of the government's macroeconomic stabilization policies has been so crude or emotive. Many observers have focused instead on the huge distortions and iniquities in the national economy that undermine enterprise and business activity. They point to a system of allocation that little resembles that of a market, characterized as it is by the reality that funds and even 'demand' go to the politically well-connected rather than economically deserving (Andrei Illarionov, in *Kommersant-Daily*, 27 December 1995, p. 2). And they highlight Russia's wholly inadequate finance-credit system and capital markets which, deformed by the lucrative trade in short-term, high-yield treasury bonds (GKOs) (Latynina, 1997, p. 4; also Ericson, 1997, p. 26), have led to skyrocketing interest rates that place commercial borrowing beyond the grasp of potentially viable enterprises and businesses.

The common thread running through the opposition to hard-line stabilization policies is the belief that, at least in Russia, the 'market' alone is not capable of determining the value of production. Only three months into the post-Soviet era, Gorbachev's former chief economic advisor Nikolai Petrakov (1992, p. 4) and other economists from the USSR Academy of Sciences were already complaining that, far from leading to a 'weeding out of marginal producers', the Gaidar reforms were in fact crippling 'entire sectors of the economy that are vitally important to the country: agriculture, the processing industry, health care and others'. The sub-text of such remarks, reiterated many times in subsequent years, is that the 'usefulness' of labour and 'need' for output cannot be measured by profit alone. There are strategic and national priorities – such as housing and infrastructural projects (roads, railways, etc.) – for which there is an objective social need and for which money needs to be found (Yavlinsky, 1996, p. 5). In this schema, the issue of labour productivity continues to be highly pertinent.

Shock therapy versus gradualism

The main rationale behind 'shock therapy' – defined by Illarionov (1994, p. 2) as a 'tough monetary and financial policy' conducted in conditions of hyperinflation or near-hyperinflation – was that the extremely grave socioeconomic situation inherited from the Soviet Union necessitated far-reaching and fast-acting measures. Aslund's (1991, p. 221) earlier comment that 'in conditions of severe economic decline, gradualism equals a prolongation of suffering,' appeared even more apposite to the post-Soviet context. In terms of specifics, what was envisaged was the reduction of the monthly inflation rate to 2 to 3 per cent in order to eliminate 'artificially supported demand', the establishment of a 'more or less stable price relationship' and 'rational price indicators', and forcing enterprises to begin 'a rapid process of adapting to the new economic conditions' (Illarionov, 1994, p. 2). Advocates of 'shock therapy' attached special importance to breaking up the old collusive relations between enterprise managers, as well as ingrained habits of dependency and irresponsibility. In their view, failure to achieve this objective would enable 'the most formidable vested interest of the transition period' to undermine reform by easing the pressure to work for money, respond to demand and find markets (Aslund, 1995, pp. 186–7). A further justification for shock therapy was that its introduction would demonstrate the seriousness of the government's commitment to comprehensive reform, thereby facilitating policy implementation. Previous Soviet economic policy measures had been crippled by their lack of credibility – the (justified) belief that 'things would settle down' after an initial brief flurry of activity. Genuine shock therapy, it was hoped, would convince enterprise managers about the irreversibility of reforms and the corresponding need to change their behaviour (Yasin, 1994, p. 7).

The counter-argument for gradualism has derived from several major premises. The first is that shock therapy asks too much change of an economy in too short a space of time. Shortly after the introduction of the first Gaidar reforms, senior Academician economists led by TsEMI director Nikolai Fedorenko (1992, p. 3) claimed that in no country had there ever 'occurred an instant transition ... from an administratively managed economy to an economy of market entrepreneurship'. There needed to be an intermediate 'commercialization' stage, during which enterprises would be put on a 'strict regimen of self-financing and self-management of all current operations and investment activities'. The import of Fedorenko's remarks was that, with the best will in the world,

Russian enterprises needed time to adapt to the new economic environment; it was unrealistic to expect them to function immediately as effective market entities. Far from stimulating attitudinal change, shock therapy would lead only to the indiscriminate destruction of enterprises virtually regardless of performance. In similar vein, a report published by Yavlinsky's Epicentre (1992, p. 11) argued that the government's obsession with financial stabilization meant that it was waging a struggle 'not against the illness – the inefficiency of the economy – but against its symptoms in the financial sphere'. More generally, shock therapy was widely blamed for Russia's increasingly serious socio-economic problems: the slump in GDP and industrial production, the rupture of economic ties, and the restriction of the population's effective demand (comments by Chernomyrdin to the Russian Supreme Soviet, *Rossiiskaya gazeta*, 29 January 1993, p. 2).

The debate over the respective merits of shock therapy and gradualist approaches has been further muddied by the issue of whether the government's economic policies – even in the heyday of 1992–93 – ever amounted to genuine shock therapy. Indeed, there is a compelling case to argue that the early Yeltsin reforms were 'neither shock nor therapy'. As Boris Fyodorov (1994, p. 2) pointed out in a report entitled *Russia's Finances in 1993*: 'A policy under which a budget deficit amounting to 10 per cent of the gross domestic product was financed through emission, inflation for the year came to 900 per cent, the population's cash income and average wages in all branches of the economy rose faster than prices, unemployment remained at the level of 1 per cent, and there were no enterprise bankruptcies or shutdowns, cannot be called shock therapy by any criteria.'

The price of reform and political risk

The issue of risk is one of the more important and misunderstood elements in the formulation of socioeconomic policy in the Yeltsin era. Players and commentators alike have frequently used it to explain and excuse government prevarication and inconsistency on a whole range of politically and socially sensitive issues. In its starkest form, risk refers to the alleged threat of a mass 'social explosion' in response to 'tough' economic policies and their consequences – falling living standards, rising unemployment, the loss of savings, etc. As such, it provides the regime with a ready alibi to delay or even kill off the implementation of potentially unpopular prescriptions, on the grounds that to push them through would be 'inhumane' and jeopardize its political survival.

In fact, while neo-liberals such as Chubais (*Literaturnaya gazeta*, 24 May 1995, p. 1) have occasionally admitted to fears that 'social tension would erupt', anecdotal and sociological evidence suggests this 'threat' has been greatly exaggerated. Even strident critics of the regime such as the Marxist commentator Boris Kagarlitsky (1996, p. 7) have ruled out the possibility of 'revolution', while various opinion polls highlight massive popular apathy and disillusionment rather than an active rebelliousness. Despite talk about the people's patience having 'reached its limit' (Yeltsin's 1997 State of the Nation address, *Rossiiskie vesti*, 11 March 1997, p. 2), recent surveys indicate that most people see no alternative to the regime despite their 'very strong feelings of alienation' from it (Popov, 1998, p. 8).

Notwithstanding its sham character, the question of political risk has nonetheless exerted a powerful influence on policy formulation and implementation in the Yeltsin era. Many of the zigzags in economic policy since 1991 have clearly been in response to 'messages' from the electorate – such as the communist and nationalist gains in the parliamentary elections of 1993 and 1995. The latter vote had particular resonance because it highlighted the extent of Yeltsin's personal unpopularity (8 per cent approval rating in January 1996[8]) and the need for major concessions to pave the way for a second term in the mid-1996 presidential elections. It was consequently no surprise that, over the succeeding six months, Yeltsin dismissed Chubais for having 'embittered the people' (*Segodnya*, 27 January 1996, p. 1), 'confessed' that the government had 'forgotten' wage-earners and pensioners (*Rossiiskaya gazeta*, 24 February 1996, p. 2), and, most importantly, loosened fiscal discipline in order to pay off pension and wage arrears.[9]

Yeltsin's 'bread and circuses' concessions prior to the 1996 Presidential elections were symptomatic of the way the administration's fear of political risk has often translated into a failure of political will and policy constancy. Unable and unwilling to take long views or distinguish between affordable and unaffordable political risk, it has from the outset offered a series of compromises and concessions amounting to virtual policy paralysis. The refusal to accept even a modicum of political risk has been especially evident in the administration's handling of labour-related issues. On the one hand, it is true that bankruptcies have increased, some enterprises are restructuring their operations, and unemployment is now assuming serious dimensions. However, as under Gorbachev, much of this has occurred in spite of government policies rather than because of them. For example, the number of bankruptcies in Russia remains exceptionally small given that, even before the August 1998 crash, only about 25 per cent of enterprises were considered to be 'operating in a stable fashion', while as many as 30 per cent had 'collapsed' (interview with Minister of Economics Yakov Urinson, *Novye Izvestiya*, 4 June 1998, pp. 1, 5). According to *Moskovskii komsomolets* (22 August 1998, pp. 1–2), fewer enterprises had been declared bankrupt in Russia during the past eight years than in the past week in the United States. Similarly, much of the enterprise restructuring that has taken place has been overwhelmingly defensive in nature. Ickes and Ryterman's (1993, p. 245) play on words, the 'survival-oriented enterprise' (SOE – in lieu of 'state-owned enterprise'), captures very well the essence of 'negative restructuring' (Blasi *et al.*, 1997, pp. 131–2), whereby enterprises have reacted to changing demand, not by reorienting their production, but by laying off workers and reducing the work hours and wages of still others.

The influence of political risk-aversion on government decision-making has been especially pronounced in the area of employment policy. In effect, the Yeltsin administration has continued in the white-washing spirit of its Soviet predecessors. Although acknowledging the existence of some unemployment, it has worked hard to (a) perpetuate the myth that the problem is by no means as serious or widespread as critics suggest; (b) 'show' that the government is doing everything to contain the social impact of unemployment; and (c) buck actual policy responsibility for alleviating the problem. In the first place, the government has argued that the size of the shadow economy is such that relatively few people are actually 'unemployed' (Verda, 1997, p. 6). Second, it has regularly emphasized its 'restraint' and solicitude for the people. Typical of this approach was Deputy Prime Minister Yurii Yarov's presentation of a Presidential decree, 'On the sale of debtor enterprises', as a measure primarily intended to minimize the social consequences of bankruptcies, namely mass unemployment *Segodnya*, 4 June 1994, p. 1). *Segodnya's* lampooning commentary accurately captured the disingenuousness of the government's approach: 'The simplest way to secure the "prevention of insolvency"...is to issue the greatest possible number of resolutions, decrees and other acts, preferably of a vague nature, accompanied by lengthy addenda and subject to discussion in parliament...All this is much better than taking decisive but risky measures and closing down economically ineffective production facilities...'

In addition to dragging its feet over formulating and implementing workable bankruptcy procedures, the Yeltsin administration has attempted to sidestep the problem of political risk by passing responsibility for dealing with unemployment to enterprises. In doing so, it has demonstrated that it is less concerned about falling labour productivity than the spectre of millions of unemployed for whom it has made no proper provision.[10] As Connor (1996, p. 173) has pointed out, the post-Soviet state, 'whatever its inclinations, does not have the resources to construct a strong safety net as yet, to sustain the under- and unemployed while they await new job opportunities'. In these circumstances, the government has given tacit approval to 'hidden unemployment', whereby millions of Russian workers perform no work, but remain nominally attached to their enterprises.[11] The growth of this phenomenon has allowed the administration to maintain the fiction that the 'real' rate of unemployment is not so very high, and ensures that enterprises rather than the state continue to assume most of the financial and 'moral' burden of maintaining the unemployed (official and otherwise).

From labour productivity to labour containment

In many respects, the wheel originally pushed by Andropov has turned full circle. As under Brezhnev, the nominal job has become a 'welfare entitlement' (Connor, 1991, p. 192) rather than a vehicle for performing productive labour. Only a few years ago, Guy Standing (1996, pp. 358–60) made the perfectly reasonable judgement that overcoming 'stagnant labour productivity' was the 'fundamental labour-market challenge of the early 1990s'. However, the experience of the post-Soviet era suggests just the opposite. Such have been the distortions of the Russian economy in the Yeltsin era that one of the principal (albeit *de facto*) object- ives of his administration has, paradoxically, been to *contain* labour productivity and its socioeconomic consequences. In the current cli- mate, improving efficiency at most Russian loss-making firms would merely lead to an increase in hidden unemployment and, in time, the pressure for large-scale redundancies. Such an outcome would compli- cate life for firms for whom it is cheaper to put workers on unpaid leave than to dismiss them (Standing, 1996, p. 139). But it would be much worse for the government which is completely unready to deal with the consequences of large-scale labour release, whether through the provi- sion of adequate unemployment benefits or job training/retraining;[12] this at a time when alternative spheres of employment – small business, private farms, the services sector – are simply too small and fragile to absorb redundancies from loss-making medium- and large-sized enter- prises. Labour productivity may be worse than ever,[13] but few have an interest in improving it for the foreseeable future. On the contrary, the reluctance of enterprises to downsize their establishments has allowed employees to 'adjust slowly to the restructuring of the economy' (Blasi *et al.*, 1997, p. 112), and afforded the government some leeway in fudging the issues of growing unemployment and poverty in society, not to mention the more general question of its economic mismanagement.

The evolution of economic attitudes

The continuing problem of labour productivity – in one form or another – begs questions about the extent of attitudinal change in post-Soviet society on such closely interrelated questions as the value and meaning of labour, economic accountability, competition and competitiveness, and the nature of the state's responsibilities to its citizens. To what extent have elements of a new economic culture emerged in post-Soviet Russia? Is it possible to talk in terms of a new 'ideology' – a set of organizing and widely accepted principles – in place of the traditional Soviet labour ideology that underwent such radical transformation during the last decade of the USSR's existence? Has a new set of understandings and conventions arisen to replace the old Brezhnevian 'social contract' with its promise of 'cradle-to-grave security' and *uverennost v zavtrashnem dne* ('confidence in tomorrow')?

Paternalism, populism and the Russian *spetsifika*

For much of the Yeltsin era, many Western politicians and commentators have been apt to argue that pessimism about Russia's difficult progress towards political democracy, a market economy and a civil society should be counterbalanced by recognition that the country has travelled a remarkably long way in a brief space of time. In this section, and with the benefit of writing after the August 1998 financial crash, it will be argued that the extent of attitudinal change in Russia has been significantly overstated, particularly in respect of core ideological values and understandings.

The post-Soviet ideological context is an extraordinary mish-mash, encompassing the neo-liberalism of the Gaidar reformers, the social democracy of Grigorii Yavlinsky,[14] the conservative-centrist tradition embodied in ex-Prime Minister Chernomyrdin, the semi-authoritarian nationalism of figures as diverse as Moscow mayor Yurii Luzhkov and Krasnoyarsk governor Aleksandr Lebed, and the new-old Communism of Gennadii Zyuganov. In varying degrees, these contrasting ideological strands have contributed to shaping the Yeltsin administration's approach to labour-related issues and to socioeconomic questions in general. Even more critically, they have conspired to ensure that, eight years after the fall of the Soviet state system, the 'new' Russia is still groping for a political, economic and social identity and governing ethos. What has emerged instead is an incoherent 'vision' of new and old, in which buzzwords such as the market and entrepreneurship are casually juxtaposed with traditional notions of paternalism and nationalism. Meanwhile, this is all taking place, indeed being nourished, by an environment in which political opportunism and populism exercise an ever growing influence.

Paternalism

This ideological imbroglio is reflected most interestingly in the evolution of paternalism in the post-Soviet era. Initially, it was believed that, notwithstanding the conventional wisdom that 'state paternalism reflects the essence of our country's traditions' (Lantsman, 1994, p. 3), its erosion in the later Gorbachev years would be further accelerated under his successor. And indeed the early indications, such as the comprehensive price liberalization of January 1992, appeared only to confirm these expectations. As we have seen, however, the pace of economic reform slowed dramatically after the first few months. Collapsing production, hyperinflation, falling living standards, the threat of mass unemployment, and mounting political pressures, all combined to dilute and then stall the original liberal market programme. This policy *revanchisme* was accompanied by the rejuvenation of traditional paternalist concepts which, despite periods of varying political fashionableness, have continued to exercise a major influence on government policy ever since. Many of Yeltsin's major speeches have reflected the ingrained nature of Soviet/Russian paternalism. In early 1993, he (*Rossiiskie vesti*, 23 March 1993, p. 2) called for the organization of 'public works' for the unemployed, as well as the strengthening of employment guarantees for employees of state enterprises declared bankrupt. At the broader level, his 1995 State of the Nation speech (*Rossiiskie vesti*, 17 February 1995, p. 5) announced '(a) real turn towards a social orientation in the economic reform', while his 1996 address declared 'a policy of direct state support' to Russian enterprises – both financial and political (promoting Russian exports) (*Rossiiskaya gazeta*, 24 February 1996, p. 2).

The continuing importance of state paternalism is particularly well illustrated in the handling of labour-related issues, such as the problem of enterprise bankruptcy. Here, the government's inability to establish effective and equitable procedures has highlighted an enduring 'social contract' mindset, a deficient understanding of the concept of 'negative reward', and a profound reluctance to make tough decisions. The explanation for this failure lies less in the claim that 'there is not and never has been a political opportunity to put a policy emphasizing bankruptcy into effect' (Yavlinsky, *Segodnya*, 22 April 1995, p. 3), than in the reality that President Yeltsin, trapped within the old Soviet paternalist paradigm, has been extremely reluctant to accept with any degree of consistency the sociopolitical costs of resolute economic decision-making. Despite much propaganda about the need for a functioning bankruptcy process – beginning with Yeltsin's 1992 decree, 'On measures for the support and recovery of insolvent enterprises (bankrupts) and the application of special measures to them' (*Izvestiya*, 16 June 1992, pp. 1–2) – the government has shown virtually no *active* interest in the 'creative destruction' of enterprises.[15]

Much of the administration's brand of paternalism is undoubtedly coloured by expectations inherited from the Soviet period. That said, the defining characteristic of paternalism under Yeltsin has been its fundamentally passive/reactive character. Remarkably little has been done to arrest the collapse in living standards or construct a new social welfare net according to fresh principles. Instead, the emphasis has been on trying to contain the short-term effects of difficult socioeconomic problems rather than find long-term solutions. For example, in allowing enterprises to accumulate debts and wage arrears – rather than calling them to account through the real threat of bankruptcy – the Yeltsin administration has kept them alive so that they can continue to 'employ' the many 'workers' who would otherwise be released and forced to struggle on the open labour market (*Kommersant-Daily*, 12 July 1994, p. 8). Likewise, the provision of budgetary and extra-budgetary funds to some sectors represents a form of indirect social welfare, enabling the continued allocation of enterprise-based benefits (albeit at lower levels) to large numbers of the population who would otherwise suffer even more than at present. Finally, the rising tide in favour of trade protectionism is not so much about making Russian goods and services 'competitive' in world markets – a forlorn hope in all but a very few sectors – than about protecting them so that they can *survive* and their workers remain on the books (and thereby enjoy at least some access to enterprise-based social benefits).

Populism

Post-Soviet state paternalism has been accompanied and reinforced by the administration's regular resort to the politics of populism. In addition to the issue of risk – in which the threat of adverse political outcomes prompts policy compromises – the populism of the Yeltsin administration has also been stimulated by 'broader problems of social justice and low living standards' (Connor, 1996, pp. 179–80). For example, Yeltsin's (*Rossiiskie vesti*, 11 March 1997, p. 2) 1997 State of the Nation address, which abused 'Russia's authorities' as 'spineless and indifferent, irresponsible and incompetent in resolving the state's problems', reflected a more generalized frustration at the continuing failure to arrest declining living standards, further pension and wage arrears, and the seemingly intractable problems of Russia's military. In doing so, it also betrayed a very real (and justified) concern that his historical legacy was being tainted and minimized with every policy failure.

   This generalized adherence to the politics of populism, combined with the regime's passive/reactive paternalism, has arguably constituted the most critical barrier to attitudinal change in the post-Soviet era. The problem here is less the presence of an urgent political imperative that forces the dilution or reversal of a particular policy prescription, than an overall lack of vision and a crisis of identity. Even at the outset of reform, Zaslavskaya (1997, p. 5) has rightly observed, Yeltsin 'did not have a deep, well thought-out strategy'. Beyond a vague desire for political democracy and a market economy, and a corresponding dislike for 'socialism', the President has never outlined a clear vision of the shape of post-Soviet Russia and the principles underpinning the new society. Correspondingly, he has shown no consistency of purpose except on the narrow, but paramount, objective of retaining and consolidating political power. Caught between his twin personae as 'great revolutionary' and 'traditional Russian ruler', Yeltsin has often tried to be all things to all people, never making a clear choice regarding reform and continually pursuing contradictory strategies (Aslund, 1995, pp. 95–96).

The Russian *spetsifika*

The third major impediment to attitudinal change at the level of the state has been the growing popularity of the idea of Russia's *spetsifika*. In the economic context, this principally embraces the notion that 'a real changeover to a market is impossible without taking into consideration the national traditions and special features of a given country' (Volsky, *Rabochaya tribuna*, 17 November 1992, pp. 1–2). Throughout the Yeltsin era, regime policies have rarely been able to escape the limitations imposed by the Russian *spetsifika* or what James Millar (1995, p. 13) has termed 'Slavophilism': 'When the going gets tough, one can always decide there should be a "third way", neither market nor communist, to set up an economy in Russia.' In practice, *spetsifika* has been used as an all-encompassing apologia for regressive economic policies, enterprise conservatism and poor work habits – excusing rather than accusing Russian enterprises and workers, blaming outside forces (and their allies, the so-called 'comprador bourgeoisie') for undermining Russia's stature and prosperity, and contending that 'foreign' economic prescriptions are inapplicable to the Russian economy. This alibi has been, and continues to be, a significant factor in the Yeltsin administration's inability to pursue a coherent economic strategy. It has always been easier to blame 'Western' economic prescriptions (Shmelev, 1996, p. 3), than to accept the unpalatable truth that it is the failure to implement a single policy vision – neo-liberal, social democratic, socialist or other – in a consistent and rigorous manner that lies at the heart of Russia's socioeconomic problems.

The nationalism represented in the idea of Russia's *spetsifika* has complemented the passive/reactive paternalism and populism of the Yeltsin administration by reinforcing deeply insular and protectionist tendencies in the national economy. In concrete terms, this has translated into calls to arrest Russia's 'deindustrialization' (Yeltsin speech to the Seventh Congress of Russian People's Deputies, *Rossiiskaya gazeta*, 2 December 1992, p. 4); support for greater state intervention in 'regulating the market' (State of the Nation address, *Rossiiskie vesti*, 11 March 1997, p. 2); and advocacy of 'sensible protectionism' (*Rossiiskaya gazeta*, 2 December 1992, pp. 3–4), including controls on the foreign competition faced by Russian goods producers (Yeltsin's State of the Nation address, *Rossiiskaya gazeta*, 24 February 1996, p. 2).

Towards a new enterprise culture?

The resultant policy confusion afflicting government economic decision-making has severely retarded the development of a new enterprise culture in Russia. In particular, the political nature of allocation, the haphazard implementation of hard budget constraints, and the continuing absence of equitable mechanisms of 'negative reward', have greatly inhibited the inculcation of 'Western' notions of market accountability, competition, and transparency at the enterprise level. In a climate characterized by 'regime uncertainty' (Ericson, 1997, p. 26), state paternalism and naked political opportunism, it is hardly surprising that firms have been slow to embrace Western management methods. The inconstancy and consequent lack of credibility of government policy have meant that most have been slow to understand that the times and the system have really changed (Aslund, 1995, p. 176). Yavlinsky's (1994, p. 4) comment that the government was failing because it could not 'force economic agents to play by any kind of established rules' nor 'refrain from changing the rules of the game every day', remains pertinent to this day. Enterprises could hardly avoid being confused by the obvious lack of realism in the government's mutually antagonistic promises to 'ensure the structural reform of the national economy without a substantial easing in financial policy or a threatening increase in the number of unemployed' (*Kommersant-Daily*, 12 July 1994, p. 8).

Added to the difficulties caused by the government's inconsistent policy direction, there were also more 'physical' impediments to a restructuring of attitudes at the enterprise level. In the first place, structural inflexibilities such as the length of production chains (the vertical integration inherited from the command–administrative economy) have limited the extent to which enterprises can be effectively downsized (Yasin, 1993, p. 7). As in Soviet times, the size and complexity of production links has meant that it remains exceptionally difficult to evaluate good and bad performance, and therefore identify which links in the production chain need to be restructured. Similarly, the widespread phenomenon of 'one-company towns'[16] has created an environment where 'the enterprise is coextensive with the community' and 'the welfare system and the enterprise are intertwined' (Millar, 1995, p. 10). Closure or large-scale redundancies in this context amounts to destruction of the community, not just the factory.

Faced with these and other problems such as uncertain markets, a paucity of investment (caused by a highly illiquid financial system), and the continuing burden of enterprise-based welfare, it is hardly surprising that managers have continued to rely on familiar Soviet methods of coping (see Kuznetsov and Kuznetsova, 1996, p. 1177). As the practice of 'negative restructuring' shows, the only realistic objective for the vast majority of enterprises is survival. In an environment where good and bad performance are often inequitably rewarded, even relatively successful enterprises must needs adopt short-term and small-scale strategies (Ericson, 1997, p. 26). Consequently, the paternalism that is already 'deeply embedded in the structure of social relations of the enterprise' (Clarke *et al.*, 1994, p. 183) has become further reinforced in Russia's increasingly uncertain economic climate. There is now more, not less, collusion between management and workers where both have a vital interest in combating the *deus ex machina* of impersonal state policy or the threat of outside ownership (or even participation). The new spirit of survival relations between workers and managers is well encapsulated by Standing's (1996, p. xxv) adapted phrase, 'you pretend to need us, we pretend to be workers'. Enterprise directors have even taken over many of the functions that in a market economy would normally be performed by trade unions. Thus, *Moskovskie novosti* commented that the bosses, who had 'a better idea than the workers of how to wring money from the higher-ups', had taken over as 'the vanguard of the strike movement' (Burtin and Kostenko, 1996, p. 4).

In short, Russian enterprise managers and workers are a long way from developing a new market economic culture. It is certainly true that several years of post-Soviet 'market reforms' have disturbed some of the complacency of both intra-enterprise and inter-enterprise relations, and some firms at least have become more responsive and flexible to the changing nature of demand. But the overwhelming picture is one of attitudinal stasis. The vast majority of enterprises are not restructuring in any significant way (Blasi *et al.*, 1997, p. 183) and the trend is if anything towards the reestablishment of traditional relationships in the production sphere (Clarke *et al.*, 1994, p. 210). The major change wrought by the introduction of quasi-capitalism thus far is a negative one, whereby some enterprise managers 'are applying the worst habits of former times in a big way. To put it simply, they are stealing' (Yeltsin, *Rossiiskie vesti*, 11 March 1997, p. 2).

A post-Soviet conception of labour

Shortly after the collapse of the USSR, Chubais (*Izvestiya*, 26 February 1992, p. 2) ventured the statement that '(n)ot everyone should be a proprietor at his workplace ... There are many people who are competent, skilled, strong and knowledgeable but who cannot, and do not choose to, play that role'. Chubais's comments were directed at what he called the 'Bolshevik mentality,' embodied in the notion of *chuvstvo khozyaina* so strongly emphasized under Gorbachev. His remarks foreshadowed the advent of a new state philosophy of economic behaviour in place of the traditional labour ideology that had formerly underpinned the Soviet state. Centring on the modern individual entrepreneur, it set out to discard much of the old ideological baggage, as well as counter alternative socialistic visions based on collective ownership and the concept of a discrete working class with its own particular interests.

The subsequent history of the Yeltsin administration has shown such neo-liberal hopes to have been misplaced. First, the emergence of a new breed of entrepreneurs has been counterbalanced by the narrowness of this stratum. The FIGs and the mafia may have flourished, but small business in urban and rural areas alike has continued to struggle. Second, while collective ownership is indeed a comparative rarity in modern-day Russia, in very many cases the workforce has nevertheless succeeded in retaining a significant say in the everyday operation of the privatized enterprise. Labour may be weak (Connor, 1996, p. 171) in the sense that workers have very limited capacity to extract concessions through organized industrial action such as large-scale strikes or slow-downs. But the insular nature of the post-Soviet economy with its strong bias towards insider ownership, and the continuance of old-style collusive relations and practices at the workplace, have ensured that workers are by no means as impotent as they have been portrayed. Continuing problems of burgeoning wage arrears and hidden unemployment are counterbalanced by the comparative lack of bankruptcies and disproportionately high putative employment – enabling access to enterprise-based social welfare – relative to levels of actual production. Traditional labour ideology may be dead, but at least some of its underpinning socioeconomic conventions and understandings live on.

The closest approximation to an 'official' post-Soviet labour ideology is to be found in the 1993 Russian ('Yeltsin') Constitution. Article 37, for example, declares that 'labour is free'. In defining this as the individual's 'right to freely dispose of his or her capabilities for labour and to choose a type of activity or occupation', the current Russian Constitution differs markedly from the 1977 Brezhnev Constitution in that it imposes no obligation to work on the individual citizen: 'Forced labour is prohibited.' However, the new Constitution is similar to its predecessor in one very important respect – its disconnection from reality. Thus, while Article 34 states that '(e)veryone has the right to the free use of his or her capabilities and property for entrepreneurial or other economic activity not prohibited by law', the practice of Russian economic life quite clearly demonstrates the opposite. There is enormous illegal economic activity, while the government has signally failed in establishing a legal and economic climate that encourages and protects honest entrepreneurial activity. Similarly, Article 37 declares that '(e)veryone has the right to work in conditions that meet the requirements of safety and hygiene, the right to remuneration for work without any kind of discrimination and not below the minimum wage established by federal law, and also the right to protection from unemployment' (*Konstitutsiya Rossiiskoi Federatsii...*, 1995, p. 272). Yet industrial and agricultural working conditions are on the whole appalling, wage arrears and hidden unemployment continue to be key features of economic life, and there is very little effective provision for the unemployed, who suffer from wholly inadequate benefits and minimal possibilities of retraining in conditions of a severely contracted labour market.

In the end, Jowitt's (1993, p. 27) characterization of the relationship between regime and society (under Brezhnev) as a 'protection racket' is even more applicable to the current era. The population 'scavenge', surviving by exploiting the loopholes in the new 'system' – secondary employment, non-payment of taxes – while the role of 'parasite' is played by a bewildering array of actors – the state, the FIGs, the bureaucracy, trade unions and criminal elements. Even more cynically than in the Soviet Union, ideology provides only the flimsiest conceptual framework within which virtually all things are permitted to the elite. Capitalism, market responsiveness, competition, liberalization, transparency, all these are part of today's economic lexicon, potential building blocks in the construction of a post-Soviet conception of labour. But for the time being their real purpose is to legitimize – with rather greater sophistication than in Soviet times – the distortion and exploitation of economic conditions in modern-day Russia.

Ideological change and political legitimacy

In his definition of legitimacy as 'uncoerced support' for a regime or government, Stephen White (1979, p. 189) distinguished between two different types: the 'come rain or come shine' version of liberal democracies; and the Soviet model which, being based more narrowly upon 'performance' criteria, made the regime politically vulnerable to deteriorating economic circumstances. It has been a central thesis of this book that the search for labour productivity – and the ideological transformation that accompanied it – undermined the legitimacy of the Soviet state system by accelerating rather than arresting the economic decline of the USSR. The question therefore arises as to the implications of the Yeltsin administration's failure to alleviate Russia's economic problems for (a) its legitimacy and capacity to rule; (b) the prospects for Western-style political democracy and civil society in Russia; (c) the future shape and nature of legitimacy in post-Soviet Russia.

Economic crisis, legitimacy and the capacity to rule

Hillel Ticktin (1992, p. 18) once wrote that the failure of Soviet ideology lay in 'the inability of a failed regime to establish a believable justification.' In the post-Soviet era, the Yeltsin administration has faced a very similar challenge. From the outset, the Russian President presented himself as the representative of a new ideological nexus – political democracy, market economics, civil society – in opposition to the moribund and generally reactionary Communist Party establishment and its failed past. As the political embodiment of a modern democratic Russia, Yeltsin sought a popular legitimacy that was intended to be the diametric opposite of the old Soviet legitimacy based on the 'commitment of enormous powers of coercion, control and manipulation at the disposal of the regime' (Bialer, 1988, pp. 269–70).

Today it is clear that the attempt to find new forms of legitimation has been at best only partially successful. While post-Soviet Russia has undoubtedly enjoyed some of the trappings of a Western-style, popular legitimacy – for example, more open parliamentary and presidential elections – the evidence indicates that the Yeltsin administration has yet to convince the population that the basis on which it exercises power differs fundamentally from that of its Soviet predecessors. A 1998 survey conducted by the Bureau of Applied Sociological Research revealed that only 3.8 per cent of respondents named 'being able to participate in free elections' as an important feature of 'life in a democratic state'. Of those surveyed, 70 per cent were pessimistic about the 'possibility of influencing the authorities in Russia', while only 23 per cent of people thought they could 'really influence affairs in the country by participating in elections' (Popov, 1998, p. 8). What these figures suggest is that the government's authority derives less from a legitimizing mandate – Yeltsin's victory in the 1996 presidential elections – than through its inherited control of the basic instrumentalities of state power such as the armed forces, the security apparatus and the bureaucracy, to which it has since added mutual support arrangements with the FIG monopolies.

Paradoxically, the failure to introduce a *new* type of legitimacy in post-Soviet Russia has acted to preserve the Yeltsin administration from the consequences of the ongoing socioeconomic crisis of the last eight years. It is difficult to think of any other country in the world where a combination of plummeting living standards, hyperinflation, rising unemployment, the periodic wiping out of the population's savings, huge salary and pension arrears, and appalling conditions in the military, would have provoked such a mild reaction as in Russia. Although the government has often shown weakness and indecision, several factors have conspired to protect its hold on power: a disunited and often morally bankrupt opposition; continuing direct and indirect state control of the electronic media; the paucity of properly functioning democratic institutions through which protest can be channelled (Albats, *Kommersant-Daily*, 18 July 1998, p. 3); a discredited trade union movement; a disillusioned but largely apathetic population; and few traditions of mass revolt. While the forms and labels of post-Soviet state legitimacy may have changed, the fundamental realities of power have not. Ultimately, Yeltsin's personal 'legitimacy' – and therefore his continuing hold on power – has come to depend far more on the extent of his political will (and mental capacity) in coercing, controlling and manipulating institutions and vested interests.

The prospects for Western-style political democracy and civil society in Russia

The prospects for the emergence of a new political culture in post-Soviet Russia do not appear at the time of writing (1999) to be particularly promising. Even before the August 1998 financial crash struck a body blow to the liberal reformist cause, Zaslavskaya (1997, p. 5) was already opining that a civilized society in Russia was unlikely to develop in the next 30 to 40 years: 'Our society is deeply amoral, but there's nothing you can do about [it] – people are what they are, the way society moulded them. A law-based state has to emerge, but it is hard for me to say how many generations that will take.'

One of the principal problems is the intimate association between political democracy and market reforms in post-Soviet Russia. In the later Gorbachev years this nexus did not necessarily discredit democracy because Yeltsin and others were able to argue, in the circumstances of the USSR's accelerating economic decline, that the real problem was that the country had too few rather than too many political and economic freedoms. Once in power, however, the Yeltsin administration found itself under far greater pressure to respond to the popular expectations that had been accumulating since *perestroika*'s first promises. The more power Yeltsin acquired – particularly after the October 1993 putsch and the introduction of the new Russian Constitution – the greater the popular onus was on him to deliver. Consequently, the failure of his administration to achieve lasting solutions to Russia's socioeconomic problems has discredited not only market reform but also the associated idea of political democracy. As Nikolai Popov (1998, p. 8) has remarked, democratic political leaders 'did not take into account the fact that people had developed false notions about democracy and pinned unjustifiably high expectations on its establishment. When those expectations were not met, the idea itself turned into a symbol of deception of the people.'[17]

Recent developments have only aggravated this state of affairs. The August 1998 financial crash had a catastrophic impact on the cause of political democracy in Russia. In the first place, it has greatly strengthened the historically popular view that Russia 'needs a strong hand', particularly in times of crisis.[18] Semi-authoritarian nationalist politicians like Luzhkov and Lebed now have greater scope to reinforce the conventional wisdom that Western economic and political prescriptions are 'inappropriate' to Russia's particular *spetsifika*. Second, the crisis virtually wiped out much of the country's nascent middle class, previously identified by Nemtsov (*Nezavisimaya gazeta*, 17 March 1998, p. 8) as 'the buttress of the development of a democratic state'.[19] Third, the immediate economic effects of the crash – such as the wiping out of savings deposits – have meant that already low popular confidence in the utility of democracy[20] has declined even further.

The future shape and nature of legitimacy in post-Soviet Russia

In the circumstances of the current crisis of liberalism and liberal values, it seems probable that state legitimacy in post-Soviet Russia will re-acquire certain Soviet-era characteristics. Although elements of political democracy (elections), market economics (basic supply and demand relations) and the civil society (alternative political parties and the legal system) are likely to be preserved, the short- to medium-term outlook is for power to remain the principal determinant of legitimacy. As before, the ability to retain legitimacy will continue to depend principally on the leadership's ability to coerce, control and manipulate.

There are, however, several variables which may tilt the balance back in favour of a new type of democratic society, in which liberal market economics and a civil society play important roles. The first is that years of worsening socioeconomic conditions have steadily eroded the people's 'reserve of social patience'. Although the liberal democrats have been severely discredited as a result of the failure to arrest falling living standards, the same challenge – and possibly fate – awaits all who would hold power in post-Soviet Russia. A more authoritarian nationalism may well be in vogue at the moment, but there is no guarantee this will continue to be the case. The nexus identified by White (1979, p. 189) between legitimacy and economic performance remains as valid as ever. Would-be 'strong-man' Presidents will need to deliver on their promises, and within a considerably shorter time-frame than that which has been afforded to Yeltsin. Indeed, the cause of Russian democracy – including more democratic institutions and a better balance of power between executive and legislature – may be unwittingly served by

Russia undergoing a short, failed experiment with a semi-authoritarian regime, opening the way for a more enlightened system of government in the future.

A second important difference between the new legitimacy and its Soviet predecessor is that Russia now has political institutions through which protest and resistance to the authorities can be channelled. While these are still undeveloped and weak, they nevertheless provide a potential framework for future challenges to state legitimacy. The old Soviet mould of sham representative institutions has been broken, so that opposition to the ruling elite can no longer be so easily neutralized. The process of *glasnost* in society initiated by Gorbachev in 1986–87 may suffer setbacks from time to time, but the overall trend is likely to be towards a more open society in which the authorities are more rigorously called to account.

This is, in turn, likely to be facilitated by generational shifts. Although Zaslavskaya may be right about the 'amorality' of post-Soviet society, it is equally valid to suppose that present and future generations will be less tolerant and patient than their USSR-conditioned predecessors about continuing government failures in socioeconomic policy. The collapse of the Soviet state system dispelled the aura of regime invincibility and set a precedent for successful opposition to state authority. The population may be passive and consumerist, but at least they are no longer so easily intimidated.

Finally, the de Tocqueville paradox, whereby 'the most dangerous moment for a bad government is generally that in which it sets about reform (see Partington, 1992, p. 699), is as applicable to the post-Soviet political future as it was in the Gorbachev years. Faced by the pressure of Russia's continuing socioeconomic problems, but lacking any real idea of how to address these successfully, an authoritarian nationalism may well follow the same path as the Soviet leadership during the last decade of the USSR: fine-tuning incremental reforms, then intra-systemic change, and finally total ideological abdication and accompanying political surrender or collapse. It is one thing to demonstrate 'political will' and 'strength' in a localized environment or in opposition; it is quite another to retain the political self-confidence essential to legitimacy in the face of the numerous and complex policy challenges that Russia is likely to face in the coming years.

Notes

Chapter 1 – Introduction

1. As will be seen in Chapter 5, Gorbachev understood 'democratic centralism' more in terms of administrative devolution, than its original Leninist definition of 'freedom of discussion, unity of action' (Lenin, *Collected Works*, Volume 10, p. 380).
2. Filtzer (1994, p. 4) alleges that the Soviet elite introduced *perestroika* and *glasnost* in order to restore to itself 'greater control over the process of surplus extraction'. He argues further that 'reforms were unavoidable if the elite *as a social group* was to retain power over society'. Subsequently, the workers 'brought society to a state of stalemate', on the one hand making the elite's reform prescriptions 'unworkable', but at the same time failing to provide an alternative to the disintegration of Soviet society (ibid., p. 122).
3. Gorbachev can hardly have failed to be mindful of the example of the 1965 Kosygin economic reform. Several writers, such as Anders Aslund (1991, p. 12) and Archie Brown (1997, p. 136), have rightly linked its failure to the problem of political context.
4. Aslund (1995, pp. 214–15) claims that the USA 'consciously pursued an arms race that the USSR could not keep up with, neither economically nor technologically. In response, the USSR had been compelled to reform, only to realize too late that it was not reformable'.
5. Kotz and Weir (1997, p. 5) assert that the 'desertion of the state socialist system by the party–state elite did not happen because of the demise of the old system. The reverse is true – the demise of the system occurred because the party-state elite deserted it'.
6. Kornai (1992, p. 197) defined 'forced growth' as that which has been 'compelled from above', (rather than 'arising from an integral, self-propeled movement in society'), and at a tempo faster than is natural or good for the economic system.
7. Aslund (1991, pp. 27–58) employed the labels radical reform, half-hearted reform, technocratic rationalisation, socialist morality and conservative programme, to define competing economic prescriptions considered by the Politburo between 1985 and 1990. Radical reform encompassed far-reaching marketization and considerable expansion of cooperatives and private enterprise; half-hearted (or 'moderate') reform grudgingly accepted the need for marketization, but continued to rely heavily on the central economic bodies and the central planning agency, Gosplan; technocratic rationalization was based on streamlining (rather than reforming or 'marketizing') the existing system; socialist morality emphasized disciplinary measures; and the conservative programme sought a minimum of change.
8. Aslund (1991, p. 36) commented on the significance of political relativity and popular perceptions in determining 'radicalness' or 'conservatism'. In this regard, he noted Gorbachev's apparent move from a 'very radical

position to an ever more conservative one in relation to public opinion', even while his 'overt position' became more radical during 1985 to 1990.
9. Lane's (1988, p. 236) thesis of a 'loyalty–solidarity' system was founded in a similar belief in the primacy of ideological/political considerations. Like Pravda, Lane argued that ideology acted very much as a force for continuity rather than change: 'Any major change in the system of motivational commitments and integration processes would lead to the breakdown of the complex set of institutional interests and exchanges'.
10. Avoidance of the term, 'social contract', may have been motivated by the consideration that its use implied an arrangement between two discrete entities. This might be seen as undermining the intimate identification between the people as owners of the means of production and the government as its representative and the instrument of its will. In omitting mention of the 'welfare state', the authorities may have wished to emphasize the quintessential Soviet idea of the workers' state, based on the performance of work rather than the receiving of welfare.
11. On a slightly more abstract level, Peter Hauslohner (1991a, p. 35) characterized the 'social contract' further as a set of 'norms' or 'implicit conventions' which emphasized egalitarianism, stability and security.

Chapter 2 – Andropov and the intensification of labour

1. The notion of the USSR as a 'workers' state' was of prime importance in Soviet labour ideology. However, analysts have differed considerably in their explanations of the essence and especially role of this concept. Some consider that the idea of working class as leading class, if not literally true, at least reflected the considerable security and leeway enjoyed by Soviet workers. The emphasis given by Lane and others to the 'loyalty–solidarity system', the social contract, and the full employment doctrine, indicates a conviction that workers' vested interests were of major account in the development and implementation of labour policies. Other commentators, such as Alex Pravda and Frank Parkin, have dismissed the notion of a clearly delineated vested interest represented by the working class. Pravda (1982, p. 115) contended that the idea of a homogeneous 'working class' was a political myth cultivated by Soviet ideologists in order to legitimize Communist Party rule, while Parkin (1979, p. 137) argued that the benefits that accrued to workers under socialism were incidental. Although regime policies might benefit workers, the regime opposed the idea of autonomous classes: 'The party-state strips away the capacity of social classes to organize in defence of their collective interests and replaces open distributive struggle by a centralized system of allocation'.
2. In *Value, Price and Profit*, Marx (see Marx and Engels, 1985, p. 134) defined surplus value as profit or 'that part of the total value of the commodity in which the surplus-labour or unpaid labour of the working man is realised'.
3. According to Gladky (1986, p. 5), just over 100,000 people were engaged in non-agricultural individual labour activity in 1986. Even after non-state forms of labour became legitimized following the Laws on Individual Labour Activity (1986) and Cooperatives (1988), the numbers of people engaged in

such activity remained very small. Goskomstat figures for 1989 showed that, out of 139 million people employed in the national economy, 120.3 million worked in the public sector, 11.6 million on collective farms, 2.9 million in cooperatives (excluding second jobs), 4 million on private smallholdings, and 0.3 million in individual labour activity (see Kolosov, 1991, p. 45).

4. The maxim, 'from each according to their ability, to each according to their work', has commonly been applied to what Marx (see Marx and Engels, 1989, p. 87) described, in the *Critique of the Gotha Programme*, as 'the first phase of communist society as it is when it has just emerged after prolonged birth-pangs from capitalist society'. In the subsequent 'higher phase of communist society', labour would become 'not only a means of life but life's prime want', valued for itself, and not simply as a means of satisfying everyday needs.

5. According to the *CIA's Handbook of Economic Statistics* (1991) (cited in Moskoff, 1993, p. 9), economic growth averaged 4.8 per cent annually in the decade 1961 to 1970. The average rate of growth then fell by half to 2.4 per cent p. a. for the following decade, and declined further to 1.7 per cent p. a. in the period 1981 to 1985. Shmelev and Popov (1990, pp. 298–9) gave 'alternative (i.e., unofficial) estimates' of national income, indicating growth rates of 4.1 per cent p. a. during 1965 to 1970 and 3.2 per cent p. a. during 1971 to 1975, declining dramatically to 1 per cent p. a. in the period 1976 to 1980 and 0.6 per cent p. a. during 1981 to 1985.

6. There has been considerable disagreement over whether 'labour shortage' was a real or fictitious problem. The majority view under Brezhnev asserted that labour resources were insufficient, in that labour supply lagged behind the effective demand for it. Some (generally reformist) commentators contended, on the other hand, that resources were completely adequate, but were utilized irrationally and wastefully. There was no shortage in the absolute sense, but only regional and localized shortages.

7. In the pre-reform period, labour turnover (*tekuchest*) and 'rolling stones' (*letuny*) were widely blamed for disruptions to the work rhythm of the factory as well as being seen as an indication of a feckless, unstable mentality.

8. Mark Mikhailov (1981, pp. 105–6) described *vedomstvennost* as 'a method of thinking ... and a way of management that diverges from the general interest ... (it is) economic egoism in all its forms'.

9. The essence of the so-called Shchekino experiment, which originated in 1967 at the Shchekino Chemical Combine in Tula, was the reduction of the number of employees while keeping the total wage fund intact, thereby increasing the earnings of the remaining personnel and the collective's stake in higher output and labour productivity (Tolstikov, 1968, p. 2). The experiment also involved the combining of two or more jobs (*sovmeshchenie*) by workers for which they received wage increments. The Shchekino method fell victim to the perennial tension between directive planning with its emphasis on detailed, 'scientific' management by the centre, and indicative planning allowing enterprises greater autonomy.

10. Job Placement Bureaux (JPBs) were established in 1967 to help redeploy workers whose release was anticipated in the wake of the Kosygin economic reform. Organized under the Council of Ministers of the Republics, their

main function was to provide information about employment vacancies and give appropriate advice to job applicants (Lane, 1987, p. 50). Although they have been described as 'labour exchanges' (Porket, 1989, p. 99), their principal focus was to alleviate labour demand ('shortage') in enterprises, rather than assist the individual in finding work. Unlike their Western counterparts, JPBs were neither coordinated on a nationwide basis nor did they perform any social welfare function. They were also understaffed, poorly financed and their 'customers' were generally viewed as hopeless cases who were unable to find work through 'normal means' (that is, by applying directly 'at the factory gate').

11. SOL was a largely self-explanatory concept that was considerably influenced by Taylorist principles of time-and-motion efficiency. Although Lenin (1952, pp. 229–30) criticized Taylorism for embodying the 'refined brutality of bourgeois exploitation', he nevertheless credited it with 'a number of the greatest scientific achievements in the field of analysing mechanical motions during work, the elimination of superfluous and awkward motions, the elaboration of correct methods of work, the introduction of the best system of accounting and control...'. Using Taylorism as an essential point of reference, Lenin claimed that 'the possibility of building socialism depends exactly upon our success in combining Soviet power and the Soviet organization of administration with the up-to-date achievements of capitalism. We must organize in Russia the study and teaching of the Taylor system, and systematically try it out and adapt it to our own needs'.

12. Hewett (1988, p. 283) noted that '[f]or the neoconservatives the computer is the vehicle through which the Soviet Union can recreate the efficiently run, centralized system of the 1940s'.

13. Berliner (1976, p. 24) used the term, 'ratchet effect', to describe a situation where central planners reacted to plan overfulfilment by enterprises by raising production growth targets for the next period to the level attained during the current period. The ratchet effect was the natural outcome of 'planning from the achieved level' (or 'benchmark planning'), which was the practice of determining plans simply on the basis of production levels in the previous year or plan period. Such planning was largely driven by the need to keep up economic appearances – Selyunin's (1967, p. 11) 'infinite expansion of output' – and took little or no account of real requirements or changing production circumstances. To maintain the illusion of a prosperous economy, 'planning from the achieved level' almost invariably meant increasing production targets every year and plan period.

14. Dembinski (1991, pp. 76–9) analysed power in terms of the regime's capacity to achieve its objectives. Condign power was 'dissuasive power, based upon penalties', compensatory power was based on reward, and conditioned power derived its strength from ideological commitment.

15. Lenin (1951, p. 160) equated *khozraschet* with state enterprises operating on 'commercial foundations' (*kommercheskie osnovaniya*), and linked its implementation with the 'vital need to increase labour productivity, and achieve the financial viability (*bezubytochnost*) and profitability (*pribylnost*) of every state enterprise'. Although Lenin was apt to refer to *khozraschet* rather than *polny khozraschet*, the implication was the same: enterprises had a responsibility to be productive, solvent and, to a large degree, economically

self-reliant. Later, under Andropov and Gorbachev, *polny khozraschet* came to denote 'real *khozraschet'*, as opposed to the discredited 'formal–administrative' version (Lisichkin, 1967, p. 183) of the *zastoi* years.

16. 'Profit' (*pribyl*) might be loosely defined as the income notionally left to an enterprise after it had discharged its financial obligations to the Ministry of Finance, respective industrial ministries, and to other enterprises. Ellman (1969, p. 289) distinguished between the Soviet conception of profit as 'a guide to the efficient allocation of resources', and its Western capitalist definition as 'the income of property owners'. However, as Shmelev and Popov (1990, p. 174) pointed out, the size of enterprise profit did not even reflect production efficiency, but rather 'unavoidable miscalculations in price setting'. 'Profitability' (*pribylnost/rentabelnost*), according to Shmelev and Popov (ibid., p. 310), was the 'ratio of profit to value of capital stock and material assets'.

17. This was the practice whereby enterprises 'forgave' each other for their failure to fulfil reciprocal production, supply and payment obligations. Since in many cases enterprises were equally culpable, few were in a position to apportion specific blame without at the same time drawing the attention of central authorities to their own poor performance. In essence, enterprises engaged in a collusive relationship, the outcome of which was that the real debt was borne by the state budget.

18. *Ediny naryad* ('single contract') was characterized by allocation of a production task to the brigade as a whole, rather than assigning individual members with specific, sub-divided duties. Since pay and bonuses would be earned by the brigade and not directly by the individual, good workers had an interest in assisting those who found it difficult to fulfil production requirements. It was hoped, also, that this interdependence would enhance production discipline, since good workers would not tolerate slackness and incompetence by others that impinged upon their own financial position (see Connor, 1991, p. 180).

19. The official attitude towards sociology under Brezhnev was typified in comments made by the Director of the USSR Academy of Sciences' Institute for Sociological Research, M. Rutkevich. Rutkevich (1973, p. 3) criticized the use of empirical survey methods, censured some academics for subscribing to 'the theoretical conceptions of bourgeois sociology', and emphasized that sociology was a 'party science'. The comparative neglect of sociology under Brezhnev was remarked upon ten years later by a senior member of the Soviet Sociological Association (Zdravomyslov, 1983, p. 3), who deplored the dilatoriness of the Ministry of Higher and Secondary Specialized Education in introducing a 'sociology specialization' in university philosophy and economics faculties.

20. Figures provided by L. Volchkova and G. Sarkisian (cited in Connor, 1991, p. 139) indicate the strength of levelling tendencies in wages distribution. The latter wrote that the wage advantage of engineering–technical over general industrial workers declined from 45.9 per cent in 1965 to 15.9 per cent by 1979, while the former observed that the average–minimum wage ratio fell from 3.47:1 in 1964 to 1.81:1 in 1968. Connor (ibid., p. 111) has also noted other Soviet estimates that the average–minimum wage ratio narrowed further to 1.5:1 by 1976.

21. Kurashvili (1983, p. 48) cited the example of Hungary's 1972 law on economic planning. According to this law, state bodies could demand that enterprises act 'in accordance with the general aims of the state plan', but they had no right to set 'concrete and compulsory plan assignments'.

Chapter 3 – Soviet labour ideology during the Chernenko interregnum

1. Soviet labour ideology did not accept that 'antagonistic' contradictions could occur under socialism. Such ideas were implicit in comments made by *Kommunist* editor Kosolapov (1984, p. 3) about the large-scale economic experiment. Kosolapov claimed that the experiment's combining of autonomy and responsibility as 'mutually conditional opposites' excluded the possibility of their being in 'conflict' with one another. A more general 'non-antagonistic contradiction' of socialism in practice was highlighted by Andropov (1983, p. 13) in his article, *'Uchenie Karla Marksa...'*, when he observed that the existing economic mechanism no longer met 'the demands arising from the material-technological, social and spiritual level of development attained by the Soviet people' (see Chapter 2). This contradiction was, however, entirely reconcilable by reviving the Soviet labour ethic, automating and mechanizing production, and restoring people's interest in working productively (ibid., pp. 14–19).
2. Chernenko's speeches indicate strongly that he equated 'organization' more with 'order' and 'discipline' than with the 'scientific organization of labour'.
3. One of the best keys to understanding this peculiarly Soviet phenomenon was provided by Berliner (1976, pp. 120–1) when he suggested that in the Soviet context the term, 'competition', in fact meant 'contest': 'For the outcome of a socialist contest does not affect the interenterprise flow of resources. The losing enterprises suffer no loss of business or revenue. Customers enjoy no direct benefit from socialist competition among the producers of their inputs, although there are indirect benefits to the extent that production may be increased and quality improved'.
4. Whitefield (1993, p. 66) notes that by 1985 eight TPCs had been established, chiefly in the north, Central Asia and Siberia. He cites a 1985 *EKO* editorial which indicated that TPCs were intended to provide a 'complex and unified approach to a wide variety of forms of production, technology and integration, allowing for the creation of a single complex of productive and social infrastructure, to combine in a complex enterprises of different specialization, and to utilize combined and co-operative production'. Parfenov (1984, p. 2) proposed combining branch and territorial management because this would enable the wider application of 'economic methods of management', the 'perfection' of inter-branch links, and the freeing of highly qualified specialists from mindless and useless paper-shuffling.
5. The *raionnoe agro-promyshlennoe obedinenie (RAPO)* was established as part of the 1982 Food Programme with the purpose of integrating the management of Soviet agricultural production. RAPOs encompassed not only direct farming activity, but also the supply of agricultural inputs and the processing of agricultural produce. Although aimed at simplifying the administration of

rural industries by breaking down interdepartmental barriers, the introduction of RAPOs in fact created additional layers of bureaucracy (see Aslund,
1991, p. 100; Dyker, 1992, p. 107).
6. Whitefield (1993, pp. 90–1) cites figures showing that the bureaucracy in
ministries and state committees (*apparat organov upravleniya ministerstv i
vedomstv*) increased from 1,356,000 in 1975 to 1,623,000 in 1985. He identifies a 'tendency towards an overall acceleration in personnel growth', with
the largest increases taking place at the 'lower levels'.
7. One of these exceptions was Karagedov's (1984, p. 2) article, 'Posle pervogo
analiza', which claimed that the large-scale economic experiment introduced
under Andropov had brought no tangible results. The writer focused, in
particular, on the instability of enterprise production plans, continued
bureaucratic interference in enterprise activity (the 'inertia of the old style
of economic management'), and acute problems in the supply of production
inputs. Karagedov called for the experiment to enter a 'second stage' during
which enterprise rights and responsibilities would be expanded significantly.
8. In its discussion of the preliminary results of the large-scale economic experiment, the Politburo deplored the fact that the 'possibilities created by the
new conditions of management have not been fully utilized thus far', and
called for the 'more active restructuring (*perestroika*) of economic work and
the perfecting of management style and methods'. It was envisaged that
expansion of the experiment – now to encompass 2,300 enterprises making
up 12 per cent of Soviet industrial production (Aslund, 1991, p. 94) – would
lead to increased economic accountability, the acceleration of STP and the
better application of labour, material and financial resources in participating
enterprises (*Pravda*, 24 August 1984, p. 1).
9. A 1985 article by Philip Hanson (1992, p. 81) described a meeting of the
social sciences section of the USSR Academy of Sciences, which discussed the
possibility of censuring *EKO*'s editors for publishing 'weak' and 'primitive'
articles.
10. In his Memoirs, Gorbachev (1996, p. 217) reaffirmed his criticisms of Soviet
economists, accusing most of them of having 'been broken of the habit of
serious and unbiased research'.

Chapter 4 – Ideological transformation under Gorbachev: The moderate intra-systemic phase, 1985–87

1. Writing in 1987, Colton (1991, p. 68) argued that it was unreasonable to
equate systemic reform in the Soviet context with 'something diametrically
opposed – a textbook capitalist economy with private ownership and un-
fettered markets'. Instead, he claimed: 'To speak of systemic reform, in
the Soviet Union or elsewhere, is to speak of something which is more
profound than tinkering or superficial reform but, by the same token, is
less all-encompassing than revolution. A definition that does not leave
room for the persistence of certain basics of the unreformed system is a
misconstruction.' While Colton's points were well made, his view of systemic
reform has not stood the test of time. With hindsight, it can be seen that the
'radical intra-systemic reform' undertaken by the regime after June 1987

would, under the terms of his definitional framework, be considered 'systemic reform'. Such an interpretation leaves no room for reform that is extra- or trans-systemic, but which does not aim to establish 'a textbook capitalist economy'; in other words, Colton's interpretation neglected the possibility of a mixed, 'socialist market', economy emerging in the Soviet Union.

2. It was not until his Memoirs that Gorbachev (1996, p. 152) unequivocally acknowledged his debt to Andropov: 'Among the leaders of the country, there was no-one else with whom I had such close and old ties, and to whom I owed so much.'

3. Sales of alcohol fell by 25 per cent during the last seven months of 1985, by 37 per cent in 1986, and by another 13 per cent in 1987 (*Pravda*, 26 January 1986, 18 January 1987, 24 January 1988 – figures cited in Aslund, 1991, pp. 78–9).

4. Gorbachev (1996, p. 221) was later to disavow even this 'achievement'. In blaming Ligachev and Solomentsev for taking implementation 'to the point of absurdity', he identified the anti-alcohol campaign as 'one more sad example of how faith in the omnipotence of command methods, extremism and administrative zeal can ruin a good idea...'

5. Cohen (1991, p. 65) theorized that the nature of Soviet politics over the previous 25 years had been encapsulated by the conflict between 'reformism' and 'conservatism'. He defined the former as 'that outlook, and those policies, which seek through measured change to improve the existing order without fundamentally transforming existing social, political, and economic foundations or going beyond prevailing ideological values'. Unlike radicalism, reformism was based on the premise that 'the potential of the existing system and the promises of the established ideology... have not been realized'. Conservatism, on the other hand, was founded on 'a deep reverence for the past, a sentimental defense of existing institutions, routines and orthodoxies... and an abiding fear of change as the harbinger of disorder and of a future that will be worse than the present as well as a sacrilege of the past'. In asserting that conservatism had held sway since the fall of Khrushchev in 1964, Cohen (ibid., p. 73) concluded that the major obstacle to future reform was 'the profound conservatism' that dominated Soviet society from top to bottom.

6. Although the importance of profit had been stressed by the Brezhnev administration following the 1965 industrial reform, Ellman (1969, p. 295) rightly pointed out that the Soviet Union remained 'very far away indeed from a system in which the authorities leave each factory to produce what it likes, the factories strive to maximise their profits, the state takes its share of the profits in the form of taxes and allows the enterprise to do what it likes with the remaining profits'. The Gorbachev administration linked profit much more closely to the devolution of rights and responsibilities to enterprises.

7. Interestingly, these fears do not appear to have been realized in post-Soviet Russia. Guy Standing (1996, p. 300) notes there was even a 'slight strengthening' of female employment during 1990 to 1994. Penny Morvant (1995, p. 7) has observed that, while women are more likely than men to register as unemployed, this does not mean they are more liable to be actually unemployed.

8. Statistics on Soviet economic performance are notoriously unreliable and/ or contradictory, but those relating to labour productivity indicate a relative then absolute decline in performance after 1970. According to figures used by Hewett (1988, pp. 52, 54–5), labour productivity growth 'in all material production' fell from a high of 6.8 per cent in the period 1966–70, to 3.1 per cent in 1981–85. Moskoff (1993, p. 90), on the other hand, suggests that labour productivity growth was as high as 5.5 per cent in 1988, but declined to 2.3 per cent in 1989 and −3 per cent in 1990.

9. The theme of a massive conservative bureaucracy acting out of concerted self-interest is a very common one in Soviet literature. However, some writers have challenged the conventional stereotyping of the bureaucracy as a single, homogeneous institutional identity. George Breslauer (1991, p. 644) noted that party and state apparatuses comprised reformists and centralists, while Jerry Hough (1988, pp. 100–2, 106) challenged the assumption that the bureaucracy must be immutably conservative; even if labels accurately typified institutional interests in a particular period, there was no guarantee this would always be the case as interests and ideology adapted to changing political and economic circumstances.

10. Aslund (1991, pp. 191–2) has given figures showing that in the twenty years before 1986, the Union budget deficit remained at about 2 to 3 per cent of GNP. In 1986 it jumped to 6 per cent, before reaching 10 per cent in 1988.

11. Although Gorbachev (*Pravda*, 22 June 1987, p. 1) indicated that he agreed with much of Shmelev's analysis of the critical state of the Soviet economy, he censured the latter's remarks regarding the acceptability, even utility, of 'a little unemployment'. In this context, he emphasized that 'socialism gives each of us the right to work, to education, free medical care and accessible housing. These are real values of our society in which the individual is socially protected. Today and in the future'.

Chapter 5 – Ideological transformation under Gorbachev: The radical intra-systemic phase, 1987–90

1. Christopher Smart (1990, pp. 13–14) has made this point generally, arguing that Gorbachev identified his overall course with 'a return to the genuine Lenin whose ideas (had) been abused and distorted by both Stalin and Brezhnev'. More specifically, Smart (ibid., pp. 17–18) links Gorbachev's tolerance of cooperatives and his emphasis on the 'human factor', with Lenin's own position on these questions.

2. In declaring that 'there is nothing more erroneous than confusing democratic centralism with bureaucratism', Lenin (1952, p. 181) stressed the need to implement the former in the national economy in order 'to ensure absolute harmony and unity' between enterprise activity, and 'centralism...in the genuinely democratic sense'. He attached particular importance to 'the full and unimpeded development...of local initiative' in the task of reorganizing Russia's economy.

3. The Kosygin industrial planning reform attempted to introduce *polny khozraschet* and profit principles in Soviet enterprise activity. But, as Nove (1992,

pp. 383–4) pointed out, the overwhelming importance of quantitative targets, together with the negligible influence of demand/need on prices, meant that the emphasis on profit (and, by extension, the economic viability of enterprises) was more nominal than real. *Khozraschet*'s 'formal–administrative variation' (Lisichkin, 1967, p. 165), based on the 'need to establish good norms' (ibid., p. 183), dominated the relationship between enterprises and planners.

4. Some writers, such as Archie Brown (1997, p. 137), have viewed the use of the term 'commodity-money relations' in the early Gorbachev period as a 'euphemism for a market'. If this is true, then it is only so in the broadest and most generous sense of the market – i.e., connoting supply and demand relations where financial levers play a role. To imply, as Brown appears to do, that Gorbachev's use of the term showed that he had from the outset a vision of a market economy is difficult to sustain. In this context, it is pertinent that in his Memoirs Gorbachev (1996, p. 350) refers to this concept in a pre-market economy sense only, as part of the learning process towards market socialism.

5. The notion of equivalence involved equalizing living conditions between city and countryside. In this context, Gorbachev (1990a, p. 27) declared to an agrarian conference in October 1988 that the 'economic relations existing today in the countryside clearly do not stimulate creative, active and enterprising labour'. He (ibid., pp. 27–8) attributed much of the sense of alienation and consequent population efflux from the countryside, to the backwardness of social development in rural areas.

6. At the Second Congress of People's Deputies, Ryzhkov (1990a, p. 219) stated unambiguously the government's view that, since the manager (*rukovoditel*) at state enterprises was 'the state's representative as owner [*sobstvennik*] of the means of production', it was 'evident that he should not be elected, but appointed'.

7. The literal translation of *samookupaemost* is 'self-repayment'. Although this term was often used more or less interchangeably with *samofinansirovanie*, it described (in theory) the more modest objective of simply covering production and labour costs.

8. Kuznetsova (1991, pp. 282–3) identified three distinct stages in the development of private cooperatives. In the first period (summer 1986 to May 1988), there was fairly rapid but geographically limited (large cities, the Baltic republics, Armenia) development in the areas of consumer services, recycling resources, catering and consumer goods production. The second phase (summer to autumn 1988), in the first few months following adoption of the Law on Cooperatives, was marked by their further rapid sectoral and geographical expansion. The third stage was initiated by the USSR Council of Ministers' decision to restrict certain types of cooperative activity, and saw the enactment of regulations on the taxation of cooperatives as well as other measures controlling their operation.

9. Both Kuznetsova and Tikhonov (head of the Union of USSR Cooperatives) understood cooperatives as 'new cooperatives'. Kuznetsova (1991, p. 281) described the new type of cooperative as 'an organic component of the new society itself', while Tikhonov (1990, p. 41) claimed that they were 'in effect a new phenomenon'. Central to such views was the idea that a genuine cooperative movement had ceased to exist following Stalin's forced

collectivization in the 1930s (see Tikhonov, 1990, p. 4; also Kuznetsova, 1991, p. 277).

10. Although Julian Cooper (1991, p. 49) argued that conversion had made significant progress between 1988 and 1991, particularly in regard to the production of medical equipment, he observed that it had been less successful in providing equipment for the food and consumer industries. Performance had also varied across the military–industrial complex. For example, the nuclear and aviation industries had performed better than Ministry of Defence establishments that normally produced tanks, artillery and munitions. In the latter, there was evidence of 'a lack of entrepreneurial initiative' (ibid., pp. 49–50).

11. Official opposition to *uravnilovka* had a long history. In a famous speech to economic managers in 1931, Stalin (1945, p. 334) blamed the high incidence of *tekuchest* on 'incorrect organization of pay, a flawed (wage) tariff system, and "leftist" (*levatskii*) *uravnilovka* in the area of pay'. As indicated in note 21 to Chapter 2, levelling tendencies in the Soviet economy occurred principally under Brezhnev.

12. At the January 1988 Plenum, for example, Gorbachev (1989, p. 36) identified as one of the benefits of the anti-alcohol campaign, the increase in the number of births from 4.9 million in 1980 to 5.6 million per annum during 1986–87.

13. As at the end of 1989, non-agricultural cooperatives employed only 4.9 million or 6.4 per cent of the working-age population (Kuznetsova, 1991, p. 289; Tikhonov, 1990, p. 7).

14. The official political–legal commentary on the Constitution (*Konstitutsiya...*, 1982, p. 187) directly addressed the charge that the Soviet citizen's obligation to work contravened Article 8 of the ILO Convention on Civil and Political Rights, regarding the unacceptability of forced labour: 'it is specified in the (ILO) Pact that the definition of such labour does not cover military service; compulsory service in states of emergency or calamity; and – what is especially important – any work or service that comes under civic duties. As can be seen from the above, the Soviet Constitution and Soviet laws conform entirely with the Pact's provisions'.

15. In July 1989, miners' strikes broke out in the Kuzbass, Vorkuta and Donetsk regions. The immediate origins of the strikes appear to have been socioeconomic: discontent over wages and conditions of service, scarcity of basic consumer items, etc. As the strikes unfolded, however, economic demands were supplemented by calls for the mines to be given economic independence, and for regions to be granted political and economic autonomy (see Rutland, 1991, pp. 291–313; 1992, p. 215; Moskoff, 1993, pp. 190–4; Clarke *et al.*, 1993, pp. 128–40).

16. Brown (1997, p. 95) dismisses as a 'common misconception' the idea that Gorbachev turned to significant political reform only after the failure of *uskorenie*. Gorbachev's Memoirs, however, reveal a more complex picture. On the one hand, he (1996, p. 349) claims that the leadership 'never retreated from the planned goal of democratic transformation'. Later, however, Gorbachev (ibid., p. 569) offers the following rationalization for the democratization that began in the spring of 1988: 'Having realized that a cosmetic job alone or even a major repair would not do, and that no

innovative economic measures would work without a radical reconstruction of the political system, we introduced free elections, a parliament, and a multi-party system ... '.

Chapter 6 – Ideological transformation under Gorbachev: The extra-systemic phase, 1990–91

1. Goskomtrud Chairman Shcherbakov (1990a, p. 2) claimed that shock therapy would lead to the immediate release of 30–35 million people, thereby making the situation 'unmanageable'. By contrast, the government's more gradual approach would 'make it possible to avoid unemployment altogether'.
2. An allegiance which he appears to have retained to this day (see Gorbachev, 1996, p. 603).
3. Abalkin's (1989, p. 7) four stages of economic reform were:
   (i) 'Stage 1 – preparing the implementation of simultaneous measures for the creation of an economic mechanism for the transition period – 1990'. This stage would see the introduction of laws on taxation and Gosbank; preparation of price, wage and social welfare reform, including the introduction of income indexation; the dissolution of all loss-making industrial enterprises and their conversion into leasing, cooperative and joint-stock companies; and laws granting greater economic autonomy to republican and local administrations;
   (ii) 'Stage 2 – the implementation of simultaneous measures and the launching of an economic mechanism for the transitional period – 1991–1992'. In this stage, the legislative acts introduced during the first stage would come into effect. The introduction of income indexation would enable the government to proceed with price and wage reform. Abalkin foreshadowed in this period the liquidation of all loss-making *sovkhozy* and *kolkhozy* and their transformation into farms (*fermerskie khozyaistva*) and cooperatives; the adaptation of enterprises to the new taxation system and to a more rigorous credit environment; and the development of various forms of financial and stock exchanges (*tovarnye birzhi, kommercheskie tsentry, fondovaya birzha*). During this phase, the first results of improved consumer goods production should make themselves felt;
   (iii) 'Stage 3 – fine-tuning the economic mechanism of the transitional period, and implementation of the program for the development of reform – 1993–1995'. Here Abalkin anticipated completing the process of restoring financial soundness to the economy; the implementation of an 'anti-monopolist program'; creation of a two-tier banking system operating on the basis of credit levers and interest policies; balancing the consumer market; a marked increase in foreign commercial links, including attracting foreign investment; the partial convertibility of the rouble; and the development of real economic competition (*konkurentsiya*). Abalkin warned against trying to achieve high growth and investment rates during this period of stabilization;
   (iv) 'Stage 4 – the establishment and development of a new economic system, and the completion of structures of production and socioeconomic

relations in accordance with this system – 1996–2000 and beyond'. Abalkin did not elaborate on specific measures in this phase, saying only that 'strong, effective stimuli for economic growth and increasing people's welfare' would be created.

4. This comprised three stages of one, five and thirty years respectively. The first stage would be characterized by 'entry into the market', involving the freeing of some prices, the introduction of initial (*pervye*) financial exchanges, and establishing a system of commercial banks. The state's role during this period would be 'quite significant' (Abalkin, 1991, p. 3).

   Abalkin claimed that the full transfer to 'economic methods of management' would require a second stage of 'no less than five years'. This time was necessary in order to carry out the demonopolization of the economy, and to convert the rouble into an 'adequately' hard currency.

   The third and final stage, involving the development of a fully-fledged market with all its mechanisms, required 'at least a generation' because of the time needed to create an 'enterprise psychology' among people still accustomed to the state taking care of business.

5. It is a measure of the fluidity and instability of ideological labelling that the constituency in favour of 'shock therapy' has split since the fall of the Soviet Union. The former arch-radical Yavlinsky has now become one of the strongest critics of the neo-liberal, Gaidar model of shock therapy.

6. Aslund (1991, p. 137) defines these as 'a kind of joint venture between the state and shareholders-employees'. Joint-stock companies represented a form of ideological compromise based on principles of destatization (*razgosudarstvlenie*) and democratization, while avoiding privatization and its too overt abandonment of the collectivist principles underpinning traditional Soviet labour ideology.

7. Lest it be thought that Ivashko was a diehard conservative, Gorbachev (1996, p. 368) describes him as 'an advocate of reforms, who maintained moderate political views'.

8. The Shatalin economic programme arose out of the agreement between Gorbachev and Yeltsin (then Chairman of the RSFSR Supreme Soviet) to set up a joint working group 'On the preparation of a concept of a union treaty for the transition to a market economy as a foundation of a Union treaty'. The group, named the Shatalin group after its Chairman, also included Nikolai Petrakov, the original authors of Yeltsin's 400-day programme for transition to a market economy – Yavlinsky, Mikhail Zadornov and A. Mikhailov – as well as Boris Fyodorov (later Yeltsin's First Deputy Prime Minister). Abalkin was invited to participate, but apparently refused because 'he did not share such radical views' (Aslund, 1991, p. 208).

   The Shatalin programme provided much of the philosophical and practical inspiration for the later Yavlinsky 500-day plan ('Transition to the Market'). This is unsurprising given that the list of contributors was virtually identical, with the only significant differences being Yavlinsky's displacement of Shatalin at the head of the working group, and Fyodorov's 'promotion' from eleventh to second in the authorship credits.

9. Socialist paternalist views on this question were shared by writers such as Ernest Mandel (1991, p. 153), who considered that a 'genuine' labour market could not function without a reserve army of the unemployed.

10. These conditions included 'obligatory fulfillment of the labor legislation rules securing the interests of citizens regarding employment guarantees, working conditions, and compensation' (Yavlinsky *et al.*, 1991, pp. 101–2).

11. Hauslohner (1991a, p. 46) argued in his 1987 article, 'Gorbachev's Social Contract', that official denials that individual redundancies were sometimes an 'inevitable concomitant' of the search for economic efficiency, would 'postpone the day when massive, covert opposition to redundancy no longer is the major obstacle to technological progress that it is alleged to be at present'.

12. Part IV of the 1991 Employment Law (Articles 25 to 37), 'Social guarantees in the event of loss of work' (*Vedomosti...*, 1991, pp. 191–6), covered redundancy, training, unemployment and emergency benefits. Article 27 (p. 193) limited the amount of benefit payable during training/retraining to a maximum of 70 per cent of the Soviet average wage. However, this could also be as low as 50 per cent of the person's wages at their previous place of work. Although Article 28 (pp. 193–4) left the issue of specific time-scales to the discretion of individual republics, it decreed minimum payment periods of 26 weeks only for people who had lost their jobs, and 13 weeks for first-time job-seekers. Moreover, under Article 33 (p. 195), unemployment benefit for those in the latter group could be as low as 75 per cent of the USSR minimum wage. Finally, Article 36 (p. 196) provided for the suspension or even termination of benefit if the recipient refused two offers of 'suitable work' (*podkhodyashchaya rabota*) after completing training or retraining.

13. Moskoff (1993, pp. 200–1) refers to the RSFSR textile workers' strike in December 1990. Worried about the collapse of several moribund enterprises and the flow-on effects on consumer item availability, the regime opted to meet the strikers' wage demands. Moskoff (ibid., p. 201) rightly points out that the outcome of this industrial dispute 'exemplified the government's consistent unwillingness to test the law on strikes against the resolve of workers when a strike was threatened'.

14. This ideological uncertainty was evident in Gorbachev's (mis)handling of the debate over the various blueprints for economic reform put forward by Shatalin, Ryzhkov and Aganbegyan in September-October 1990. Unable to decide between Shatalin's economic programme emphasizing rapid marketization, and Ryzhkov's programme (to which Abalkin was a major contributor) which set greater store on the introduction of 'stabilization' measures, Gorbachev asked Aganbegyan to develop a compromise draft. When this turned out to be virtually indistinguishable from the Shatalin plan, Gorbachev continued to prevaricate by proposing that a further compromise programme be developed on the basis of the three existing blueprints. The eventual outcome, 'The Basic Guidelines for the Stabilization of the Economy...', leant heavily towards the more cautious Ryzhkov/Abalkin approach (see Aslund, 1991, pp. 208–10).

15. As Moskoff (1993, pp. 109–10) has pointed out, it is very difficult to come up with a standard definition of what constitutes poverty. Even government institutions found it hard to agree; in 1988 Goskomtrud claimed that 105 roubles a month represented the poverty line, while Goskomstat estimated it instead at 75 roubles. Had the Goskomtrud figure been chosen – the final agreed poverty line was 78 roubles – 90 million people (one-third of the

population) would have been officially classed as living in poverty. Moskoff (ibid., pp. 110–11) also mentions a popular survey in August 1991 that determined a subsistence minimum of 328 roubles a month, a figure leaving 84 per cent of people below the poverty line.

Chapter 7 – Labour and legitimacy in post-Soviet Russia

1. Advocates of tight money are apt to quote Sokolnikov's famous aphorism, 'Emission is the opium of the national economy', in support of their views. For example, Boris Fyodorov used it directly as the title of an article ('Emissiya – opium dlya narodnogo khozyaistva', *Izvestiya*, 15 September 1993, p. 4).
2. Rutland (1994, p. 1120) noted that privatization did not lead to a reduction in subsidies for industry (around 22 per cent of GDP) or agriculture (7 per cent). The *OECD's Review of Agricultural Policies: Russian Federation* (1998, p. 236) provides data on producer subsidy equivalents (PSEs) showing that these fell from 98 per cent in 1986 to a low of −105 per cent in 1992, before rising steadily during the post-Soviet period to 32 per cent in 1996.
3. According to Russia's leading public-opinion research company, VTsIOM, 31 per cent of workers were not paid on time with another 39 per cent being not paid at all (Varoli, 1997, p. 9). More recent figures show that government wage arrears increased from an estimated 4 billion roubles at the beginning of 1998, to 16 billion roubles by year's end (OECD report on Liaison Committee Meeting between the Russian Federation and the OECD, 5 March 1999, p. 5).
4. The rouble fell from 6 to the US dollar on the eve of the financial crash, to 20:1 by the beginning of December (*Russian Economic Trends*, 1998, p. 35). At the time of writing (1999), it has fallen further to 25 roubles to the dollar. The CPI increased by 38.4 per cent in September 1998, the highest monthly growth rate since February 1992. During October and November, CPI grew by around 5 per cent a month (ibid., p. 11).
5. According to Aslund (1995, p. 158), Gaidar had intended to free energy prices by 1 March 1992. However, strong lobbying by the energy and other industrial sectors, and mounting political pressures on the government, succeeded in blocking the freeing of energy prices. Furthermore, Gaidar's Minister for Fuel and Energy, Vladimir Lopukhin, was sacked for his advocacy of energy price liberalization, while Gazprom's Viktor Chernomyrdin was appointed Deputy Prime Minister for Energy.
6. Somewhat remarkably, Aslund (1995, p. 3) asserts that after the August 1991 putsch, the Russian economy had become 'emancipated from politics'.
7. Vitalis (1999, pp. 5–6) highlights the growing incidence of regional price controls, even in so-called 'progressive' areas such as St Petersburg and Nizhny Novgorod.
8. According to *VTsTOM* figures, in January 1996 Yeltsin (7.9 per cent) ranked only sixth among preferred candidates in a putative first round of presidential elections, behind Zyuganov (21.2 per cent), Yavlinsky (11.2 per cent), far-right leader Vladimir Zhirinovsky (11 per cent), Lebed (10.4 per cent) and the eye surgeon and independent Svyatoslav Fyodorov (8 per cent).

9. For example, by establishing a special presidential 'social fund' to pay off wage arrears (Service, 1998, p. 538).

10. Current provisions allow for unemployment benefits up to 75 per cent of monthly salary for the first three months, up to 60 per cent for the next four months (but no more than 3,107 roubles – about USD 125), 45 per cent of the last salary for the twelve months after that, and then down to the minimum monthly salary – a risible 890 roubles (less than USD 40) in September 1999 (Ognev, 1999, p. 31). Dmitriev and Sourkov (1999, p. 6) note that, in the period 1995–98, significant arrears were increasing in the area of unemployment benefits. They make the point that, due to decentralization of the employment fund, 'regions the worst affected by recession and unemployment were the least capable of financing unemployment benefits.' Finally, they (ibid., p. 26) include 1998 Goskomstat figures which reveal the considerable gap between the percentage of unemployed as defined by ILO criteria – 11.7 per cent – and the number of registered unemployed – 2.6 per cent.

11. In 1996 'some 6.7 million people were forced to take administrative leave for various lengths of time (and about 3 million of those "on vacation" didn't get a single kopek), while another 3.2 million citizens worked only part-time (*Trud*, 31 December 1996, p. 5).

12. Blasi *et al.* (1997, p. 112) note that fewer than 5 per cent of laid-off workers received retraining in 1995.

13. Blasi *et al.* (1997, pp. 137–8) reveal that, although the average Russian firm reduced its personnel by 23 per cent between 1992 and 1995, during the same period it was working at only 55 per cent of capacity; Clarke *et al.* (1994, p. 210) also note that 'lay-offs . . . have nowhere exceeded the decline in production, so lay-offs have not led to any increase in productivity or significant changes in working practices'.

14. See note 5, Chapter 6.

15. It is no surprise that the rate of bankruptcy proceedings increased markedly after the state abdicated control of the process in early 1998. Federal Bankruptcy Service director Georgii Tal (*Izvestiya*, 28 October 1998, p. 4) noted that in the seven months since the most recent bankruptcy law came into effect (on 1 March 1998), 3,831 processes had been launched compared to a total of 4,035 in the previous five years. Moreover, only 6 per cent of the new cases were initiated by the state; the vast majority were pursued by creditors who saw the revised bankruptcy process as a most convenient means of acquiring property. Significantly, new bankruptcy procedures led also to markedly different outcomes: whereas in the past some 60 per cent of cases had led to the 'reorganization' or 'financial rehabilitation' of the enterprise – that is, they were bailed out – the 1998 law led to liquidation of the bankrupt enterprise in 80 per cent of cases.

16. Aslund (1995, pp. 153–4), has noted that '[a]lmost half of all Russian towns have only one industrial firm'.

17. Gaidar (interview in *Trud*, 28 March 1997, p. 5) has claimed that Russia has no 'democratic traditions'. In his view, since 'the first shoots appeared in the midst of an extremely grave postsocialist crisis', it is hardly surprising that the concept of 'democracy' had 'largely negative associations'.

18. Already in 1993, a nationwide survey found that most respondents listed Yurii Andropov and Margaret Thatcher as their 'ideal' political figure by a considerable margin (Klyamkin, 1993, p. 4).
19. This recalls Barrington Moore's (1969, p. 418) famous aphorism, 'No bourgeois, no democracy.'
20. The pre-crash poll conducted by the Bureau of Applied Sociological Research found that only 5.6 per cent of people saw democracy as a unifying idea for Russia (Popov, 1998, p. 8).

Bibliography

Abalkin, Leonid (1983a), 'Ekonomicheskie funktsii sotsialisticheskogo gosu-darstva', *Pravda*, 12 May, pp. 2–3.

Abalkin, Leonid (1983b), 'Teoreticheskie voprosy khozyaistvennogo mekha-nizma', *Kommunist*, no. 14 (1240), September, pp. 28–38.

Abalkin, Leonid (1989), 'Radikalnaya ekonomicheskaya reforma: pervoochered-nye i dolgovremennye mery (material dlya obsuzhdenie), *Ekonomicheskaya gazeta*, no. 43, October, pp. 4–7.

Abalkin, Leonid (1991), 'Versiya Abalkina: intervyu posle otstavki', interview in *Izvestiya*, 14 March, p. 3.

Adam, Jan (Ed) (1987), *Employment in the Soviet Union and Eastern Europe* (2nd revised edition, Macmillan Press, Basingstoke and London).

Adam, Jan (1993), *Planning and Market in Soviet and East European Thought* (St. Martin's Press, New York).

Aganbegyan, Abel (1973), 'Upor na intensivnye metody', *Pravda*, 12 November, p. 2.

Aganbegyan, Abel (1987), 'Otstupat nekuda', interview in *Izvestiya*, 25 August, p. 2.

Andreeva, Nina (1990), 'Esli my pridem k vlasti...', interview in *Argumenty i fakty*, no. 22, 2–8 June, pp. 4–5.

Andropov, Yurii (1983), 'Uchenie Karla Marksa i nekotorye voprosy sotsialisti-cheskogo stroitelstva v SSSR', *Kommunist*, no. 3 (1229), February, pp. 9–23.

Antosenkov, Yevgenii (1991), 'A New Employment Concept in Soviet Labour Legislation' in Standing (1991), pp. 63–79.

Aslund, Anders (1991), *Gorbachev's Struggle for Economic Reform* (second edition, Cornell University Press, Ithaca, New York).

Aslund, Anders (1995), *How Russia Became a Market Economy* (The Brookings Institution, Washington DC).

Batalin, Y. (1984), 'Puti rosta proizvoditelnosti truda', *Pravda*, 4 September, p. 2.

Belousov, Rem (1984), 'Demokraticheskii tsentralizm i khozyaistvennaya samos-toyatelnost', *EKO*, no. 1, January, pp. 3–21.

Berliner, Joseph S. (1976), *The Innovation Decision in Soviet Industry* (The Massa-chusetts Institute of Technology, Boston).

Bialer, Seweryn (1988), 'The Conditions of Stability in the Soviet Union' in Thompson and Sheldon (1988), pp. 254–71.

Birman, Aleksandr (1983), 'Tonny, shtuki, rubli', *EKO*, no. 9, September, pp. 42–61.

Birman, Igor (1985), 'The Soviet Economy: Alternative Views', *Soviet Survey*, vol. 29, no. 2 (125), Summer, pp. 102–15.

Birman, Igor (1996), 'Gloomy Prospects for the Russian Economy', *Europe-Asia Studies*, vol. 48, no. 5, pp. 735–50.

Blasi, Joseph R., Kroumova, Maya and Kruse, Douglas (1997), *Kremlin Capitalism: Privatizing the Russian Economy* (ILR Press/Cornell University Press, Ithaca and London).

Bleaney, Michael (1988), *Do Soviet Economies Work? The Soviet and East European Experience* (Basil Blackwell, Oxford).

Blyakhman, Leonid and Zlotnitskaya, Tatyana (1984), 'Differentsiatsiya zarabotnoi platy kak faktor stimulirovaniya truda', *Sotsiologicheskie issledovaniya*, no. 1, pp. 39–47.

Bondarev, Yurii (1991), 'Moya pozitsiya', letter to *Literaturnaya Rossiya*, no. 35 (1491), 30 August, p. 3.

Bordukov, A. (1983), 'Chelovek na rabote', *Pravda*, 26 July, p. 2.

Breslauer, George W. (1991), 'Thinking about the Soviet Future' in Dallin and Lapidus (1991), pp. 635–57.

Brezhnev, Leonid (1970), 'Delo Lenina zhivet i pobezhdaet' (speech on the 100th Anniversary of Lenin's birth), *Pravda*, 22 April, pp. 2–5.

Brezhnev, Leonid (1976), 'Otchet TsK KPSS i ocherednye zadachi partii v oblasti vnutrennei i vneshnei politiki' (speech to the 25th Party Congress), *Pravda*, 25 February, pp. 2–9.

Brezhnev, Leonid (1977), 'O proekte Konstitutsii (osnovnogo zakona) SSSR i itogakh vsenarodnogo obsuzhdeniya', *Pravda*, 5 October, pp. 2–3.

Bronshtein, Mikhail (1990), 'Tsena promedleniya', *Izvestiya*, 10 June, p. 2.

Brown, Archie (1997), *The Gorbachev Factor* (Oxford University Press, Oxford and New York).

Buinovsky, Viktor (1988), 'Dela vsem khvatit', interview in *Izvestiya*, 21 January, p. 3.

Bunich, Pavel (1984), 'Ekonomicheskoe stimulirovanie vysokikh konechnykh rezultatov', *EKO*, no. 2, February, pp. 3–25.

Burtin, Aleksandr and Kostenko, Dmitrii (1996), 'Bunt odinochek', *Moskovskie novosti*, no. 44, 3–10 November, p. 4.

Chapman, Janet G. (1991), 'Recent and Prospective Trends in Soviet Wage Determination' in Standing (1991), pp. 177–202.

Cheban, I. (1980), 'Trudovoi spor', *Pravda*, 1 October, p. 3.

Chekalin, A. (1983), 'Samostoyatelnost', *Pravda*, 22 June, p. 2.

Chernenko, Konstantin (1984a), speech at the Extraordinary Party Plenum, *Pravda*, 14 February, pp. 1–2.

Chernenko, Konstantin (1984b), speech at the Party Plenum, *Pravda*, 11 April, pp. 1–2.

Chernenko, Konstantin (1984c), speech to workers at the Moscow metallurgical factory, 'Serp i molot', *Pravda*, 30 April, pp. 1–2.

Chernenko, Konstantin (1984d), 'Vysokii grazhdanskii dolg narodnogo kontrolera', speech to the All-Union Conference of People's Controllers, *Pravda*, 6 October, pp. 1–2.

Chernenko, Konstantin (1984e), 'Dostoino zavershit pyatiletku, uskorit intensifikatsiyu ekonomiki', speech to the Politburo, *Pravda*, 16 November, pp. 1–2.

Chernenko, Konstantin, (1985a), 'Ravnenie na vysshie trebovaniya sotsializma', summary of Chernenko's article, 'Na uroven trebovanii razvitogo sotsializma. Nekotorye aktualnye problemy teorii, strategii i taktiki KPSS', *Pravda*, 17 January, pp. 2–3.

Chernenko, Konstantin (1985b), campaign speech for the Supreme Soviet elections, *Pravda*, 23 February, pp. 1–2.

Chizhova, Liliya (1983), 'Sbalansirovannost resursov truda c potrebnostyami ekonomiki', *Voprosy ekonomiki*, no. 5, May, pp. 61–9.

Churakov, Vladimir (1983), 'Sbalansirovannost rabochikh mest i trudovykh resursov', *Voprosy ekonomiki*, no. 10, October, pp. 88–96.

Clarke, Simon, Fairbrother, Peter, Burawoy, Michael and Krotov, Pavel (1993), *What About the Workers? Workers and the Transition to Capitalism in Russia* (Verso, London and New York).

Clarke, Simon, Fairbrother, Peter, Borisov, Vadim and Bizyukov, Peter (1994), 'The Privatisation of Industrial Enterprises in Russia: Four Case-Studies', *Europe-Asia Studies*, vol. 46, no. 2, pp. 179–214.

Cohen, Stephen F. (1991), 'The Friends and Foes of Change: Reformism and Conservatism in the Soviet Union' in Dallin and Lapidus (1991), pp. 64–80.

Colton, Timothy J. (1991), 'The Politics of Systemic Economic Reform' in Hewett and Winston (1991), pp. 65–90.

Connor, Walter D. (1991), *The Accidental Proletariat: Workers, Politics, and Crisis in Gorbachev's Russia* (Princeton University Press, New Jersey).

Connor, Walter D. (1996), *Tattered Banners: Labor, Conflict, and Corporatism in Postcommunist Russia* (Westview Press, Boulder, Colorado).

Cook, Linda J. (1992), 'Brezhnev's Social Contract and Gorbachev's Reforms', *Soviet Studies*, vol. 44, no. 1, pp. 37–56.

Cooper, Julian (1991), *The Soviet Defence Industry: Conversion and Reform* (Royal Institute of International Affairs/Pinter Publishers, London).

Dallin, Alexander and Lapidus, Gail W. (eds) (1991), *The Soviet System in Crisis* (Westview Press, Boulder and Oxford).

Dembinski, Pawel H. (1991), *The Logic of the Planned Economy: The Seeds of the Collapse* (Clarendon Press, Oxford).

Demchenko, I. (1988), 'Kem teper byt', *Moskovskaya Pravda*, 2 March, p. 2.

Dmitriev, Mikhail and Sourkov, Sergei (1999) 'Patterns of Incomes, Consumption, Poverty, and Social Transfers in Russia during 1994–1998', (unpublished paper).

Dunaeva, Vera (1983), 'Zakon povyshayushcheisya proizvoditelnosti truda i strukturnye izmeneniya v sotsialisticheskoi ekonomike', *Voprosy ekonomiki*, October, pp. 3–14.

Dyker, David A. (1992), *Restructuring the Soviet Economy* (Routledge, London and New York).

Efimov, A. (1984), 'Ekonomika: proportsionalnost i sbalansirovannost', *Pravda*, 18 May, pp. 2–3.

Ellman, Michael (1969), 'Economic Reform in the Soviet Union' in PEP (London), vol. XXXV, Broadsheet 509, April, pp. 283–371.

Ellman, Michael and Kontorovich, Vladimir (eds) (1992), *The Disintegration of the Soviet Economic System* (Routledge, London and New York).

Ericson, Richard E. (1997), 'The Future of Market Transformation and the Yeltsin Succession', *Problems of Post-Communism*, November/December, pp. 23–8.

Ezigaryan, Gevork (1983), 'Sovershenstvovanie khozyaistvennogo mekhanizma v promyshlennosti', *Voprosy ekonomiki*, no. 5, May, pp. 49–60.

Fedorenko, Nikolai *et al.* (1992), 'Shturm rynochnykh redutov poka ne udalsya', *Izvestiya*, 18 March, p. 3.

Filev, Viktor (1983), 'O dalneishem vnedrenii shchekinskogo metoda', *Voprosy ekonomiki*, no. 2, February, pp. 58–68.

Filtzer, Donald (1994), *Soviet Workers and the Collapse of Perestroika: The Soviet Labour Process and Gorbachev's Reforms, 1985–1991* (Cambridge University Press).

Frolov, Ivan (1984), 'Vysokoe soprikosnovenie – o nekotorykh sotsialnykh problemakh na novom etape razvitiya NTR', *Pravda*, 23 November, pp. 2–3.

Fyodorov, Boris (1993a), 'Dobivaem finansy, a kivaem na kurs rublya', *Segodnya*, 16 March, p. 10.

Fyodorov, Boris (1993b), 'Emissiya – opium dlya narodnogo khozyaistva', *Izvestiya*, 15 September, p. 4.

Galbraith, John Kenneth (1987), *A History of Economics: The Past as Present* (Hamish Hamilton, London).

Gladky, Ivan (1986), 'O proekte Zakona SSSR ob individualnoi trudovoi deyatelnosti', speech to the Supreme Soviet, *Pravda*, 20 November, p. 5.

Gladky, Ivan (1988), 'Pravo na trud garantiruetsya', interview in *Trud*, 28 January, pp. 1–2.

Glaziev, Sergei (1994), 'Soglasie ili soglashatelstvo?, *Rossiiskie vesti*, 21 October, p. 2.

Glaziev, Sergei (1996), 'Ekonomika strany vse eshche daleka ot podema', *Nezavisimaya gazeta*, 11 November, pp. 1, 5

Gorbachev, Mikhail (1987a), *Izbrannye rechi i stati*, vol. 2 (Politizdat, Moscow).

Gorbachev, Mikhail (1987b), *Izbrannye rechi i stati*, vol. 3.

Gorbachev, Mikhail (1987c), *Izbrannye rechi i stati*, vol. 4.

Gorbachev, Mikhail (1988a), *Perestroika: New Thinking for Our Country and the World* (Fontana/Collins, London).

Gorbachev, Mikhail (1988b), *Izbrannye rechi i stati*, vol. 5.

Gorbachev, Mikhail (1989), *Izbrannye rechi i stati*, vol. 6.

Gorbachev, Mikhail (1990a), *Izbrannye rechi i stati*, vol. 7.

Gorbachev, Mikhail (1990b), speech on 15 March 1990 published in *Vneocherednoi tretii sezd Narodnykh Deputatov SSSR, 12–15 mart 1990 g., stenograficheskii otchet*, vol. 3 (Izdanie Verkhovnogo Soveta SSSR, Moscow), pp. 56–69.

Gorbachev, Mikhail (1990c), 'Politicheskii otchet TsK KPSS XXVIII Sezdu KPSS i zadachi partii' (delivered on 2 July 1990), published in *Materialy XXVIII Sezda KPSS* (Politizdat, Moscow), pp. 3–51.

Gorbachev, Mikhail (1996), *Memoirs* (Doubleday, London).

Grotseskul, G. (1983), 'Ostaetsya v deistvii – shchekinskii metod: opyt i rezervy', *Pravda*, 18 October, p. 2.

Gvishiani, Dzhermen and Milner, Benstion (1983), 'Organizatsionnye rezervy upravleniya', *Voprosy ekonomiki*, no. 11, November, pp. 3–12.

Hanson, Philip (1992), *From Stagnation to Catastroika: Commentaries on the Soviet Economy, 1983–1991* (Praeger/Center for Strategic and International Studies/Radio Free Europe-Radio Liberty, Washington DC).

Hauslohner, Peter (1991), 'Gorbachev's Social Contract' in Hewett and Winston (1991), pp. 31–64.

Hewett, Ed A. (1988), *Reforming the Soviet Economy: Equality versus Efficiency* (The Brookings Institution, Washington DC).

Hewett, Ed A. and Winston, Victor H. (eds) (1991), *Milestones in Glasnost and Perestroyka: Politics and People* (The Brookings Institution, Washington DC).

Hough, Jerry F. (1988), *Russia and the West: Gorbachev and the Politics of Reform* (Simon and Schuster, New York).

Hough, Jerry F. (1991), 'Understanding Gorbachev: The Importance of Politics' in Hewett and Winston (1991), pp. 465–84.

Ickes, Barry W. and Ryterman, Randi (1993), 'Roadblock to Economic Reform: Inter-Enterprise Debt and the Transition to Markets', *Post-Soviet Affairs*, vol. 9, no. 3, pp. 231–52.

Illarionov, Andrei (1994), 'V Rossii shokovoi terapii ne bylo', *Izvestiya*, 1 February, p. 2.

Ivanov, S. (1983), 'Pravo na trud i obyazannost truditsya', *Pravda*, 18 March, p. 2.

Ivashko, Vladimir (1990), speech on 8 October 1990, 'O polozhenii v strane i zadachakh KPSS v svyazi s perevodom ekonomiki na rynochnye otnosheniya', published in *Materialy plenuma TsK KPSS, 8–9 oktyabrya 1990 g.* (Politizdat, Moscow, 1990), pp. 15–34.

Jowitt, Ken (1993), *New World Disorder: The Leninist Extinction* (University of California Press, Berkeley and Los Angeles).

Kagarlitsky, Boris (1996), 'Vozmozhno li v Rossii reformy?', *Nezavisimaya gazeta, NG-Stsenarii*, no. 9, 19 December, p. 7.

Kamenitser, S. and Milner, B. (1967), 'Stimulirovat, a ne prinuzhdat', *Literaturnaya gazeta*, no. 5, 1 February, p. 10.

Karagedov, Raimundas (1983), 'Ob organizatsionnoi strukture upravleniya promyshlennostyu', *EKO*, no. 8, August, pp. 50–69.

Karagedov, Raimundas (1984), 'Posle pervogo analiza', *Pravda*, 9 August, p. 2.

Klyamkin, Igor (1993), 'Tetcher, Pinochet ili Andropov?', *Izvestiya*, 4 November, p. 4.

Kolosov, Valerii F. (1991), 'The New Employment Policy in the USSR' in Standing (1991), pp. 45–61.

Konstitutsiya Rossiiskoi Federatsii: Entsiklopedicheskii slovar (1995), (Nauchnoe izdatelstvo, Moscow)

Konstitutsiya SSSR: Politiko-pravovoi kommentarii (1982), (Politizdat, Moscow).

Korelsky V. and Rozhno, I. (1984), 'Distsiplina: prava i otvetstvennost', *Pravda*, 24 January, p. 2.

Kornai, Janos (1980), *Economics of Shortage* (North-Holland Publishing Company, Amsterdam, New York and Oxford).

Kornai, Janos (1992), *The Socialist System: The Political Economy of Communism* (Oxford University Press).

Kosolapov, R. (1984), 'Sotsializm i protivorechiya', *Pravda*, 20 July, pp. 2–3.

Kostakov, Vladimir (1986a), 'Odin kak semero', *Sovetskaya kultura*, 4 January, p. 3.

Kostakov, Vladimir (1986b), 'Man and Progress', *Sovetskaya kultura*, 1 February, p. 3, cited in *CDSP*, vol. XXXVIII, no. 3, pp. 4–5, 23.

Kostakov, Vladimir (1987), 'Zanyatost: defitsit ili izbytok?', *Kommunist*, no. 2 (1300), January, pp. 78–89.

Kostakov, Vladimir (1991), 'Labour Surplus and Labour Shortage in the USSR' in Standing (1991), pp. 81–105.

Kostin, Leonid (1987), 'Perestroika i zarplata', interview in *Izvestiya*, 11 September, p. 2.

Kosygin, Aleksei (1966), 'Zayavlenie pravitelstva SSSR ob osnovnykh voprosakh vnutrennei i vneshnei politiki', *Pravda*, 4 August, pp. 1, 3–4.

Kotlyar, Aleksandr (1983), 'Polnaya zanyatost i sbalansirovannost faktorov sotsialisticheskogo proizvodstva', *Voprosy ekonomiki*, no. 7, July, pp. 106–17.

Kotlyar, Aleksandr (1991), 'Regulating Employment in the Context of Mobility' in Standing (1991), pp. 107–19.

Kotz, David with Weir, Fred (1997), *Revolution from Above: The Demise of the Soviet System* (Routledge, London and New York).

KPSS – v rezolyutsiyakh i resheniyakh sezdov, konferentsii i plenumov TsK, tom 15, 1985–88 (1989), (Politizdat, Moscow).

Kurashvili, Boris (1983), 'Sudby otraslevogo upravleniya', *EKO*, no. 10, October, pp. 34–57.

Kurashvili, Boris (1985), 'Kontury vozmozhnoi perestroiki', *EKO*, no. 5, pp. 59–79.

Kux, Ernest (1987), 'The Leadership Crisis in the Soviet Union' in Veen (1987), pp. 287–98.

Kuznetsov, Andrei and Kuznetsova, Olga, (1996), 'Privatisation, Shareholding and the Efficiency Argument: Russian Experience', *Europe-Asia Studies*, vol. 48, no. 7, pp. 1173–85.

Kuznetsova, Tamara (1991), 'The Growth of Cooperatives in the Soviet Union' in Standing (1991), pp. 277–94.

Kvasha, Aleksandr (1983), 'Teoreticheskie problemy demograficheskoi politiki v SSSR', *Voprosy ekonomiki*, no. 11, November, pp. 72–80.

Kvasha, Aleksandr (1989), 'Perepis: predvaritelnye itogi', interview in *Izvestiya*, 29 April, p. 2.

Lane, David (1987), *Soviet Labour and the Ethic of Communism* (Wheatsheaf Books/ Westview Press, Brighton, UK and Boulder, Colorado).

Lane, David (1988), 'Full Employment and Labor Utilization in the USSR' in Sacks and Pankhurst (1988), pp. 221–38.

Lane, David (1991), 'The Roots of Political Reform: The Changing Social Structure of the USSR' in Merridale and Ward (1991), pp. 95–113.

Lane, David (ed.) (1992), *Russia in Flux: the Political and Social Consequences of Reform* (Edward Elgar, Aldershot).

Lantsman, Mikhail (1994), 'Kosmopolit Abalkin i pochvennik Gaidar', *Segodnya*, 1 February, p. 3.

Laptev, V. (1983), 'Khozyaistvenny dogovor kak instrument planirovaniya', *EKO*, no. 4, April 1983, pp. 34–48.

Latsis, Otto (1987), 'Individualny trud v sovremennoi sotsialisticheskoi ekonomike', *Kommunist*, no. 1 (1299), January, pp. 74–82.

Latynina, Yuliya (1996), 'Maly biznes v Rossii: menyaem svobodu na bezopasnost', *Segodnya*, 27 June, p. 3.

Latynina, Yuliya (1997), 'Dengi po-rossiiski', *Izvestiya*, 30 January, p. 4.

Lenin, Vladimir (1952), *Sochineniya*, vol. 27, (4th edition, Gospolitizdat, Moscow).

Lenin, Vladimir (1951), *Sochineniya*, vol. 33.

Lewin, Moshe (1991), 'Conclusions' in Merridale and Ward (1991), pp. 237–45.

Lewin, Moshe (1995), *Russia/USSR/Russia: The Drive and Drift of a Superstate* (The New Press, New York)

Ligachev, Yegor (1993), *Inside Gorbachev's Kremlin: The Memoirs of Yegor Ligachev* (Pantheon Books, New York).

Lisichkin, Gennadii (1967), 'Spustya dva goda', *Novy mir*, no. 2, February, pp. 160–85.

Lisichkin, V. (1990), 'Vse prodaetsya, ne vse pokupaetsya', interview in *Pravda*, 15 May, p. 2.

Loginov, Viktor (1982), 'Krepit distsiplinu', *Pravda*, 25 December, p. 2.

Malle, Silvana (1990), *Employment Planning in the Soviet Union – Continuity and Change* (Macmillan Press, Birmingham).

Malmygin, Igor (1983), 'Sbalansirovannost rabochikh mest i trudovykh resursov', *Voprosy ekonomiki*, no. 11, November, pp. 25–32.

Maltsev, G. (1974), 'Sotsialnaya spravedlivost i prava cheloveka v sotsialisticheskom obshchestve', *Sovetskoe gosudarstvo i pravo*, no. 11, November, pp. 10–18.

Mandel, Ernest (1991), *Beyond Perestroika: The Future of Gorbachev's USSR* (Verso, London and New York).

Manevich, Yevgenii (1965), 'Vseobshchnost truda i problemy ratsionalnogo ispolzovaniya rabochei sily v SSSR', *EKO*, no. 6, June, pp. 23–30.

Manevich, Yevgenii (1969), 'Problemy vosproizvodstva rabochei sily i puti uluchsheniya ispolzovaniya trudovykh resursov v SSSR', *Voprosy ekonomiki*, no. 10, October, pp. 27–40.

Manykina, Iraida (1991), 'An Assessment of Soviet Labour Statistics' in Standing (1991), pp. 401–18.

Marx, Karl and Engels, Frederick, *Collected Works*, (Lawrence and Wishart, London).

Marx, Karl and Engels, Frederick (1985), vol. 20, *Marx and Engels: 1864–68* (Lawrence and Wishart, London).

Marx, Karl and Engels, Frederick (1989), vol. 24, *Marx and Engels: 1874–83* (Lawrence and Wishort, London).

Maslova, Inga (1991), 'State Employment Programmes in the Light of the New Law on Employment' in Standing (1991), pp. 121–44.

Materialy XXVIII Sezda Kommunisticheskoi Partii Sovetskogo Soyuza (1990), (Politizdat, Moscow).

McAuley, Alastair (1992), 'Poverty and Underprivileged Groups' in Lane (1992), pp. 196–209.

Mchedlov, M. and Rozhnov, V. (1983), 'O sotsialisticheskoi tsivilizovannosti', *Pravda*, 26 August, pp. 2–3.

Menshikov, Stanislav (1991), *Catastrophe or Catharsis? The Soviet Economy Today* (Inter-Verso, Moscow and London, 1991).

Merridale, Catherine and Ward, Chris (eds) (1991), *Perestroika: The Historical Perspective* (Edward Arnold, London and New York).

Mikhailov, Mark (1981), 'Po povodu vedomstvennosti', *Kommunist*, no. 8, May, pp. 104–15.

Millar, James R. (1995), 'From Utopian Socialism to Utopian Capitalism: The Failure of Revolution and Reform in Post-Soviet Russia', *Problems of Post-Communism*, May/June, pp. 7–14.

Moore, Barrington (1969), *Social Origins of Dictatorship and Democracy* (Penguin Books, Harmondsworth, England).

Morvant, Penny (1995), 'Unemployment: A Growing Problem', *Transition*, vol. 1, no. 6, 28 April, pp. 46–50.

Morvant, Penny (1996), 'The Changing Face of Poverty', *Transition*, 12 January, pp. 56–61.

Moskoff, William (1993), *Hard Times: Impoverishment and Protest in the Perestroika Years* (M. E. Sharpe, Armonk and London).

Negoduiko, N. (1983), 'Na poroge eksperimenta', *Pravda*, 2 December, p. 2.

Nemtsov, Boris (1998), 'Budushchee Rossii – oligarkhiya ili demokratiya?', *Nezavisimaya gazeta*, 17 March, p. 8.

Nishanov, R. N. (1989), Report to the Uzbek Communist Party *aktiv*, *Pravda vostoka*, 17 June, pp. 1–2.

Nove, Alec (1992), *An Economic History of the USSR, 1917–1991* (3rd edition, Penguin Books, London).

Novoplyansky, D. (1983), 'Shalyai-valyai', *Pravda*, 3 December 1983, p. 3.

'O dopolnitelnykh merakh po rasshireniyu prav proizvodstvennykh obedinenii (predpriyatii) promyshlennosti v planirovanii i khozyaistvennoi deyatelnosti i po usileniyu ikh otvetstvennosti za rezultaty raboty', joint Party/Government Resolution, *Pravda*, 26 July 1983, p. 1.

'Ob usilenii raboty po ukrepleniyu sotsialisticheskoi distsipliny truda', Party Resolution, *Pravda*, 7 August 1983, p. 1.

'O merakh po uskoreniyu nauchno-tekhnicheskogo progressa v narodnom khozyaistve', joint Party/Government Resolution, *Pravda*, 28 August 1983, p. 1.

'O merakh po rasshireniyu khozyaistvennoi samostoyatelnosti i usileniyu zainteresovannosti proizvodstvennykh obedinenii (predpriyatii) bytovogo obsluzhivaniya v bolee polnom udovletvorenii potrebnostei naseleniya v uslugakh', Party Resolution, *Pravda*, 10 February 1984, p. 1.

'O povyshenii roli Instituta ekonomiki Akademii nauk SSSR v razrabotke voprosov ekonomicheskoi teorii razvitogo sotsializma', Party Resolution, *Pravda*, 24 February 1984, p. 1.

'Ob obespechenii effektivnoi zanyatosti naseleniya, sovershenstvovanii sistemy trudoustroistva i usilenii sotsialnykh garantii dlya trudyashchikhsya', joint Party/Government/AUCCTU Resolution, *Izvestiya*, 20 January 1988, pp. 1–2.

'O merakh po ozdorovleniyu ekonomiki, etapakh ekonomicheskoi reformy i prinstipialnykh podkhodakh k razrabotke trinadtsatogo pyatiletnego plana', USSR Congress of People's Deputies Resolution, *Pravda*, 22 December 1989, pp. 1,3.

'O neotlozhnykh merakh po obespecheniyu stabilnoi raboty bazovykh otraslei narodnogo khozyaistva', Presidential decree, *Izvestiya*, 17 May 1991, p. 2

OECD (1998), *Review of Agricultural Policies: Russian Federation* (OECD, Paris).

Ognev, Max (1999), 'Government Help Is at Hand', *The Russia Business Review*, September Vol. 7, No. 8, p. 31.

'Osnovy zakonodatelstva Soyuza SSSR i soyuznykh respublik o trude', *Pravda*, 17 July 1970, pp. 2–4.

Parfenov, Viktor (1983), 'Upravlentsy', *Pravda*, 26 December, p. 2.

Parfenov, Viktor (1984), 'Na stykakh', *Pravda*, 11 June, p. 2.

Parkin, Frank (1979), *Marxism and Class Theory: A Bourgeois Critique* (Tavistock Publications, London).

Partington, Angela (1992), *The Oxford Dictionary of Quotations* (fourth edition, Oxford University Press, Oxford and New York).

Pavlov, Valentin (1991a), 'Budem realistami', interview in *Trud*, 12 February, pp. 1–2.

Pavlov, Valentin (1991b), 'Trud. Otvetstvennost. Konsolidatsiya' (speech to the Supreme Soviet), *Pravda*, 23 April, pp. 2–3.

Perevedentsev, Viktor (1976), 'Shagni za okolitsu', *Komsomolskaya Pravda*, 28 January, p. 2.

Petrakov, Nikolai *et al.* (1992), 'Pravitelstvo utratilo kontrol nad ekonomicheskimi protsessami', *Nezavisimaya gazeta*, 6 March, p. 4

'Po voprosam, svyazannym c uporyadocheniem rezhima raboty predpriyatii, organizatsii i uchrezhdenii, zanyatykh obsluzhivaniem naseleniya', Government Resolution, *Pravda*, 18 January 1983, p. 1.

Popkova, Lydia (1987), 'Gde pyshnee pirogi?', *Novy mir*, no. 5, pp. 239–41.

Popov, Nikolai (1998), 'Po raznye storony', *Nezavisimaya gazeta*, 6 August, p. 8.

Porket, J. L. (1989), *Work, Employment and Unemployment in the Soviet Union* (Macmillan Press, London).

Pravda, Alex (1982), 'Is There a Soviet Working Class?', *Problems of Communism*, vol. XXXI, November–December, pp. 1–24.

Pravda, Alex (1988), 'Ideology and the Policy Process' in White and Pravda (1988), pp. 225–52.

Prostyakov, Igor (1988), 'Popav pod sokrashchenie ...', interview in *Pravda*, 21 January, p. 2.

Rumyantsev, A. and Bunich, P. (1967), 'Khozyaistvo i sistema upravleniya', *Izvestiya*, 16 November, p. 2.

Rutkevich, M. (1973), 'Sotsiologiya i upravleniya obshchestvom', *Pravda*, 14 September, p. 3.

Rutland, Peter (1991), 'Labour Unrest and Movements in 1989 and 1990' in Hewett and Winston (1991), pp. 287–325.

Rutland, Peter (1992), 'Economic Crisis and Reform' in White, Pravda and Gitelman (1992), pp. 200–26.

Rutland, Peter (1994), 'Privatisation in Russia: One Step Forward: Two Steps Back?, *Europe-Asia Studies*, vol. 46, no. 7, pp. 1109–31.

Rutland, Peter (1997), 'Russia's Flawed Market Transition', *Problems of Post-Communism*, November/December, pp. 29–33.

Ryzhkov, Nikolai (1986), 'Ob osnovnykh napravleniyakh ekonomicheskogo i sotsialnogo razvitiya SSSR na 1986–1990 gody i na period do 2000 goda', published in *XXVII sezd KPSS, 25 fevralya-6 marta 1986 goda, stenograficheskii otchet v trekh tomakh*, vol. 2 (Politizdat, Moscow), pp. 4–48.

Ryzhkov, Nikolai (1990a), speech on 13 December 1989, published in *Vtoroi sezd narodnykh deputatov SSSR*, vol. 1 (Politizdat, Moscow), pp. 209–49.

Ryzhkov, Nikolai (1990b), 'Ob ekonomicheskom polozhenii strany i kontseptsii perekhoda k reguliruemoi rynochnoi ekonomike', published in *Tretya sessiya Verkhovnogo Soveta SSSR, stenograficheskii otchet*, part 14, 23–25 May 1990, bulletin no. 51 (Izdanie Verkhovnogo Soveta SSSR, 1990), pp. 88–134.

Sacks, Michael Paul and Pankhurst, Jerry G. (eds) (1988), *Understanding Soviet Society* (Allen and Unwin, Winchester, USA).

Sadikov, I. (1983), 'Pochemu brakodelu ne stydno', *Pravda*, 25 February, p. 3.

Schmidt-Hauer, Christian (1987), 'The Power Centre' in Veen (1987), pp. 265–86.

Schroeder, Gertrude E. (1987), 'Managing Labour Shortages in the Soviet Union' in Adam (1987), pp. 3–26.

Selyunin, Vasilii (1967), 'Our Daily Work', *Moskva*, no. 7, July, pp. 173–86, cited in *CDSP*, vol. XIX, no. 38, pp. 6–13.

Selyunin, Vasilii (1988), 'Istoki', *Novy mir*, no. 5, pp. 162–89.

Service, Robert (1998), *A History of Twentieth-Century Russia* (Penguin Books, Harmondsworth, England).

Severinov, Yurii (1984), 'V khode raboty vyyasnilos...', *Pravda*, 17 October, p. 2.

Shafarevich, Igor (1991), 'Rossiya naedine s soboi', *Pravda*, 2 November, pp. 1, 3.

Shatalin, Stanislav (1986), 'Sotsialnoe razvitie i ekonomicheskii rost', *Kommunist*, no. 14 (1294), September, pp. 59–70.

Shatalin, Stanislav *et al.* (1990), 'Chelovek, svoboda, rynok', *Izvestiya*, 4 September, p. 3.

Shcherbakov, Vladimir, (1986), 'Kazhdomu – po trudu', interview in *Trud*, 30 August, p. 2.

Shcherbakov, Vladimir, (1989), 'Uravnyat shansy, no ne zarplaty', interview in *Izvestiya*, 16 October, p. 2.

Shcherbakov, Vladimir, (1990a), 'Sotsialnaya zashchita v usloviyakh rynka', interview in *Izvestiya*, 7 August, p. 2.

Shcherbakov, Vladimir, (1990b), 'Mery sotsialnoi zashchity v usloviyakh rynka', *Izvestiya*, 8 August, pp. 1–2.

Shcherbakov, Vladimir, (1991), 'The Labour Market in the USSR: Problems and Perspectives' in Standing (1991), pp. 19–44.

Shirokov, V. (1989), 'Chelovek bez raboty', *Pravda*, 31 October, p. 2.

Shishkov, S. (1985), 'Strogo, neotvratimo, po spravedlivosti', *Pravda*, 12 February, p. 3.

Shlapentokh, Vladimir (1988), *Soviet Ideologies in the Period of Glasnost: Responses to Brezhnev's Stagnation* (Praeger, New York).

Shmelev, Nikolai (1987), 'Avansy i dolgi', *Novy mir*, no. 6, June, pp. 142–58.

Shmelev, Nikoai (1996), 'Chego my khotim – ischeznut s karty mira', *Literaturnaya gazeta*, 4 December, p. 3.

Shmelev, Nikolai and Popov, Vladimir (1990), *The Turning Point: Revitalizing the Soviet Economy* (I. B. Tauris, London).

Sitaryan, Stepan (1984), 'Poisk prodolzhaetsya', interview in *Pravda*, 2 October, p. 2.

Smart, Christopher (1990), 'Gorbachev's Lenin: The Myth in Service to Perestroika', *Studies in Comparative Communism*, vol. XXIII, no. 1, Spring, pp. 5–22.

Smith, Hedrick (1991), *The New Russians* (Vintage, London).

Stalin, Iosef (1945), 'Novaya obstanovka – novye zadachi khozyaistvennogo stroitelstva', speech to industrial managers on 23 June 1931, published in Iosef Stalin, *Voprosy Leninizma* (11th edition, Gospolitizdat), pp. 331–49.

Standing, Guy (ed.) (1991), *In Search of Flexibility: The New Soviet Labour Market* (International Labour Office, Geneva).

Standing, Guy (1996), *Russian Unemployment and Enterprise Restructuring: Reviving Dead Souls* (Macmillan Press, Basingstoke and London/St Martin's Press, New York).

Steele, Jonathan and Abraham, Eric (1983), *Andropov in Power* (Martin Robertson, Oxford).

Subotsky, Yurii (1983), 'Kak ispolzovat preimushchestva?', *EKO*, no. 3, March, pp. 17–37.

Sutela, Pekka (1991), *Economic Thought and Economic Reform in the Soviet Union* (Cambridge University Press, Cambridge).

Taylor, Michael (1991), 'Non-wage Labour Costs in the USSR and the Role of the Trade Unions' in Standing (1991), pp. 237–58.

Teague, Elizabeth (1988), *Solidarity and the Soviet Worker* (Croom Helm, Beckenham).

Thompson, Terry L. and Sheldon, Richard (eds) (1988), *Soviet Society and Culture: Essays in Honor of Vera S. Dunham* (Westview Press, Boulder and London).

Ticktin, Hillel (1992), *Origins of the USSR: Essays on the Political Economy of a Disintegrating System* (M. E. Sharpe, Armonk and London).

Tikhonov, V. A. (1990), 'Cooperatives as a Form of Free Enterprise in the USSR' (Melbourne University Centre for Soviet and East European Studies Discussion Papers, no. 1).

Tolstikov, Y. A. (1968), 'Shchekinskii eksperiment', *Sovetskaya Estoniya*, 18 September, p. 2.

Varoli, John (1997), 'Economic Reform Casts a Long Shadow in Russia', *Transition*, 21 March, pp. 6–10, 56.

Vedomosti Verkhovnogo Soveta SSSR (1987), st.385, no. 26 (2412), 1 July (Izdanie Verkhovnogo Soveta SSSR, Moscow), pp. 427–63.

Vedomosti Sezda narodnykh deputatov i Verkhovnogo Soveta SSSR (1990), st. 906, no. 44, 31 October (Izdanie Verkhovnogo Soveta SSSR), pp. 1088–123.

Vedomosti Sezda narodnykh deputatov i Verkhovnogo Soveta SSSR (1991), st.111, no. 5, 30 January, pp. 180–97.

Veen, Hans-Joachim (Ed) (1987), *From Brezhnev to Gorbachev: Domestic Affairs and Soviet Foreign Policy* (Berg, Leamington Spa).

Verda, Aleksei (1997), 'Rynok truda v Rossii', *Nezavisimaya gazeta*, 21 October, p. 6.

Veretennikov, Vladimir (1991), 'Wage Differentials: The Trade Union View' in Standing (1991), pp. 221–36.

Vitalis, Vangelis (1999), 'Second Level Regional Policies in the Russian Federation and The Multilateral Trade Rules Affecting such Policies, paper presented to an OECD Seminar on the Interface between the Central and Sub-National Levels of Government in Russia's Trade Policy, Novgorod, 11–12 March 1999.

Wegren, Stephen K. and Durgin, Frank A. (1995), 'Why Agrarian Reform Is Failing', *Transition*, 20 October.

White, Stephen (1979), *Political Culture and Soviet Politics* (Macmillan Press, Basingstoke and London).

White, Stephen and Pravda, Alex (eds) (1988), *Ideology and Soviet Politics* (Macmillan, Basingstoke and London, 1988).

White, Stephen, Pravda, Alex and Gitelman, Zvi (eds) (1992), *Developments in Soviet and Post-Soviet Politics* (2nd edition, Macmillan, Basingstoke and London).

Whitefield, Stephen (1993), *Industrial Power and the Soviet State* (Clarendon Press, Oxford).

Yadov, Vladimir (1983), 'Otnoshenie k trudu: kontseptualnaya model i realnye tendentsii', *Sotsiologicheskie issledovaniya*, no. 3, pp. 50–62.

Yakovlev, A. and Miryushchenko, L. (1984), 'Na svoi dengi', *Pravda*, 6 February, p. 2.

Yarygina, Tatyana (1991a), 'Predmet ne pervoi neobkhodimosti', *Moskovskie novosti*, 21 April, p. 10.

Yarygina, Tatyana (1991b), 'Chto za dushoi u lyudei, idushchikh k rynku', *Izvestiya*, 6 December, p. 6.

Yasin, Yevgenii (1991), 'Chto nas zhdet, esli ...', *Ogonek*, no. 6, February, pp. 20–2.

Yasin, Yevgenii (1993), 'Reforma po gaidaru: 500 dnei spustya', *Rossiiskie vesti*, 6 April, p. 7.

Yasin, Yevgenii (1994), 'Programma, kotoruyu nevozmozhno realizovat', *Rossiiskie vesti*, 9 February, p. 2.

Yavlinsky, Grigorii (1994), 'Inaya reforma', *Nezavisimaya gazeta*, 10 February, p. 4.

Yavlinsky, Grigorii (1996), 'Vmesto byudzheta krizisa i dolgov – byudzhet reform i razvitiya', *Nezavisimaya gazeta*, 15 December, pp. 4–5.

Yavlinsky, Grigorii, Zadornov, Mikhail and Mikhailov, Aleksei (1991), 'Plyus "Bolshaya semerka" : programma organizovannogo vozvrashchenie v mirovuyu ekonomiku', *Izvestiya*, 20 May, p. 3.

Yavlinsky, Grigorii et al. (1991), *500 Days: Transition to the Market* (St. Martin's Press, New York).

Yavlinsky, Grigorii *et al.* (1992), 'Reformy v Rossii, vesna-92', *Moskovskie novosti*, pp. 9–16.

Zakharova, Nataliya, Posadskaya, Anastasiya and Rimashevskaya, Natalya (1989), 'Kak my reshaem zhenskii vopros', *Kommunist*, no. 4 (1338), March, pp. 56–65.

Zaslavskaya, Tatyana (1986), 'Chelovecheskii faktor razvitiya ekonomiki i sotsialnaya spravedlivost', *Kommunist*, no. 13 (1293), September, pp. 61–73.

Zaslavskaya, Tatyana (1990), *The Second Socialist Revolution: An Alternative Soviet Strategy* (I.B. Tauris, London).

Zaslavskaya, Tatyana (1997), 'V politike tsinik luchshe romantika', interview in *Nezavisimaya gazeta*, 9 December, p. 5.

Zaslavsky, Igor (1991), ''My khotim znat o cheloveke vse'', interview in *Pravda*, 1 February, p. 2.

Zdravomyslov, A. (1983), 'Sotsiologiya: problemy i perspektivy', *Pravda*, 23 September, pp. 2–3.

Zemtsov, Ilya (1989), *Chernenko, The Last Bolshevik: The Soviet Union on the Eve of Perestroika* (Transaction Publishers, New Brunswick, New Jersey).

Index

labour-saving technology 59, 72–4
land ownership/allocation 112, 162
large-scale economic experiment *see* economic experiments
Law on Employment (1991) 153, 158, 160, 209
Law on Individual Labour Activity (1986) 85–6
Law on Labour Collectives (1983) 57–8
Law on the State Enterprise (1987) 3, 67–8, 100, 102, 105–6, 107, 112–13, 121, 136, 152
leasing 109–10, 112, 121, 148, 207
Lebed, Aleksandr 183
legality, socialist (*sotsialisticheskaya zakonnost*) 58
legitimacy 6, 7, 9, 14–15, 132, 133, 165–6, 168–9, 191–3, 194–5
Lenin, Vladimir 105, 144, 199–200, 204–5
liberalization
economic 133, 167–8, 172–5, 191
political 7, 8, 9, 98, 133
Ligachev, Yegor 95, 158, 203
liquidation of enterprises 106–7, 121, 131–2, 149, 156, 157, 207, 209, 211
living standards 6, 110, 131, 137, 139, 142, 144, 162, 184, 185, 186, 194
localism (*mestnichestvo*) 94
Lopukhin, Vladimir 210
loss-making enterprises 13, 86, 105–6, 120, 121, 131–2, 142, 146, 147–8, 156, 157, 161, 164, 167, 182, 207
loyalty-solidarity system 4, 197
Luzhkov, Yurii 183

mafia 190
Manevich, Yevgenii 32
market (*rynok*) 111, 165
'all-Union' 152
conceptions/notions of the 15, 111, 134–45, 168, 169–75, 194
economy 131, 144, 169, 186
prescriptions 5
regulated 137, 139–40, 150

relations and mechanisms 68, 87–8, 88, 100, 103, 104, 131, 135, 139, 151, 175
socialism 15, 142–3, 144, 205
market (*sbyt*) 105
marketization 15, 88, 137, 157, 164, 196
Marx, Karl 24, 144
Marxism 12, 176
Marxism-Leninism 47, 59, 65
materialism 138
maternity (and child) benefits 80, 81, 118, 126, 159
maximization of labour 126
mechanization *see* production
mediocrity, culture of 116–17
messianism 12
middle class 194
migration 155
military-industrial complex 114, 170, 206
miners 131–2, 151, 160, 206
minimum wage 44, 112–13
ministries, government/branch *see* bureaucracy
moderate-radical path of economic reform 142–3
modernization 14
modernization of production *see* production
monetary emission and policies *see* emission
monetary overhang 91, 115
morality, socialist *see* socialist
moral-ideological methods/attitudes towards labour 57, 93, 159
moral-psychological factors in labour 42–3

nationalism 184, 194
negative restructuring *see* restructuring
negative reward/incentives 57, 89, 96, 103, 148, 172, 185, 187
Nemtsov, Boris 174, 194
neo-liberalism 183, 187, 189
networking 170, 173
New Economic Policy (NEP) 23, 42, 47, 101, 105
'new man' (*novy chelovek*) 29–30